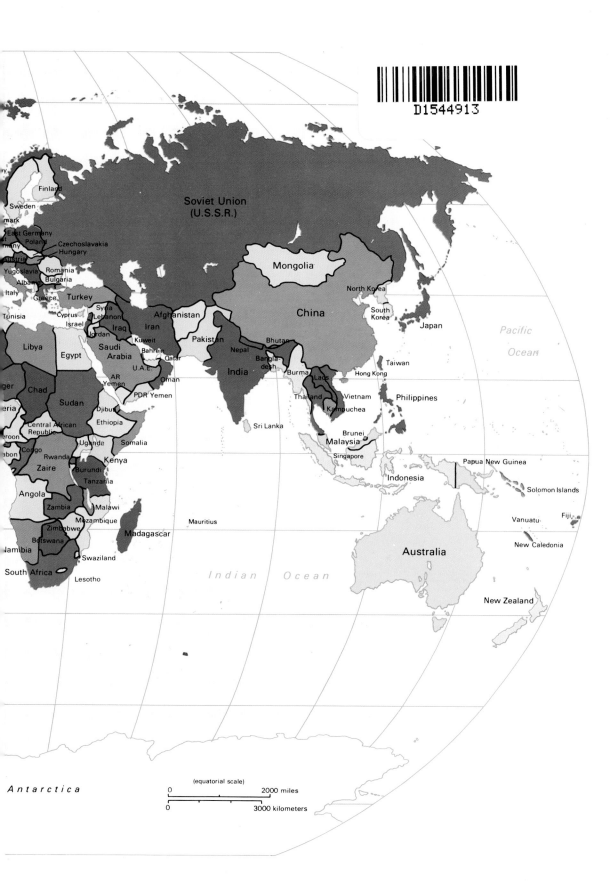

Finland

Sweden

mark

East Germany

many Poland

Austria Czechoslovakia

Yugoslavia Hungary

Albania Romania

Italy Bulgaria

Greece Turkey

Tunisia Cyprus Syria

Israel Lebanon

Jordan Iraq

Libya Egypt Saudi
Arabia

ger

Chad Sudan AR
Yemen

Central African
Republic Djibouti

eroon Ethiopia

abon Congo Uganda Somalia

Rwanda

Zaire Burundi Kenya

Angola Tanzania

Zambia Malawi

Zimbabwe Mozambique

Botswana

Jamibia

South Africa Lesotho Swaziland

Madagascar

Antarctica

Soviet Union
(U.S.S.R.)

Mongolia

North Korea

China

South
Korea

Afghanistan

Iran

Kuweit

Bahrein

Qatar

U.A.E.

Oman

PDR Yemen

Pakistan

India

Nepal

Bhutan

Bangla-
desh

Burma

Laos

Thailand

Sri Lanka

Japan

Taiwan

Hong Kong

Vietnam

Kampuchea

Philippines

Brunei

Malaysia

Singapore

Indonesia

Papua New Guinea

Solomon Islands

Vanuatu

Fiji

New Caledonia

Australia

New Zealand

Pacific

Ocean

Mauritius

Indian   Ocean

(equatorial scale)

0   2000 miles

0   3000 kilometers

D1544913

TOURISM
The International
Business

Robert Christie Mill

School of Hotel and Restaurant Management
University of Denver

PRENTICE HALL, Englewood Cliffs, New Jersey 07632

Library of Congress Cataloging-in-Publication Data

Mill, Robert Christie.
    Tourism : the international business / by Robert Christie Mill.
        p.   cm.
    Bibliography: p.
    Includes index.
    ISBN 0-13-926296-2
    1. Tourist trade.   I. Title.
G155.A1M52   1990
338.4'791—dc20

89-35809
CIP

> *This book is dedicated
> to Robyn, Jeff, Michael,
> David, and Kimberley.*

Editorial/production supervision and
    interior design: **Julie Boddorf**
Cover design: **Lundgren Graphics**
Cover photograph: **Dennis Hallinan (Hong Kong Harbor)/FPG**
Manufacturing buyer: **Laura Crossland/Dave Dickey**

© 1990 by **Prentice-Hall, Inc.**
A Division of Simon & Schuster
Englewood Cliffs, New Jersey 07632

Printed in the United States of America

10 9 8 7 6 5 4 3 2 1

ISBN   0-13-926296-2

PRENTICE-HALL INTERNATIONAL (UK) LIMITED, *London*
PRENTICE-HALL OF AUSTRALIA PTY. LIMITED, *Sydney*
PRENTICE-HALL CANADA INC., *Toronto*
PRENTICE-HALL HISPANOAMERICANA, S.A., *Mexico*
PRENTICE-HALL OF INDIA PRIVATE LIMITED, *New Delhi*
PRENTICE-HALL OF JAPAN, INC., *Tokyo*
SIMON & SCHUSTER ASIA PTE. LTD., *Singapore*
EDITORA PRENTICE-HALL DO BRASIL, LTDA., *Rio de Janeiro*

CONTENTS

PREFACE

People travel for business, for pleasure, or for a combination of the two. The vast majority of these people travel to specific destinations, which represents the building blocks of tourism. Once individuals have the time, money, and motivation to travel and have decided where to go, they need some means to get there. Once at the destination, these tourists, as they are now called, require some place to stay, some place to eat and drink, something to do (sightseeing, tennis, golf, skiing, for example), and something to buy as a remembrance of the trip. This is where the transportation, lodging, food and beverage, sightseeing, recreation, and retailing industries come in.

The shortsighted operator believes that business begins when the customer walks in the front door. The smarter manager understands that there is a vast world outside the front door—called travel and tourism—that determines the shape of demand for the business that one is engaged in. Thus, the airlines realize that to sell airline tickets it is necessary to sell a destination for someone to fly to; the hotel operator realizes that the fortunes of the property are dependent upon the fortunes of the destination of which it is a part.

That is what this book focuses on. By understanding what travel and tourism is all about, those who operate businesses that rely on the visitor will be in a better position to take a pro-active role in securing that business for themselves.

The text is divided into four sections: an overview of tourism, the development of tourism, the marketing of tourism, and the future of tourism.

The first section explains what tourism is. In Chapter 1, the history of tourism is explored so that managers can get a perspective on where we have come from. Tourism, as we know it today, is defined and the factors that make up tourism are outlined. Careers in travel and tourism are highlighted for the reader's consideration.

Chapter 2 explores the tourist in more detail. The reasons for travel are examined and various segments of the market are covered. The general principles explaining tourist movements are uncovered. By studying the factors that influence where tourism takes place, destinations can begin to determine their chances for attracting tourists. They can then go on to see where potential tourists will come from.

The means that tourists use to get to their destination are examined in Chapter 3. Airways, railways, waterways, highways, and local transit are covered in relation to their size and importance, who owns them, how they are financed, and the characteristics of the market that uses them. The way that transportation companies are regulated is dealt with, and the marketing of passenger transportation is examined in some depth.

The destinations that tourists go to are the subject of Chapter 4, which explores the various tourism destinations of the world. This geography of the world concentrates on the tourist attractions of various countries and regions.

Chapter 5 looks at how tourism is organized. The chapter considers tourism organization in both the private and the public sectors. In the public sector the international agreements necessary for tourism to flourish lead to an examination of the various international organizations that facilitate tourism. Various national models are explored. The private-sector businesses that make up tourism are summarized.

At this point the reader should have a good grasp of what tourism is all about—how it developed, what we mean today when we discuss tourism, why people travel, where they travel to, how they get there, and how the system is organized from the international to the local level.

The second section of the text covers the development of tourism. Chapter 6 answers the question, "Why develop tourism?" The goals of tourism are looked at from the perspective of the tourist, the destination, and the host community. The pluses and minuses of tourism development are closely examined from an economic, social, cultural, and environmental viewpoint. Methodologies that measure the impact of tourism and priorities are suggested.

Once a destination is convinced of the desirability of developing tourism, a plan is needed. Thus, tourism planning is the subject of Chapter 7. The importance of planning is explained, and the role of data collection and analysis as a basis for decision making is outlined. The various ways of collecting data for use in planning tourism are also examined.

The actual development of a destination is the topic of Chapter 8. Readers are taken through the steps involved in developing a destination for tourism from the preliminary analysis of tourist potential to the preparation of areawide master plans and the determination of financial feasibility.

Having developed tourism it is then necessary to manage it. In Chapter 9 we examine the requirements of a tourism "industry." Leadership must be developed in the community if tourism is to prosper. Coordinating this effort requires developing communications, tourist centers, a visitor services program, as well as conducting ongoing research into visitor satisfaction. Education and training for the host businesses are important as are promotional campaigns to lure tourists and a public awareness effort to educate local citizens about the benefits that tourism has for them. Lastly, this must somehow be paid for. Various community strategies for funding tourism are examined.

The reader by now will understand the benefits of developing tourism, the pitfalls to avoid, and methods used to collect research data as a basis for planning tourism. A step-by-step process for developing a destination and means to set up and fund a system for organizing tourism at the community level have been laid out.

The third section of the text covers tourism marketing. In Chapter 10 the subject of promotion is covered. Readers are taken through the procedures involved in creating an effective promotional plan for a community. The role of both national and state government tourist offices is delineated. Advantages of direct promotion is contrasted with the use of various middlemen in the distribution of tourism.

Chapter 11 focuses on the way travel is distributed to the public. A distinction is made between direct and indirect channels of distribution. The role of tour wholesalers in the marketing of tourism is examined and the reasons people take tours are explored. The chapter looks at the workings of the wholesale business from the economics of operation to the preparation and operation of a typical tour.

The part that retail travel agents play in distributing travel is the subject of the remainder of the chapter. The structure of the industry and the regulations that govern it are examined. A discussion of the functions of the agency and how the agency makes money completes the chapter.

The final section of the text is comprised of only one chapter—the future of tourism. The demand for tourism will be influenced by changes in population, income, leisure, and consumer tastes. The impact of these changes on both pleasure and business travel is pointed out in some detail.

Three appendices complete the text. Appendix 1 leads the reader to the major information sources for travel and tourism. Appendix 2 is a glossary of common tourism terms. Appendix 3 is a listing of major trade abbreviations.

It is hoped that by the time they finish reading this book readers will understand what tourism is and will have a clear idea of how to develop and market a tourism destination. That knowledge can then be used to get a piece of the international pie called *tourism*.

1

TOURISM: ITS HISTORICAL DEVELOPMENT

LEARNING OBJECTIVES

At the end of this chapter the reader will be able to:

■ Understand the contributions to travel and tourism made throughout various eras.

■ Realize the role transportation has played and continues to play in shaping tourism.

■ Identify the four major dimensions of tourism.

■ Identify the factors necessary for the development of travel and tourism.

■ Realize the various career opportunities available in travel and tourism.

■ Define and correctly use the following terms:

Grand Tour	U.S. Travel Data Center
Spas	Travel
Grand Hotels	Recreation
Tourism	Trip
Domestic Tourist	Attractions
International Tourist	Facilities
Domestic Visitor	Infrastructure
International Visitor	Transportation
Excursionist	Hospitality
Maslow's Hierarchy of Needs	

TOURISM THROUGH THE AGES

Introduction

As we prepare for an annual vacation or a weekend trip we take for granted how easy present-day travel is. We do not realize the conditions necessary for present-day tourism to flourish. Consider what we require to travel. First, we must have the free time to engage in leisure pursuits. Second, we must have the money to go somewhere. Where we go is affected by the means of transportation. A combination of time, money, and availability of transportation determines where we will go. When we get there (wherever "it" is) we must have a way of paying for our purchases. And, while the joy of travel is enhanced by a certain amount of risk, the route and the destination must be sufficiently safe to encourage our travel. It is only by surveying where we have come from that we can truly appreciate where we are now and plan for where we might want to be.

Early Travel

Early peoples tended to stay in one place. Travel was essentially to seek food or to escape danger.

The Bible, however, makes reference to travel for purposes of trade. In ancient times we began to see the development of routes for the purpose of facilitating trade and the creation of specialized, if somewhat crude, vehicles specifically for traveling. The growth of cities along waterways such as the Nile River and the Mediterranean Sea encouraged the development of water travel.

The Empire Era

Egyptians. As empires grew, we began to see the development of the conditions necessary for travel. At the peak of the Egyptian era, travel

2

Figure 1–1   Present-day travel by water. (Courtesy Jamaica Tourist Board.)

for both business and pleasure began to flourish. Travel was necessary between the central government and the outlying territories. To accommodate travelers on official business, hospitality centers were built along major routes and in the cities. Egyptians also traveled for pleasure, and public festivals were held several times a year. Herodotus, sometimes called the first travel writer, observed:

> The Egyptians were also the first to introduce solemn assemblies, processions, and litanies to the gods; . . . The following are the proceedings of the assembly at Bubastis. Men and women come sailing all together, vast numbers in each boat, many of the women with castanets, which they strike, while some of the men pipe during the whole time of the voyage; the remainder of the voyagers, male and female, sing the while, and make a clapping with their hands. When they arrive opposite any of the towns upon the banks of the stream, they approach the shore, and while some of the women continued to play and sing, others call aloud to the females of the place and load them with abuse, while a certain number dance, and some standing up expose themselves. After proceeding in this way all along the river-course, they reach Bubastis, where they celebrate the feast with abundant sacrifices. More grapewine is consumed at this festival than in all the rest of the year besides. The number of those who attend, counting the men and women and omitting the children, amounts, according to the native reports, to 700,000.[1]

Figure 1-2   (Courtesy Egyptian Office of Tourism.)

Travel also satisfied people's curiosity. The earlier Pharoahs used the good building stone of the Nile to construct great tombs and temples as early as 2700 B.C. Over a thousand years later the Egyptians found themselves surrounded by this historical treasure chest. Writers noted that visitors left messages to show they had been there (graffiti?) and took home remembrances of the trip (souvenirs?).

Assyrians and Persians.   Assyria comprised the area now known as Iraq. As the empire expanded from the Mediterranean in the west to the Persian Gulf in the east, the means of travel were improved, largely for military use. Roads were improved, markers were established to indicate distances, and posts and wells were developed for safety and nourishment. Even today we see the influence of military construction aiding pleasure travel. The recently completed U.S. interstate highway system was developed initially to facilitate transportation in the event of a national emergency.

The Assyrian military traveled by chariot, others by horse, while the donkey was the principal mode of transportation of the common people.

The Persians, who defeated the Assyrians, continued improvements in the travel infrastructure. New kinds of wagons were developed including a four-wheeled carriage for the wealthy.

Greeks.   While previous civilizations had set the stage for the development of travel, it took the Greeks and, later, the Romans to bring it all together.

The Greeks continued in the tradition of the great traders. Because water was the most important means of moving commercial goods, Greek cities grew up along the coast, thus ensuring that travel was primarily by sea.

Travel for official business was less important as Greece was divided into city-states that were fiercely independent. Pleasure travel did exist in three areas: for religious festivals, for sporting events (most notably the Olympic Games), and to visit cities, especially Athens.

Travel was advanced by two important developments. First, through currency exchange. Previously travelers would pay their way by carrying various goods and selling them at their destination. The money of Greek city-states was now accepted as international currency, eliminating the need to travel with a retinue of goods. Second, the Greek language spread throughout the Mediterranean area, making it easier to communicate as one traveled.

Romans.   Travel flourished in Roman times for several reasons. The control of the sprawling Roman Empire stimulated trade and led to the growth of a large middle class with the money to travel; Roman coins were all the traveler had to carry to finance the trip; the means of transportation—roads and waterways—were excellent; communication was relatively easy as Greek and Latin were the principal languages; and the legal system provided protection from foreign courts, thereby ensuring the safety of the traveler.

The sporting games started by the Greeks were copied in the fights-to-the-death of the Roman gladiators. Sightseeing was also popular, particularly trips to Greece. Greece had recently become a part of greater Rome and was now the place to see. Pausanias, a Greek, wrote a 10 volume *Guide to Greece,* aimed at Roman tourists, in A.D. 170. In his 10 volumes he describes in great detail the monuments, sculptures, and the stories and myths behind them.

Touring was also popular to Egypt, site of the Sphinx and the Pyramids, and to Asia Minor, scene of the Trojan War. Aristotle visited Asia Minor before establishing his famous school.

It was at this time that an unknown scholar developed the idea of the Seven Wonders of the World.

A final development was that of second homes and vacations associated with them. Villas spread from Rome south to Naples, near the sea, to the mountains, and to mineral spas.

Europeans

Pilgrims.   As the Roman Empire collapsed in the fifth century, roads fell into disuse and barbarians made it unsafe to travel. Whereas a Roman courier could travel up to 100 miles a day, the average daily rate of jour-

Figure 1–3   Visits to religious sites remain popular—Segovia Cathedral (Courtesy National Tourist Office of Spain.)

ney during the Middle Ages was 20 miles. It was not until the twelfth century that the roads became secure again. This was due to the large numbers of travelers going on pilgrimages.

Pilgrims traveled to pay homage to a particular site or as an atonement for sin. Those who heard confessions often required the sinner to travel barefoot. In other cases pilgrims journeyed to fulfill a promise made when they were sick. Sir John Mandeville is credited with writing a fourteenth-century manual for pilgrims to the Holy Land. In it we see the early signs of the destructive nature of tourists:

> You must understand that when men arrive in Jerusalem they make their first pilgrimage to the church which is the Sepulchre of Our Lord. . . . Not long ago the Sepulchre was quite open, so that men could kiss it and touch it. But because some men who went there used to try to break bits of the stone off to take away with them, the Sultan had a wall built around the Tomb so that nobody could touch it except on the left side.[2]

Beginning in 1388 King Richard II required pilgrims to carry permits, the forerunner of the modern passport.

Renaissance.   The next important factor in the history of travel was the Renaissance. As society moved from a rural to an urban base, wealth grew and more people had the money to travel. Pilgrimages were still important although journeys to Jerusalem declined because of the growth of Protestantism in Europe. The impetus to travel in order to learn was aided by the arrival of Renaissance works from Italy. Stable monarchies helped assure travelers' safety, although, as can be seen in the writings of this sixteenth-century traveler, certain precautions still had to be taken:

> A traveller has the need of a falcon's eye, a monkey's face, a merchant's words, a camel's back, a hog's mouth, a deer's feet. And the traveller to Rome—the back of an ass, the belly of a hog, and a conscience as broad as the king's highway.
>
> Line your doublet with taffetie, taffetie is lice-proof.
>
> Never journey without something to eat in your pocket, if only to throw at dogs when attacked by them.
>
> Carry a note-book and red crayon.
>
> When going by coach, avoid women, especially old women; they always want the best places.
>
> At sea, remove your spurs; sailors make a point of stealing them from those who are being seasick. Keep your distance from them in any case; they are covered with vermin.
>
> In an inn-bedroom which contains big pictures, look behind the latter to see they do not conceal a secret door, or a window.
>
> Women should not travel at all and married men not much.[3]

Grand Tour.   The beginning of the sixteenth century saw a new age of curiosity and exploration that culminated in the popularity of the Grand Tour. This was initially a sixteenth-century Elizabethan concept brought about by the need to develop a class of professional statesmen and ambassadors. Young men accompanied ambassadors throughout Europe in order to complete their education.

The practice developed into the seventeenth and eighteenth centuries until it became almost routine. No gentleman's education was complete until he spent from one to three years traveling around Europe with a tutor. This practice was undoubtedly influenced by the writings of John Locke, who believed that human knowledge came entirely from external sources. Once one environment was "exhausted" it became necessary to travel on to another. Thus, travel became a requirement for those seeking to develop the mind and accumulate knowledge.

The Grand Tour began in France, where French was studied together with dancing, fencing, riding, and drawing. Before Paris could corrupt one's morals or ruin one's finances, the student would head for Italy to study sculpture, music appreciation, and art. The return was by way of Germany, Switzerland, and the Low countries (Holland, Belgium, and Luxembourg).

Travel was by coach and could be rather uncomfortable. It was also necessary to "prove" one's culture and sophistication by returning home armed with paintings and sculptures, many of which were frauds foisted on unsuspecting travelers.

While travel was primarily by the English—some 20,000 people a year—the aristocracy of Scandanavia and Russia soon followed the Grand Tour practice.

Though fewer in number, some notable Germans also took the Grand Tour. One such was the writer Goethe. One of his experiences illustrates the differences in cultural values between host and guest:

> "Where is the privy?" inquired Goethe at Torbole.
> "In the courtyard, signore."
> Goethe surveyed the courtyard but could see no likely doorway.
> "Where exactly in the courtyard?" he asked.
> "Oh, anywhere you like, signore," was the affable reply.[4]

The Grand Tour reached its peak of popularity in the mid-eighteenth century, but was brought to a sudden end by the French Revolution and the Napoleonic Wars.

The Victorian Age

In the late eighteenth and early nineteenth centuries two major factors affected the development of tourism. Increased industrialization accounted for both of them. First, the Industrial Revolution accelerated the movement from rural to urban areas. This produced a large number of people in a relatively small area. The desire to "escape," even for a brief period, was present. Associated with this was the development of steam engines in the form of trains and steamships. This allowed the means to escape.

Because of the proximity of the coast to the major urban areas, it was only natural that train lines were extended in these directions. However, the vast majority of visitors to the seaside were day-trippers. It was well into the second half of the nineteenth century that the working classes were able to get regular holidays and sufficient income to use their leisure time to travel.

Development of Spas. The development of spas was largely due to the medical profession, which, during the seventeenth century, began to recommend the medicinal properties of mineral waters. The idea originated, however, with the Greeks. The Roman Empire in Britain associated health with baths and springs. The word "spa" in fact comes from "espa," meaning a fountain, and was taken from the Belgian town of Spa.

Spas on the continent of Europe were developed two hundred to three hundred years before their growth in England. Development occurred because of three factors: the approval of the medical profession; court patronage; and local entrepreneurship to take advantage of the first two.

Patronage by court figures helped establish spas as the "in" place to be. Today we talk in tourism about "mass follows class"—the idea that the masses are influenced in their choice of vacation spot by where people influential to them visit. Today, film stars seem to have taken over the role of influencer once enjoyed by royalty.

The number of people who could afford to "take the waters" was rather small. By the end of the seventeenth century the influence of the medical profession had declined and spas were more for entertainment than for health. Their popularity continued, however, into the nineteenth century. It is still possible today to drink from the mineral waters at Bath in England, while Hot Springs in Arkansas and Glenwood Springs in Colorado still attract many visitors. Additionally, many Eastern European towns proclaim the beneficial effects of mud packs and hydrotherapy.

Growth of Seaside Resorts.   The medical profession, the British court, and Napoleon all helped popularize the seaside resort. The original motive for sea bathing was for reasons of health. Dr. Richard Russell argued that sea water was effective against such maladies as cirrhosis, dropsy, gout, gonorrhea, and scurvy, and he insisted that people drink a pint of it daily. It is worth noting that the good Dr. Russell was a physician in Brighton, a resort close to London and on the water!

Brighton's fame was assured after the patronage of the Prince Regent, who later became George IV. Similarly, Southend and Cowes are associated with Princess Charlotte and Queen Victoria, respectively.

The growth of the seaside resort was stimulated by the French Revolution and the Napoleonic Wars. It will be recalled that both contributed to the demise of the Grand Tour. Those who would have taken the Grand Tour could not travel to the Continent. The now fashionable seaside resorts were the alternative.

Seaside resorts were genteel to the point of being dull. Originally people bathed in the nude. This, however, led to inquisitive onlookers. The bathers then turned to bathing machines that could be rolled out into deep waters. The sightseers countered with telescopes! This led to the wearing of bathing dresses, which revealed nothing. Visitors were led to complain:

> The ladies dressed in flannel cases
> Show nothing but their handsome faces.[5]

Figure 1-4 The ultimate "seaside resort"—Waikiki. (Courtesy Hawaii Visitors Bureau; Peter French, photographer.)

Toward the end of the nineteenth century the seaside resorts became the palaces for the working classes. This was due to the introduction of paid holidays and better wages.

The term *holiday* comes from "holy days"—days for religious observances. Ancient Rome featured public holidays for great feasting. As Europe became Christian certain saints' days and religious festivals became holy days when people fasted and prayed and refrained from work. After the Industrial Revolution, religious holidays gradually became secularized and the week's holiday emerged. The vacation was negotiated between employer and the workers and was again due to the economic and social changes brought about by the Industrial Revolution. It made sense to take the holidays during the warmer summer months. For the employer it was advantageous to close the entire factory down for one week rather than face the problems of operating with small groups of people absent over a longer period of time. Even today, certain weeks are associated with the general holidays of certain towns.

Prior to World War I the principal mode of transportation was the railway. This meant that development was concentrated at particular points. Regional development occurred with particular resorts growing to serve specific urban areas. The growth of the automobile, as will be seen later, allowed tourism to become more dispersed.

Americans

Early Travel in the U.S.   Tourism in the United States developed for the same reasons as in Europe. Travel was limited by the need for transportation. The first development of note was that of resorts. With the encouragement of physicians, resorts like Saratoga in New York State became very fashionable by the early 1800s. Ocean resorts also became attractive for health reasons initially, although amusements soon sprang up as well.

It took the development of the railway to open up the country to travelers. The completion of the Erie Railroad spurred the development of Niagara Falls as a honeymoon paradise by the 1870s.

The vast river network of the interior of the nation allowed the development of steamboat excursions, particularly gambling and amusement trips between New Orleans and St. Louis.

The industrial Revolution produced a class of wealthy people who had the time to travel. Thus, touring became popular. Many people took the Grand Tour. For most people in the South, an American-style Grand Tour to the North took a comparable amount of time and money. Three attractions were paramount: Northern cities, historical sites (those associated with the American Revolution and the Civil War), and resorts.

By the late 1800s, the West was attracting not only easterners but also Europeans to see the natural beauty and to hunt buffalo. Foreign travelers were also fascinated at this time by travel for religious reasons—to visit the important shrines of the various religious sects that had sprung up.

The 12-hour workday had been reduced to 10 hours by the end of the 1800s, and vacations were beginning to be recognized. While travel had been for the few, now it began to come within the reach of more and more people.

Tourism Today.   Today, Americans take more than 500 million trips annually to places 100 miles or more from home. Over two-thirds of these trips are pleasure-oriented. Over half of the pleasure trips are to visit friends and relatives. Approximately two-thirds of all trips are taken by auto, truck, or recreational vehicle. Weekend trips, as distinct from the traditional vacation trip, have been increasing and now represent about 40 percent of all trips taken.

For every $100 spent on trips over 25 miles from home, about $37 is spent on personal transportation, $21 on purchases, $14 on food, $13 on public transportation, $9 on lodging, and $6 on entertainment and recreation.

The major beneficiaries of tourism, in terms of dollars spent there, are California, Florida, New York, Texas, and New Jersey.

Transportation

The mode of transportation available determines the destinations to which one can travel. The location of accommodation, in turn, followed the development of transportation.

Stagecoach Travel.   Coaches were invented in Hungary in the fifteenth century. The word *coach* comes from the Hungarian town of Kocs. The first coaches were closed carriages suspended on leather straps between four wheels. The straps acted as springs that attempted to compensate for the poor condition of the roads.

The need to rest horses every few miles led to the development of post, or posting, houses where the animals could be changed or fed. This also allowed passengers the opportunity to rest their weary bones, for the poor state of most roads meant that travel was a jolting experience. In fact, the development of the English tavern was due to the need of stagecoach passengers to have overnight accommodation.

A major development in travel by road came in the early nineteenth century when John McAdam and Thomas Telford invented a new type of road surface that greatly improved the common dirt road found throughout Europe. The technique consisted of laying small broken stones over the general level of the ground with suitable drainage on each side of the road. It is said that McAdam insisted that no stone be used if it could not fit into the mouth of the laborer laying it down. The result was an increase in the comfort factor when traveling by coach.

Rail Travel.   The first railway was opened in England in 1825. While some people thought that trains went too fast for decent people, the increase in speed made day trips to the coast possible. At a cost of 1 penny a mile (cheaper than travel by coach) and a speed of 18 miles per hour, a large demand was created. The result was an accelerated growth in the popularity of English seaside resorts.

First-class cars were lighted by oil lamps and had comfortable accommodations. Second-class coaches had roofs but no sides, while third-class passengers rode in open cars. Brakes were unreliable as were the rails. Spikes often came loose from the rails, which buckled and could pierce both cars and passengers.

Food was served on American trains beginning in the 1860s. Salon cars sold buffalo, elk, beefsteak, or mutton for $1. It took George Mortimer Pullman to introduce comfortable overnight travel by rail for other than the upper classes. Sleeping berths cost $2 a night in the *Pioneer*. In Europe the Compagnie des Wagon-Lits equivalent was the *Orient Express* from Paris to Istanbul.

By the early twentieth century a private railroad car was a sign of wealth, but the 1929 stock market crash brought an end to the practice.

Figure 1–5   Aboard the *Orient Express.* (Courtesy Britrail Travel International, Inc.)

Today, some private rail cars have been renovated to their former glory for special tours.

The heyday of the railroads lasted approximately 100 years, from the 1830s to the 1930s. Railroads in the United States could not meet the challenge of the airlines, which offered speed over long distances, or buses that provided luxury coaches over shorter distances. Railroads in some cases sought to dissuade people from using rail transport. They felt there was much more profit to be made from hauling freight. Use of rail tracks by long, heavy, and slow freight trains means that American passenger trains can never reach the speeds of European and Japanese trains. Tracks are in such poor shape that speed is severely limited.

Water Travel.   Travel by water naturally preceded rail transport, but it was not until the mid-nineteenth century that the ocean liners came into prominence. Sir Samuel Cunard inaugurated the first regular steamship service between Britain and the United States in 1840. By the 1890s the trip was done in six days.

Just as the automobile and the airplane led to the decline of train travel, so too the airplane led to the demise of the ocean liner. In its peak year of 1957, over 1 million passengers crossed the ocean on liners. The following year more people crossed the Atlantic by plane than by ship. Between 1960 and 1975, passenger departures from New York fell from 500,000 a year to 50,000. Transatlantic travel by liner has almost disappeared.

Existing ships were refitted for cruising, and then newer, lighter cruise ships were built as the demand increased. The worldwide cruise market is well over 2 million passengers strong. Yet the potential is much larger. Less than 10 percent of the U.S. population has ever taken a cruise. Cruising is much more of a vacation experience than a mode of transportation.

Travel by Road. Henry Ford's Model T of 1908 started a revolution in tourism. Destination development was tied to the means of transportation. From the early posting houses to the railroad hotels and resorts and steamship ports—wherever transportation brought people was where the destinations grew. Development of tourism was concentrated in those areas. But the arrival of the automobile changed all that. Now people began to travel wherever they wanted on a road system that crisscrossed the country. Development became more dispersed rather than being concentrated in a few places. The benefits of tourism were being spread more widely.

Organizing such a system also became more complex. People could now much more readily travel *when* they wanted as well as *where* they wanted. They were no longer at the mercy of schedules put together by the transportation companies. However, they were still limited by such things as time and money.

The motel is a legacy of the automobile. It is also another example of how accommodations developed to follow the transportation routes.

Today, over 90 percent of all pleasure trips taken in the United States are done by automobile.

Air Travel. Regularly scheduled air service began in 1919 by what was to become Deutsche Lufthansa. Air service in both Europe and the United States was reserved for ferrying the mails. Seven years later Western Airlines began carrying the mail and one passenger if the weight limitations permitted.

By 1940 the travel time between Britain and the United States had been cut from six days to one, and the airlines began to take away the market from the liners. In 1958 the introduction of jet travel reduced the time from 24 hours to 8. Today, the *Concorde* crosses the Atlantic in just over 3 hours.

Accommodations

Early Inns. In earlier times, travelers stayed in private homes and were treated as part of the family. People felt an obligation to house the traveler. As travel became more popular, however, specific buildings were erected to house travelers. The first hostelries were called *ordinaries,* and they date from the mid-seventeenth century in colonial America. They later evolved into taverns and inns or houses.

An ordinary usually consisted of two small rooms. One room had a bar and was used for eating and drinking; the other room was reserved for the landlord and his family. Travelers slept on the floor of the bar and dining room.

As the amount of travel grew, so did the demand for accommodation along the way. Inns offered sleeping quarters for overnight guests while taverns consisted of places specializing in food, drink, and conviviality. It was accepted practice for travelers of the same sex to share both rooms and beds.

The Grand Hotels. The Victorian era of the early nineteenth century gave us two remarkable institutions—the railway station and the grand hotel. No longer was overnight accommodation a painful necessity. It was in the United States that the first grand hotel was developed—the City Hotel in New York City. Opened at the end of the eighteenth century, it consisted of 73 rooms on five floors.

The Tremont House, which opened in Boston in 1829, is generally regarded as the first modern hotel in America. Then the largest hotel in the world, with 170 rooms and a dining room capable of seating 200, it broke with the traditional inn in several ways: It had both single and double rooms, numerous public rooms, the stables were isolated from the rooms, and there was no signboard outside the front entrance.

The Tremont also offered several features that were novel for the times: eight baths with cold running water in the basement, a row of eight water closets on the ground floor, gas lights in the public rooms, a different key for each room, and free soap (regarded as an extravagance).

Figure 1-6 Chateau Frontenac, Quebec. (Courtesy Cunard.)

As America grew, each town sought to have its own Tremont House to symbolize how successful and prosperous it was.

By the twentieth century, as more people traveled, the nature of the hotel industry changed. The opening of the Buffalo Statler signalled the beginning of the commercial hotel concept. The hotel's slogan was "a room and a bath for a dollar and a half." But the Great Depression brought the travel industry to a virtual halt, until after World War II.

Motels. Following World War II, peacetime prosperity saw the means to travel spread to more and more people. Business people traveled by car rather than by train, and whole families were taking vacations. As middle America took off in the automobile a new class of motor hotels, or motels, sprang up to cater to their needs. However, the quality of these "mom and pop" operations was spotty.

One traveler who decided to do something about it was Kemmons Wilson. On a vacation trip with his family he found cramped, uncomfortable rooms, extra charges for children, and less than adequate restaurants. In 1952 he opened a motel that would be the first Holiday Inn. It had a swimming pool, air conditioning, a restaurant on the premises, a telephone in every room, free ice, dog kennels, free parking, and baby sitters available. As occupancy increased in motels, it decreased in hotels.

Figure 1-7 Present-day motel—Hururu. (Courtesy New Zealand Tourist & Publicity Office.)

Hotels Today.   As Holiday Inns developed in size they also added features to their properties. Rooms were better furnished; facilities were added. As they moved upscale a gap was left at the lower-priced end of the market. That gap was filled by a variety of budget chains offering a clean room without the frills required by a business person or family traveler en route to a destination.

The other end of the market opened up also with a variety of luxury properties and all-suite hotels that provided a two-room suite for families or business people.

Chains have increased their influence, and the independent is finding it increasingly harder to compete.

Today, the hotel industry is segmenting its marketing efforts to an extent not seen before. Properties are being built for specific groups of people—the upscale, the middle market, and the value conscious. Many of the chains have separate divisions competing in the marketplace.

TOURISM: A DEFINITION

A variety of definitions exist for what we call *tourism*. Thus, it is important to know exactly what we are talking about when we say "tourism" for several reasons. The development of attractions and facilities requires increasingly large amounts of money. A decision to build or not build depends upon numbers of potential users. Is there a large enough market to support such a project, be it a hotel, restaurant, or theme park? If we can arrive at a common definition of tourism, travel, and tourist then we are better able to use the numbers or data to determine whether or not to build, where to advertise, which destinations are growing or fading. In short, our business decisions will be better if they are made with a full understanding of what exactly we are talking about.

Tourism is not an industry, although tourism gives rise to a variety of industries. Tourism is an *activity* engaged in by people who travel.

International Tourist

League of Nations.   It is generally agreed that definitions of a tourist are unsatisfactory. According to the League of Nations in 1937, a "foreign tourist" is

> any person visiting a country, other than that in which he usually resides for a period of at least 24 hours.

The following individuals are considered tourists:

persons traveling for pleasure, for family reasons, for health, etc.;

persons traveling to meetings, or in representative capacity of any kind (scientific, administrative, diplomatic, religious, athletic, etc.);

persons traveling for business reasons;

persons arriving in the course of a sea cruise, even when they stay less than 24 hours (the latter should be regarded as a separate group, disregarding if necessary their usual place of residence.

The following individuals are not regarded as tourists:

persons arriving, with or without a contract of work, to take up an occupation or engage in any business activity within that country;

other persons arriving to establish a residence in that country;

students and other persons in boarding establishments or schools;

residents in a foreign zone and persons domiciled in one country and working in an adjoining country;

travelers passing through a country without stopping, even if the journey takes more than 24 hours.[6]

The definition of "foreign tourist" was largely one of time—staying in the country for more than 24 hours. Exceptions were made for those on a sea cruise. The motivations for travel, to be included as a tourist, were rather liberal. As long as people were not arriving to take up work or were not students they were called "tourists" whether their purpose was business or pleasure.

IUOTO. In 1950 the International Union of Official Travel Organizations (IUOTO), which later became the World Tourism Organization, suggested two changes to the above definition. The organization recommended that "students and young persons in boarding establishments or schools" be regarded as tourists. It also suggested that excursionists and transit travelers not be defined as tourists. The IUOTO believed that the term "excursionist" should be given to someone traveling for pleasure in a country in which he or she normally does not reside a period of less than 24 hours as long as the person was not there to work. A "transit traveler" could actually be in the country longer than 24 hours. According to the IUOTO this term referred to "any person traversing a country even for a period of more than 24 hours, without stopping, or a person traversing a country during a period of less than 24 hours, provided that the stops made are of short duration and for other than tourism purposes."[7]

United Nations' Rome Conference. In 1963 the United Nations Conference on International Travel and Tourism in Rome recommended a definition of the term "visitor" to include any person who visits a country other

Figure 1-8   (Courtesy Texas Department of Tourism.)

than the one in which he or she lives for any purpose other than one which involves pay from the country being visited. Specifically, conference members noted that visits could be for the following reasons:

1. leisure, recreation, holiday, sport, health, study, religion;
2. business, family, friends, mission, meeting.

If the person stayed for less than 24 hours, he or she would be "excursionists." If the person stayed longer, he or she would be tourists. Under this definition a tourist would be someone who traveled for business or for pleasure as long as the individual did not receive money from the country visited.

In 1968 the United Nations Statistical Commission accepted this definition but recommended that member-nations decide for themselves whether to use the term "excursionist" or "day visitor." The important point was to distinguish between visitors who did or did not stay overnight.

United Nations Department of Economic and Social Affairs.   In 1978 the Department of Economic and Social Affairs of the U.N. published guidelines that included a definition of the term "international visitor." The agency recognized that international visitors were those who visited a given country from abroad (what we might call inbound tourists) and those who went abroad on visits from a given country (outbound tourists). It indicated that the maximum period a person could spend in a country and still be called a visitor would be one year.

Most countries at the national level accept the United Nations' def-

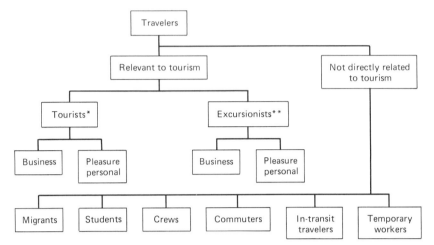

*One or more nights stay
**Arrive and depart same day

Figure 1-9   Classification of Travelers. (*Source:* Robert Christie Mill and Alastair M. Morrison, *The Tourism System: An Introductory Text*, [Englewood Cliffs, N.J.: Prentice-Hall, 1985], p. 100.

inition of visitors. The classification of travelers adopted by the World Tourism Organization is shown in Figure 1-9. Briefly, an international tourist is someone who spends at least one night, but no more than one year, in a country other than his or her own. The tourist can be there for a variety of reasons but not for pay from the country being visited. A person who meets the above criteria but who does not stay overnight is called an excursionist.

Domestic Tourist

World Tourism Organization. The World Tourism Organization has also proposed a definition for "domestic tourist" that is based on length of stay:

> any person residing within a country, irrespective of nationality, travelling to a place within this country other than his usual residence for a period of not less than 24 hours or one night for a purpose other than the exercise of a remunerated activity in the place visited. The motives for such travel may be:
>
> 1. leisure (recreation, holidays, health, studies, religion, sports);
> 2. business, family, mission, meeting.

A domestic excursionist is someone who meets the above definition but who does not stay overnight.[8]

National Tourism Resources Review Commission. In 1973 the National Tourism Resources Review Commission published its landmark study of tourism in the United States. In it, the commission proposed that a domestic tourist was one who traveled away from home for at least 50 miles one way. The travel could be for any reason except commuting to work.

The Canadian government specifies that a tourist is one who travels at least 25 miles outside his or her community.

Trip. The U.S. Census Bureau publishes the National Travel Survey every five years. In the 1963 and 1967 surveys the bureau defined a "trip" as "each time a person goes to a place at least 100 miles away from home and returns or is out-of-town one or more nights." Later surveys omitted the phrase "or is out-of-town one or more nights." This means that estimates of national tourist travel are understated as, for example, weekend trips to locations less than 100 miles away are not counted.

U.S. Travel Data Center. The prestigious Travel Data Center regularly collects, analyzes, and publishes data on travel and tourism in the United States. It has accepted the definition of the U.S. Census Bureau. Travel as part of an operating crew on a train, plane, bus, truck or ship, commuting to a place of work, or trips made by students to and from school are not included in the center's definition of a trip.

Travel, Tourism, and Recreation

For the purpose of this text, travel refers to the act of moving outside of one's home community for business or for pleasure but not for commuting or traveling to or from school.

Tourism is the term given to the activity that occurs when tourists travel. This encompasses everything from the planning of the trip, the travel to the place, the stay itself, the return, and the reminiscences about it afterwards. It includes the activities the travel undertakes as part of the trip, the purchases bought, and the interactions that occur between host and guest. In sum, tourism is all of the activities and events that occur when a visitor travels.

The term "recreation" overlaps in many ways with tourism. Recreation is what happens during an individual's leisure time. And leisure time is defined as the time people have discretion over. During leisure time, individuals can do what *they* want. The activities that people engage in during leisure time are known as recreation. Some say that to be "recreation" the activity should be constructive or pleasurable. This might involve either active or passive pursuits, indoor or outdoor activities. There is no time or distance aspect to recreation. A round of golf two miles from home after work would constitute recreation. If I packed my clubs into the car and drove 100 miles to a resort for the weekend, my round of golf would be part of tourism and I would be on a trip.

THE DIMENSIONS OF TOURISM

There are four major dimensions to tourism—attractions, facilities, transportation, and hospitality.

Attractions

Attractions draw people to a destination. As an inducer of growth they either are what first draws visitors to the area or, in terms of development, tend to be developed first.

Attraction may be a primary destination, such as Disney World, where it is attractive enough to be the primary motivation for a visit. It might also be a secondary destination—an interesting or necessary place to visit for one or two days on the way to the primary destination. Such places are also called *stopover* or *touring destinations.* A tourist driving from Washington, D.C., to Florida may, for example, stop for a day in Knoxville, Tennessee. Knoxville is the stopover destination on the way to the primary destination, Florida. From a marketing perspective it is important to know whether the visitor considers you a primary or secondary destination. Primary destinations are oriented toward the location of the market (say Disneyland) or to the site of the resource (for example, Aspen). This will be explored further in the chapters on destination development.

Attractions may be based on natural resources, culture, ethnicity, or entertainment.

Natural Resources. Every area is blessed to a certain extent with natural resources, which takes in the physical features, the climate, and the natural beauty of the area.

Each area has its own unique combination of natural resource features. The most important features for tourism are the attractiveness brought about by differences in temperature, the variety of the scenery, and the number of recreational opportunities the resources allow.

It is said that opposites attract, and that is certainly true in tourism. North Americans are drawn to the sun of Florida in winter; places that have no snow send tourists to the slopes of Colorado in winter. Because climatic changes are seasonal, it is desirable to make use of the natural resources throughout the year if possible. For years the resorts of Colorado relied totally on winter ski business. After one particularly

Figure 1–10   The importance of natural resources—Mt. Cook. (Courtesy New Zealand Tourist & Publicity Office.)

bad year ("bad" for a winter resort means little or no snow) resort owners realized that if the snowfall was poor their entire year was ruined. Now the resort areas are encouraging what is known as *multiple-use* of facilities. Mountains that provide for winter skiing can also accommodate hikers or water slides in summer.

Location, or accessibility, is very important to the success of a destination that relies upon natural resources. For most tourism destinations, there is a direct relationship between distance and demand—the farther away people are from the destination, the fewer their numbers visiting it as a proportion of total attendance.

The natural resources of a destination are very fragile. Because of its attractiveness the destination draws people. These visitors leave their marks (and sometimes their garbage) on the resource. As a result the destination becomes less attractive. Once the decline has started it is difficult to reverse. The key is to manage the resource in such a way that it will maintain its attractiveness to tourists.

Culture.   The culture of an area is the way of life of its people. It is exhibited in such things as places of historical interest, religion, the way people live, the way they are governed, and their traditions—both past and present. Part of the culture of the British is the tradition of afternoon tea and going down to the pub at night. Both are part of the attraction of visiting that country.

Ethnicity. The number one reason that people in North America take a trip is to visit friends and relatives. Because of the mobility of Americans (it is estimated that one out of five people moves each year) vacations are often used to renew ties with family and friends.

On an international level there is the desire to get back to one's homeland. Distinct travel patterns can be seen, such as the movement of Bostonians to Ireland and residents of Toronto to Scotland. There are two types of such tourists. First-generation tourists generally stay with relatives whereas later generations are more likely to stay in hotels. For the former there is a great desire to see things the way they remembered them. Later generations expect more of the creature comforts to which they have grown accustomed.

Entertainment. Tourists are often attracted to a place because of the entertainment provided. That entertainment may be a permanent feature of the destination such as a theme park or zoo. Obvious examples are Disney World, Six Flags Over Georgia, and the San Diego Zoo. The entertainment may be a temporary event such as the Superbowl or a county fair. There has been an increasing trend toward active participation in recreational activities. The attraction may not be to watch people run, for example, but to participate in the sport.

Facilities

Attractions bring people to the destination; facilities service them when they get there. Because they are away from home, the visitor requires certain things—a place to stay, something to eat and drink. Facilities support, rather than start, the growth of a destination. The major facilities are lodging places, restaurants for food and beverages, support services, and infrastructure.

Lodging. Almost half of all American tourists stay with friends and relatives when taking a trip. Despite this, lodging accounts for between one-fifth to one-fourth of total tourist expenditures.

To be successful a destination area needs sufficient accommodation of the right kind to appeal to the visitor. That may mean campsites, or bed and breakfast places in private homes, hotels, motels, or resorts. The type provided will depend upon the market being catered to.

As noted earlier in this chapter, the type of accommodation provided is, in part, determined by the transportation used by visitors to the destination. A system of bed and breakfast houses will work only if the visitors travel by car.

Food and Beverage.   The largest proportion of the tourist dollar is spent on food and beverage. A majority of tourists, when they travel, seem to want both food and drinks with which they are familiar. The British tourist craves cups of tea and fish and chips; the American wants hamburgers and ice water.

Yet some destinations have marketed their cuisine as part of the tourism experience. When destinations do this they create a demand for local products. This "backward" linkage means that other local industries share in the benefits of tourism. On the other hand, when destinations import food and beverage to meet tourists' needs, they keep less of the tourist dollar within the destination.

Support Services.   Support services for tourism include such things as souvenir or duty-free shops, laundries, guides, and recreational facilities.

Most support services for tourism are small businesses. This presents both advantages and potential difficulties for the destination. On the positive side, the fact that the businesses are small means that the tourist dollar is spread among those people within the destination. Many hosts share in the benefits of tourism. A major difficulty is that many small businesses fail because they lack the capital and/or the management expertise of larger operations.

Figure 1–11   Shopping in Hong Kong. (Courtesy Hong Kong Tourist Association.)

In many cases shopping becomes a major reason for traveling to a particular destination. Travelers will often go to Hong Kong solely for the shopping bargains. Even if shopping is not the major motivation it is important for most people to purchase gifts for those left at home as a souvenir to remind them of their trip. Souvenirs that are true to the area can serve several purposes. First, they help that "backward linkage," stimulating the economy by creating an industry of artisans. Second, souvenirs can serve as marketing devices. Tourists buy souvenirs and later display them in their home. Souvenirs act as constant reminders to them of their visit as well as being on view to visitors to their homes. Third, the making and selling of authentic souvenirs can help preserve the culture of an area. The Cuna Indians of Panama, in making *molas,* or blouses, for tourists, have kept that part of their culture alive.

It is important that support services be readily accessible to the tourist and that the services offered be of a quality and price level to meet tourists' needs.

Infrastructure.   The infrastructure of an area is comprised of the following: Water systems; communication networks; health care facilities; transportation terminals; power sources; sewage/drainage areas; streets/highways; security systems.

The attractions and facilities of a destination are not accessible to visitors until a basic infrastructure exists. However, it is not necessary that a fully developed infrastructure be in place. For some tourists in certain destinations the lack of modern highways may actually be an attraction. Several years ago the Irish Tourist Board ran a newspaper ad showing a motorist on a narrow road stuck behind a flock of sheep. The headline said: "A traffic jam in Ireland."

In most cases development of the infrastructure is the responsibility of the public sector. Any advances in the infrastructure benefit not only the tourist but also the residents of the area.

Infrastructure is costly and requires a long lead time to plan and develop.

Transportation

The basis of tourism is that people want to travel to a place that is different from that which they are used to—a different culture, different climate, different scenery. Different places are physically removed from each other. Hence the necessity to travel to them. Hence, also, the need for, and the importance of, transportation to get there—and to get there comfortably.

Conditions for Travel.   Travel between two points can be explained in terms of three factors: complementarity, intervening opportunity, and transferability.[9] For travel to take place there must be a demand in one place and supply in another. People in Scotland want sunshine (demand); the Mediterranean offers sunshine (supply); thus complementarity exists. This factor will induce travel only if no intervening opportunity is present. If the same guarantee of sunshine could be found closer to home then people from Scotland would not travel to the Mediterranean. This explains why more people from the northeastern United States travel to Florida for the sun than to California.

The third factor explaining travel is transferability—the distance between two points measured in time and money. Even if complementarity exists and there are no intervening opportunities, travel will not take place if the distance is perceived as being too far and/or the cost of travel is perceived as being too great.

There is an important relationship between transportation and tourism. The improvement of transportation facilities has stimulated tourism, whereas the expansion of tourism has increased the need for better transportation.

Saving Time.   Increasingly, people measure distance not in terms of miles or kilometers but in terms of time. They "spend" time to get from one point to another. Time can be saved in a variety of ways. New methods may be found to increase the speed by which the traveler is transported. A major factor in this regard was the introduction of jet aircraft in the 1950s. Planes could now fly at up to 600 miles per hour, effectively halving the time between destinations.

A second way of saving time is to improve such things as rail lines to allow for faster movement. Amtrak took this approach in the northeast corridor between Boston and Washington, D.C. The speed of its trains was limited not by the power and capabilities of the locomotives but by the poor condition of the track. Consequently, Amtrak spent a considerable amount of money on improving the roadbed, thereby reducing the time spent on the journey.

Time can be saved by scheduling full passenger loads. If a tour operator can guarantee an airline a full plane of tourists, the plane will leave when the operator wants it to leave. Departure times can then be scheduled that are convenient to the traveler.

As the speed of today's planes increases it often takes less time to fly between two airports than it does to get from the plane to downtown. Time is spent getting off the plane, waiting for luggage, finding ground transportation, and fighting the traffic in what is often a long journey, both in distance and time, to the downtown area. Time can be saved by considering ways to improve the travel from terminal to town by such means as high-speed rail connections. Passengers at Chicago's O'Hare and London's Heathrow airport can deplane and, without leaving cover, get on a train or tube to take them into the city.

Finally, time can be saved through the discovery and use of new

devices such as radar and automatic signalling devices. Advances in
these areas made during World War II were used after the war in the
commercial airline industry to improve service.

Hospitality

The hospitality of an area is the general feeling of welcome that tourists receive while visiting the area. People do not want to go where they
do not feel welcome. When most people think back on a trip it is not the
weather or the scenery that comes to mind. Most often it is a memory
of people—positive or negative interactions with other tourists, with the
people of the destination, or with the employees of restaurants, hotels,
and shops.

Destinations can encourage a feeling of hospitality in several ways.
First, it may be necessary to conduct a program to inform residents of
the destination of what tourism can do and is doing for their area. Too
often the residents only see the negatives—the long lines and high prices
caused, they feel, by tourists. A community awareness program can show
the benefits of both tourism and tourists. More specifically, for those who
come into contact with tourists through their work, hospitality training
may be necessary. Employees can be instructed in such things as the
importance of appearance, greeting guests, and being helpful.

Each time a tourist meets an employee or resident of a tourist area

Figure 1-12 Jamaican
hospitality. (Courtesy Jamaica Tourist Board.)

is a "moment of truth." How that employee or resident interacts with the tourist can either enhance the vacation or undo all the advertising that has gone into getting the visitor to travel to the destination.

ECONOMIC IMPORTANCE

The economic importance of tourism can be seen from the following figures:

- Global travel volume is over 4 billion arrivals; domestic tourism is about 90 percent of total travel worldwide. About 90 percent of domestic tourism occurs in Europe and the Americas.
- There are over 340 million international arrivals annually; excluding transportation, international tourism receipts were over $120 billion. Europe receives about two-thirds of all international arrivals although East Asia, the Pacific, the Middle East, and Africa are recording the highest proportional gains. International tourism receipts are over $120 billion annually.
- U.S. citizens make close to 30 million international trips a year, spending about $25 billion in the process. Over 22 million international tourists visit the United States and spend over $15 billion (including payments to U.S. flag carriers). Receipts from domestic tourism in the United States exceed $240 billion.

INFLUENCES ON TRAVEL PATTERNS

For tourism to happen, people need the time, the money, the means, and the motivation to travel.

Leisure

People spend their time in one of three ways: at work; engaged in necessary tasks (eating, sleeping, visiting sick aunts); or at leisure. Prior to the Industrial Revolution most people worked the land. The way they spent their time was influenced by the calendar and the weather.

The story is told of a farmer out with his plow on the Sabbath. He was working furiously to gather in his crops before an impending storm. His minister happened by and chided the farmer for working on the Sabbath.

"Now, Jock," said the minister, "even the Lord rested on the seventh day."

"Aye, minister," said the farmer with an eye on the approaching storm. "But he got finished and I didn't."

As people moved from the farms to the factories, time was controlled by the factory owners. Perhaps to have output on a continuous basis year-round, or perhaps to control the working classes, laborers were forced to work up to 70 hours a week. Their only day off was the Sabbath. Yet people were so tired and were paid so little that they had neither the energy nor the money to do anything or go anywhere. Moreover, the sanctity of the Sabbath was strictly enforced.

The first "holy days" were unpaid vacations. Even when an annual holiday was given, workers were not paid during the time they were off. Nevertheless, they at least had the time to spend. It took the rise in power of the trade unions in the 1920s and 1930s to fight for paid vacations. Today, the average workweek is less than 40 hours. Workers in the United States, West Germany, and Sweden have up to 40 days of paid leisure time a year. This is approximately twice that in Great Britain.

These days the demand is for blocks of time rather than reductions in the workday. The Uniform Monday Holidays Act established four three-day weekend holidays in the United States. This has an obvious impact on the opportunity for people to take a trip.

Over the years there has been much talk of a four- and eventually a three-day workweek. In reality, companies have not moved to the concept of a four-day workweek as quickly as forecasters thought. Studies that have been done indicate that, if people had more three-day weekends, they would likely take more weekend trips. However, people typically overestimate what they will do if and when they actually get the time. Studies of people who have four-day workweek jobs found that they tended to base their leisure time around the home because they were so tired from working.

Time is increasingly important to people. Unlike money, time cannot be saved. There is an increasing number of two-family households employed in the workplace. Additionally, a number of states are experimenting with year-round schooling. It will, therefore, become more difficult to find a time when all members of the family can get together for a vacation. Thus, there will be an increased demand for time-intensive activities. Such things as weekend packages and short cruises will appeal to families who have the money but not the time to travel.

Money

The second factor necessary for tourism to occur is money. Even when workers were first given an annual vacation they were not paid. As a result, few could travel. As paid vacations became the norm in the twentieth century, people had the time and the means to take a trip.

There are several aspects to the money required for travel. First, the money required is *discretionary*. That is, after obligations such as taxes,

Figure 1-13 Tourists need—and spend—money. (Courtesy Hong Kong Tourist Association.)

rent, and food are taken care of, individuals have discretion over how to spend the remainder of their money. It might be saved, it might buy a compact disk player, or it might be spent on a getaway weekend. This illustration helps us realize that the tourism dollar is in competition with other consumer products. Before we can get the tourists to our destination or facility we must first get them interested in the idea of taking a vacation.

Second, the major economic factor (outside of paid vacations) that has influenced tourism is the presence of more and more two-income families. With two spouses working outside the home more discretionary income is available. Indeed, as pointed out above, time, in many cases, is becoming scarcer than money.

Means to Travel

There are two aspects to mobility, or the means to travel. There is actual mobility, or the method people use to travel, such as air or automobile. Air and train travel tends to concentrate tourism; automobile and coach travel tends to disperse tourism development.

The second aspect to mobility is speed of movement. As people are able to travel faster, they save time and, with a limited vacation, can travel farther. As technology allows us to travel faster and faster, areas once thought inaccessible will now be within reach.

Motivation

Even if people have the time, the money, and the mobility to travel, tourism will not happen unless they have the motivation to take a trip. People buy vacations for the same reasons they buy anything else: They feel that, by making the purchase, they will satisfy their needs and wants. Motivation occurs when an individual is moved to satisfy a need.

We all have a variety of needs. Abraham Maslow identified a *hierarchy of needs.* Individuals are first concerned with physical needs—the need for food and drink, for example. As these needs are satisfied the individual's attention moves to a higher-level need—satisfaction of the need for safety, love and belonging, status, self-esteem, and self-actualization (being all that you can be). These higher-level needs are psychological rather than physical. To his original list, Maslow added two intellectual needs—the need to know and understand, and the need for aesthetics.

We may be unaware of a need but we know what we want. A couple may want a winter cruise but cannot exactly say why. The difference between a need and a want is that we are aware of our wants; we may not be aware of the underlying need we are seeking to satisfy. Too often marketers focus on advertising to the *want* without being aware of the underlying *need.* If the need can be established and advertised, the result will be a more powerful marketing appeal.

The couple who wanted a winter cruise may feel that, upon their return, they will be the envy of their neighbors (need for status). Or a single person may feel, after watching *Love Boat,* that the result will be to meet the partner of their dreams (need for love).

The point is that we buy vacations to satisfy our needs, but we may be unaware of these needs. The role of marketing is to turn needs into wants by making us aware of them. Advertisements might say "Be the envy of your friends" or "Meet the person of your dreams." This might trigger a response that, yes, we would like our neighbors to envy us or we would like to meet that special person.

The second role of advertising is to suggest some way in which the need, now turned into a want, can be satisfied. "Take this cruise . . . and be the envy of your friends." Or, "Take this cruise . . . and meet the person of your dreams." People are moved to action after seeing the message, and that is where the motivation comes in.

It should be pointed out that advertisers do not have to trumpet their message in the words noted above. The message can be given through pictures and words that get the point across without being bla-

Figure 1-14 Cruises satisfy many needs. (Courtesy New Zealand Tourist & Publicity Office.)

tant about it. One ad in Scottish newspapers showed two little girls in Canada. One is reading a letter. She turns to the other and says, "Guess what, Grandma and Grampa are coming . . . from Scotland!" Grandparents reading this have underlying needs for love, and the message makes them aware of that. Now they want to visit *their* grandchildren in Canada. They are motivated to travel. The message has not only made them aware of their need but also suggested how it can be satisfied.

When people have the time, the money, the means, and the motivation then they will become tourists.

CAREERS IN TRAVEL/TOURISM

The major industry segments associated with travel and tourism are:

- travel companies such as airlines, cruise ships, bus companies, and car rental companies;
- attractions such as theme parks and national parks;
- facilities such as hotels and food and beverage establishments;

- destination marketing such as convention centers, chambers of commerce, area associations, and states;
- channel marketing such as tour wholesalers and retail travel agents;
- other affiliated areas such as tourism research and travel journalism.

Travel

Air Lines. The domestic airlines employ over 450,000 people. Employees are classified as flight crew or ground crew. The flight crew, in turn, is made up of the flight deck crew and the cabin crew.

The flight deck crew consists of the captain or senior pilot, those responsible for operating the aircraft and supervising other crew members; the first officer or co-pilot, responsible for charting the route and computing flying time; and the second officer or flight engineer, who inspects the plane before takeoff and after landing and determines the amount of fuel needed. Newer planes are designed to require only two people in the cockpit—the pilot and the flight engineer.

A college degree is preferred for the cockpit crew. A commercial pilot's license is required. The flight engineer must have a flight engineer's rating, while pilots must have an instrument rating, an airline transport pilot's license, a radio operator's permit, and 1,500 hours of previous flight hours, usually received in the military or in general aviation.

Entrants usually begin as flight engineers. Promotion to first officer takes 5 to 10 years; to captain, an additional 10 years.

There can be up to 16 people in the cabin crew. The cabin crew is responsible for the care and safety of the passengers, and their duties range from serving food and beverages, to demonstrating safety equipment, giving first aid when required, and calming nervous flyers.

A college background is preferred for flight attendants. Training consists of a four- to six-week training program. They can aspire to positions as purser, in charge of a flight crew, training supervisor, or a variety of ground positions in sales or public relations for the airline.

Ground crew positions are in reservations and sales, passenger services, maintenance, and security. Reservation agents handle calls from passengers inquiring about flights and making reservations. Some college is preferred in addition to office experience and typing skills. Training lasts four weeks and includes lessons in the use of computers. Agents can advance to sales representative or flight attendant positions. In airline sales offices most employees work outside the office as sales representatives calling on potential customers such as travel agencies and the business travel departments of corporations.

Passenger service employees work in the airport terminal checking luggage, assigning seats, and boarding passengers.

Station managers and airport managers are found at airports. Every airline operating out of an airport employs a station manager who is responsible for the coordination of that airline's flights from that particular airport. The airport manager, on the other hand, is employed by the government authority that operates the airport and is responsible for the administration of the facility. This involves relations with the airlines, operation of the businesses within the airport, and the safety and maintenance of the aircraft. A college degree with a background in administration and an interest in air transportation or engineering is required.

Other positions are available in maintenance, security, and air traffic control.

Cruise Lines. In contrast to the airline industry, cruise lines employ approximately 10,000 Americans. The relatively low number of jobs is because most ships are registered in foreign countries and employ nationals of those countries.

Jobs can be either on board or ashore. On-board crew consist of the ship's crew and the hotel crew. For the ship's crew the captain is responsible for the operation of the ship and the safety of the crew and passengers. There are a number of officers who assist in this role. Graduation from officer training school and Coast Guard certification are required. Aspiring captains usually enter as third mate and get deck experience aboard ship.

Coast Guard experience is also required for engineers, who are responsible for the maintenance of the ship and are usually graduates of a marine academy. These qualifications are also required of the purser, the person responsible for the ship's paperwork and for handling money. The purser has a great deal of contact with ship passengers in the handling of traveler's checks, selling shore excursions, and assisting with customs and immigration requirements.

The hotel crew typically consists of a hotel manager—responsible for the operation of hotel services—various assistant managers, food and beverage managers, a cruise director and staff who arrange social and recreational activities, and a steward department responsible for the cleaning of cabins and the service of food and beverages.

People who aspire to management positions should have a college degree in hotel and restaurant management in combination with practical experience in various industry operations.

The easiest way to get into the cruise business is through a cruise line's office ashore. Entry-level positions are in reservations and sales. Sales representatives are involved in selling to others in the travel channel of distribution such as tour operators and retail travel agents. Advancement can occur to sales supervisor, fly/cruise specialist, or into marketing.

Motorcoach/Rail/Car Rental. Career opportunities in the motorcoach, railroad, and car rental industries revolve around reservations and sales positions. There are also jobs in maintenance and driving.

With the decline of passenger rail transport in the United States, positions are limited. On the other hand, deregulation has added opportunities in the motorcoach industry; car rental companies continue to grow and offer good career prospects.

Attractions

The vast majority of attractions operate in the private or the public sector. Private-sector attractions, such as theme parks and resorts, are in business to make a profit. Public-sector attractions, such as zoos, national parks, and museums, operate on a nonprofit basis.

Private Sector. In theme parks, opportunities exist in staffing the food service, gift shop, and rides. Many of these positions are seasonal, depending upon when the park is open. Often the way to a full-time position is by working as a seasonal employee.

A resort is both an attraction and a facility (see below). In addition to offering lodging and food and beverage outlets, the accent is on recreation. Instructors are required to teach the recreational activities offered at the resorts. Recreation programming or guest activity directors are needed to plan, design, and organize the guest activity programs for those staying at the resort. This position is similar to the social director aboard ship. A degree in park and recreation administration is desirable for such a job.

Public Sector. Many jobs in the public sector are civil service positions and require that the applicant pass appropriate civil service tests.

Attractions such as museums, parks, and zoos offer two kinds of positions. First, there are highly technical jobs requiring specialized knowledge and degrees. In museums a curator is responsible for locating, acquiring, and exhibiting the items on display. Advanced degrees in fine arts may be called for. A zoo director may be required to have a degree in zoology while national park specialists have degrees in botany, biology, or ecology. They should also have some knowledge of how to interpret to the visitor the nature of animals they work with in a way that is both educational and entertaining. This can be done through lectures, walks, exhibits, and displays. In parks the most visible position of this kind is the park ranger. Duties range from being an interpreter to being a police officer. A college degree and several years of experience are necessary for this position.

The second type of job is one that is of a support nature. Museums need security people; zoos require people to care for and clean up after the animals.

Facilities

Lodging.   A variety of jobs are available in the lodging industry. Within a hotel there are several departments, each with job opportunities. The major operating departments are in the front office, in housekeeping, and in food and beverage service. Typical entry-level positions would be baggage porter, desk clerk, room attendant, server, or kitchen helper. In the kitchen a specialized diploma in cooking would be required. While some managers rise to the top through on-the-job experience, the preferred route is through a specialized degree in hotel and restaurant administration followed by a period of working in the various departments.

Opportunities also exist in a number of support departments such as engineering, marketing, accounting, and convention services. While chief engineers can work their way through the ranks, specialist degrees and training are preferred in the other areas mentioned.

Food and Beverage.   Restaurant jobs are broken down into front-of-the-house and back-of-the-house. The former involves contact with the customer; the latter does not. Entry-level positions are the same for food and beverage departments in hotels. Specialized diplomas are sought for cooks and chefs. A degree is preferred for management positions.

Destination Marketing

The marketing of a destination is carried out by the staff of a chamber of commerce, convention and visitors bureau, state travel office, and, at the national level, a national tourist office.

Available jobs are mostly at the local level in a chamber of commerce or convention and visitors bureau. Most communities have one or the other, or both. A bureau can be staffed by as many as 60 people. Their job is to promote that particular destination. Much of the effort is spent on attracting conventions and groups. This requires a great deal of personal selling in addition to advertising and direct mail. A sales representative would be a typical entry-level position. The bureau's director would have a specialized degree in marketing or hospitality management.

State tourist offices average 30 employees. They are involved with planning and directing the marketing effort of the state to attract tourists. Jobs are available in research, advertising, and public relations. Specialized degrees are desired. The state travel director may be a politically appointed position.

Few job opportunities exist at the national level because of the lack of employees in the United States Travel and Tourism Administration

(USTTA). The majority of USTTA employees are assigned overseas and work primarily with the travel trade in countries with potential to send tourists to the United States.

Channel Marketing

Tour Wholesalers. Job opportunities in tour wholesaling or operation exist in operations, in tour management, and in sales and promotion. In operations, entry-level positions are receptionist and operations clerk. Receptionists handle calls from retail travel agents interested in booking tours. Receptionists can advance to the position of reservation supervisor, responsible for hiring and training new receptionists and handling group bookings and major accounts.

Operations clerks have little or no contact with retailers or the public. They handle the documentation for a tour, including passenger rosters, rooming lists, and other passenger tour documents. The operations supervisor is responsible for all operations staff.

Depending on the size of the office, specialist positions may be available for group coordinators, accountants, and costing specialists.

Negotiation of supplier prices and the creation of tours are handled either by the owner of a small company or the senior staff of a larger group.

The tour manager or director is responsible for the day-to-day operation of a tour. Opportunities exist for full- and part-time managers. The latter might be teachers who wish to lead a group during summer vacation. The tour manager must have expertise in foreign languages to lead a group overseas. Most wholesalers hire European nationals to manage a tour in Europe. The National Tour Association offers certification for people who have been in the tour industry for at least two years.

The sales representative calls on retailers and makes presentations to groups to promote the tours offered by the wholesaler.

Retail Travel Agent. Specialized training is required to get into a retail travel agency. A number of schools offer hands-on training for people interested in such work. It is also possible to move into the operations of an agency from other areas, particularly airline reservations. Such people can transfer skills and knowledge gained in working for the airlines to an agency. Another entry-level position is that of outside sales representative. This job involves selling the agency's services to individuals and groups.

Travel agents or counselors can take advanced courses from the Institute of Certified Travel Agents (ICTA). Upon completion of the program they are designated a Certified Travel Counselor (CTC). The American Society of Travel Agents (ASTA) also awards a proficiency certificate upon successful completion of an examination.

Agents may rise within an agency, go on to own their own agency, or move into a related area of travel. One such area is corporate travel management. A corporate travel manager handles the travel budget and policy for a company. This person can either work with an outside travel agency or establish an in-house travel department.

Other.   For those with specialized education and an interest in travel and tourism, opportunities exist in such areas as research for private consulting companies or public agencies, and travel writing and photography on a free-lance or salaried basis.

ENDNOTES

1. From Herodotus, *History of the Persian Wars* (440 B.C.), in *The Norton Book of Travel,* Paul Fussell, ed. (New York: W.W. Norton & Company, 1987), pp. 36–37.

2. From Sir John Mandeville, *Travels* (1356–1357), in *The Norton Book of Travel,* Paul Fussell, ed. (New York: W.W. Norton & Company, 1987), p. 67.

3. E.S. Bates, *Touring in 1600* (Boston and New York: Houghton Mifflin), pp. 58–59. Copyright 1911 by E.S. Bates.

4. Geoffrey Trease, *The Grand Tour* (New York: Holt, Rinehart & Winston, 1967), p. 13.

5. H. Robinson, *A Geography of Tourism* (London: MacDonald and Evans Ltd., 1976), p. 11.

6. *Tourism Policy and International Tourism in OECD Member Countries,* Paris: Organization for Economic Cooperation and Development, 1980, pp. 5–7.

7. *Technical Handbook on the Collection and Presentation of Domestic and International Tourism Statistics,* Introduction (Madrid: World Tourism Organization, 1981).

8. Ibid., Part 2: Domestic Tourism.

9. Robinson, *Geography of Tourism,* p. 97.

S T U D Y   QUESTIONS

1. In the days of early travel
   - why did people travel?
   - what factor encouraged the development of water travel?
2. What factors during the Empire Era encouraged travel?
3. How did the Renaissance influence travel?
4. What was the Grand Tour?
5. The Victorian era influenced travel in two significant ways. What were they?
6. What led to the development of spas and seaside resorts?

7.   How did early travel in the United States develop?

8.   Which comes first—transportation or accommodation? Give examples.

9.   Define: tourism; tourist; international tourist; domestic tourist; excursionist; domestic excursionist; trip; recreation.

10. What are the four major dimensions of tourism and the four factors necessary for people to travel?

D I S C U S S I O N   QUESTIONS

1.   What factors are necessary for the development of travel and tourism? Give examples from the various eras of travel as to how these factors contributed to tourism.

2.   How does transportation shape tourism? Give examples from the times of the stagecoach, rail, water, road, and air travel.

3.   Define the following: tourism; travel; foreign tourist; domestic tourist; foreign visitor; domestic visitor; excursionist; trip.

4.   Discuss the importance of the four major dimensions of tourism.

WHO IS
THE TOURIST?

At the end of this chapter the reader will be able to:

- Identify and discuss what motivates tourists to travel.
- Describe the characteristics of the various segments of demand for travel.
- Describe the impact that physical factors play in the development of various types of tourism.
- Identify various principles that explain travel movements.
- Define and correctly use the following terms:

Maslow's Hierarchy of Needs	Segments of the market
Regular business travel	Meeting
Convention travel	Congress
Incentive travel	Hybrid trip
Pleasure travel	

Tourists come in a variety of shapes and sizes. This chapter explores in greater detail what motivates the tourist to travel. We then go on to examine the characteristics of the market and the tourists' travel patterns.

MOTIVATIONS

As noted in the previous chapter, people take vacations because they feel that, by doing so, they will satisfy various needs and wants. Abraham Maslow identified a set of universal needs that he arranged in a hierarchy. These needs are physical, psychological, and intellectual. By understanding what makes people travel we can do a better job of advertising to them to induce them to travel. Additionally, we can do a better job of catering to their needs if we know what those needs are.

Physical

The most basic need of all is physical. When people worked 70 hours a week for 50 weeks a year they saved a little each week for their two-week break. During those two weeks they "escaped" from their everyday life. They recharged their weary bodies and did things they did not have a chance to do during the year. They ate too much, drank too much, took afternoon naps in a deckchair on the beach.

Today the escape may be more mental than physical. As the physical demands have been reduced for many people, the mental demands have increased. It is increasingly difficult for the white-collar manager to "clock out" mentally at the end of the day. It often takes several days in a vacation spot before the person seeking mental relaxation can tune-out the office.

The key words that are heard are such terms as:

GET AWAY   ESCAPE   RELAX   CHANGE OF PACE

MELLOW OUT   BREAK

Different people in different circumstances look for different ways of expressing this. The harried executive desires a secluded spot away from telephones and interruptions. The couple in a northern city want to escape the winter snow. The rural family seeks the excitement of a seaside resort. The 9-to-5 office worker longs for the adventure of an exotic getaway. The factor that explains these varied examples is "opposite." It is said that a change is as good as a rest. As noted before, opposites attract. The key in attracting and satisfying the traveler who seeks satisfaction of physical needs is to look at his or her everyday life and provide something different.

Safety

When we take care of our bodies we are helping ensure that we will live a longer life. This is a very basic motivation. It shows itself in people who travel for health or to engage in recreational pursuits.

As was seen in the previous chapter, people have long traveled for health reasons. Doctors would prescribe trips to the seaside for the beneficial effects of the bracing air. The resorts in Switzerland were predated by sanitoria where people were sent because of the unpolluted air and sunshine. Today, medical opinion is less in favor of the impact of sun on the skin. While warnings of skin cancer abound, for many the warmth of the sun is very beneficial. In fact, it is said that the area around the pool at a Florida resort is a sardine's revenge: "Many bodies, crammed into a tight space, covered in oil."

An increasing tendency these days is for people to participate in various recreational activities. The top recreational pursuits in the United States have remained popular for the past decade. They are swimming, walking, bicycling, fishing, and team sports. The past decade has seen a significant growth in canoeing, jogging, roller skating, racquetball, soccer skiing, and tennis. A major trend has been a move toward physically demanding activities.

The major words associated with participation in outdoor recreation are:

FUN   EXERCISE   KEEP IN SHAPE

OUTDOORS   HEALTH   FEEL GOOD   FRESH AIR

Belonging

The need for belonging is expressed in the desire to be with friends and family—to be part of a group, to belong. People, by and large, are social beings. They want communication and contact with others.

There are several aspects to this motivation. First, the fact that people move their residences—on average, once every five years—means that family and friends can renew relationships by using vacation time to keep in touch. The major reason given for taking a trip in the United States is "visiting friends and relatives." Typically, this type of tourism involves travel by auto. Many stay with friends and family at the destination. Hotels and restaurants along the way are the recipients of this type of travel.

Second, there is ethnic tourism—the desire to find one's roots. This involves the desire to "return to the homeland." Two segments of the market were mentioned earlier. First-generation visitors go back to see things as they remembered them. They will often stay with friends. This cuts down on the economic importance of this segment to the destination. On the other hand, little in the way of development or facilities is needed, for these tourists want to see things as they were. Later generations have grown up somewhere else and have become used to the conveniences in their country of birth. Consequently, they desire the comforts of home. That costs money for the destination in terms of the provision of facilities. On the other hand, this group is more likely to stay in hotels and to eat in restaurants. They spend more money at the destination than does the former group.

While these are the two primary segments of this market, in other

Figure 2-1 Visiting friends. (Courtesy Jamaica Tourist Board.)

cases people may travel to begin or renew relationships. Club Med is one organization that originally appealed to the singles crowd. They advertised a carefree, activity-based opportunity to meet and mingle with the opposite sex. As changing demographics brought a mini baby boom, Club Med sought to appeal to families with young children.

It is not necessary to be young to have a relationship. There are an increasing number of "empty nesters" in the marketplace. An empty nester is a couple whose children have left home. For so many years the focus of the couple's life had been the children—getting them through school, taking them to sports activities, Boy Scouts, and Girl Guides; onto dating and the senior prom. Now they are on their own. Because the focus had been on the children, parents, oftentimes, had spent little or no time on their own relationship. They may even feel apprehensive about this "stranger"—their spouse—who is, all of a sudden, the one they are spending time with. Such things as coach tours offer an opportunity to renew the relationship while being part of a larger group. The group offers the "security" of being able to mix with others rather than have the "pressure" of talking to the same person for the entire trip.

This motivation is expressed by such things as:

FAMILY TOGETHERNESS   COMPANIONSHIP

MAINTAINING PERSONAL TIES   INTERPERSONAL RELATIONS

ROOTS   ETHNICITY

SHOWING AFFECTION FOR FAMILY MEMBERS

Esteem

The two aspects to this motivation are self-esteem and esteem from others. When people travel to a conference to increase their business knowledge they are concerned with their own personal development. This translates directly into feeling more confident about their ability to perform the job. Their self-esteem is enhanced.

We also seek esteem from others. People often buy things to "keep up with the Joneses." They are concerned about what others think, and they feel that what they buy and where they go is a reflection of themselves. It has been said before that, in tourism, "mass follows class." Royalty and film stars determine where the "in places" are. Others follow in the hope that they will be seen by their friends as status people. Their egos are being massaged.

The phrases used to describe this are:

CONVINCE ONESELF OF ONE'S ACHIEVEMENTS   PRESTIGE

SHOW ONE'S IMPORTANCE TO OTHERS   STATUS

SOCIAL RECOGNITION   EGO-ENHANCEMENT

PROFESSIONAL/BUSINESS   PERSONAL DEVELOPMENT

ACHIEVEMENT   MASTERY

COMPETENCE   FASHION

Self-Actualization

Self-actualization involves being true to one's nature. It means knowing who you are and using your gifts to the fullest. If we consider leisure to be the freeing of ourselves from lower-level needs, then self-actualization is the end goal of leisure.

Self-actualization is seen in:

EXPLORATION AND SELF-EVALUATION   SELF-DISCOVERY

SATISFACTION OF INNER DESIRES

To Know and Understand

The desire for knowledge is felt in a great number of people. It is truly said that travel broadens the mind. After we have traveled to a particular place, for example, we are more interested in news items or television programs about it. Our interest is sparked by the fact that we have personal experience of it. It was the desire for knowledge that was the reason for the growth of the Grand Tour. Still today, we feel an "obligation" to visit museums and monuments at a distant destination.

By learning about other cultures we can also discover our own. Some of the ways in which this is expressed are:

CULTURAL   EDUCATION   WANDERLUST

Aesthetics

The last of Maslow's needs refers to the appreciation of beauty. Those who are concerned with the environment or who like to view scenery are expressing this need.

Maslow believed that lower-level needs had to be satisfied to some extent before the satisfaction of higher-level needs became a concern. This would mean that vacations, which were targeted toward the satisfaction of lower-level needs, would be more resistant to barriers to travel. In times of a gasoline shortage, for example, people would be less likely to put off a trip to visit friends and relatives than a drive to take a scenic tour.

If we in the business of tourism are aware of the underlying reason for taking a vacation (the satisfaction of various needs) then more effective marketing campaigns can be developed to meet those needs. More effective appeals will lead to more people buying trips. Additionally, we

Figure 2-2   Matterhorn.
(Courtesy Cunard.)

will be better able to satisfy those needs if we are aware of the (often hidden) real reason for traveling.

SEGMENTS OF THE MARKET

A *segment* of the market is a part of the market whose members have similar characteristics. In this way it is possible to market to them as a group. In tourism the major segments are business travelers and pleasure travelers.

Business Travelers

The segments of the business market are regular business travelers; business people attending meetings, conventions, and congresses; and finally, incentive travel.

Regular Business Travel.   Approximately one in every five trips taken in Canada and the United States is for business reasons. As business increasingly becomes international in scope there is an increase in inter-

Figure 2-3 Government travel is business travel—Parliament Buildings, Wellington City, New Zealand. (Courtesy New Zealand Tourist & Publicity Office.)

national business travel also. The business ties between North America and Europe have traditionally been strong. Of late, however, the focus has been on increasing business ties with the Far East. We have seen, and would expect to continue to see, an increase in international business travel between these two areas.

The bulk of North American business travel involves the airlines. Business travelers tend to be well educated, affluent, have high-level jobs, and fly often. Their profile makes them excellent prospects for pleasure as well as business travel.

Increasing numbers of women today travel on business. They presently comprise between 15 and 25 percent of the market. Women business travelers

1. are slightly younger;
2. tend to stay longer at their destinations;

3. are more apt to be unmarried;
4. are more likely to be attending a meeting or convention;
5. are more likely to book through a travel agent;
6. have a greater preference for downtown accommodations closer to their work;
7. are more concerned with the security aspects of their accommodation facilities.

Both airlines and hotels are making special efforts to appeal to this group of travelers. The cost of a trip is paid for by the company as a cost of doing business. In addition, it is often a reflection of the image the business wants to project. For example, it might impress clients to meet in a luxury property. As a result, airlines appeal to business travelers through the provision of first-class and business-class seating. These facilities offer wider seats and more leg room. Business travelers can argue to their companies that, because they have more space, they can more readily work as they travel.

Many hotels offer special executive floors and have secretarial, telex, and computer facilities available. The Meridien Hotel in New Orleans offers these and other business services on a complimentary basis seven days a week.

Frequent-flyer and frequent-stay programs have been developed to encourage the business traveler to choose one particular company. By flying a certain number of miles or staying a specific period, the traveler can choose a bonus flight or hotel stay. After 45,000 miles of travel on Continental, the TravelBank member can claim a first-class ticket within the United States, Canada, or Mexico. Each stay at a Sheraton Hotel accumulates points toward gifts from a catalog. The various sectors of the industry have also gotten together so that staying at a particular hotel, renting from a specific car rental company, and flying a particular airline will accumulate points for the one program.

As businesses have become more concerned with the bottom line they have begun to look more closely at the way their employees rack up travel prizes. An employee may have the choice of a less expensive airline but choose the one whose incentive program he or she belongs to. The Internal Revenue Service is also exploring whether or not these awards should be taxable. Lastly, a new industry has emerged consisting of companies who "buy" accumulated mileage trips and sell them to others. The airlines have become rather upset about this because it defeats the purpose of their efforts—to reward the frequent flyer.

Meetings, Conventions, Congresses.   About 20 percent of all business trips are for the purpose of attending corporate meetings or conventions. Conventions may be institutional or corporate/government. The term "institutional" means associations and other groups that have a shared purpose. The "corporate/government" segment refers to organizations that deal with specific business or government concerns. They tend to be private in nature.

A congress, convention, or meeting is defined thus:

> a regular formalized meeting of an association or body, or a meeting sponsored by an association or body on a regular or ad hoc basis. Depending on the objectives of a particular survey, this may be qualified by a minimum size, by the use of premises, by a minimum time or/and having a fixed agenda or program.[1]

Over 80 percent of American associations hold a major annual convention for their members. In addition, many businesses bring managers together with corporate staff at least once a year. This complements the numerous local and regional meetings held annually.

Conventions can be international, continental, national, or regional. International conventions involve participants from more than two foreign nations and take place in different countries each year. They are usually nongovernmental in nature. It is forecast that the number of attendees of such events will have doubled between 1973 and 1993. An example is the International Association of Scientific Experts in Tourism, which in recent years has met in Europe, Africa, and North America.

Continental conventions limit their meetings to one continent. The Travel and Tourism Research Association has meetings in the United States and Canada.

National conventions tend to be limited by their by-laws or by tradition to meeting within the country within which the parent organization is located. Usually participants are citizens of that country. National conventions may rotate around the country geographically to give representation to all its members.

Regional conventions are organized at the state, provincial, or regional level.

It is estimated that expenditures on meetings and conventions by associations run about $35 billion; over $11 billion is spent by corporations. On average in 1985, convention delegates each spent $464, staying on average four nights. Almost half was spent on lodging, 25 percent on food, and just over 10 percent for retail purchases.

Alarmed at the amount of money being spent on conventions outside the United States, the federal government has attempted to control convention expenditures. In 1976 the Tax Reform Act permitted U.S. corporations to hold only two conventions a year outside the United States. Attendees were allowed to deduct expenses from only two foreign conventions a year. In addition, detailed records had to be kept by the organization and the attendees. These regulations lasted four years. A new law is in effect that allows U.S. residents to deduct all relevant expenses in the "North American Zone," which includes Canada and Mexico.

Incentive Travel.   An increasing number of companies offer travel as a reward to their employees who have met company objectives. Travel is used as an incentive to perform. It has been noted that

> travel which is earned through effort salves not only the ego, but the conscience as well.

A company might have a sales contest to increase sales volume. Quotas are set for the sales staff. Those who surpass their quota by a set amount are eligible for the trip. The average incentive travel trip lasts five days and involves an average of 174 people. The most popular incentive travel destinations are Mexico, the Caribbean, Bermuda, and Europe. Within the United States, Hawaii, Las Vegas, Miami, Disney World, San Francisco, San Diego, and New Orleans are popular.

A number of specialized companies have developed to handle these trips. They not only design the incentive program but also organize the travel itself. Many belong to the Society of Incentive Travel Executives, or SITE. These companies act as tour wholesalers. Buying for a group, they can negotiate special rates from the airlines, hotels, and ground transportation companies they deal with. To this they add a 15 to 20 percent markup for their services and costs in packaging the trip.

Hybrid.   The hybrid trip is one in which the traveler combines business and pleasure. Business travel can be "converted" into pleasure travel in one or more of three ways. First, the traveler may bring his or her spouse along. The spouse is a pleasure traveler while the business traveler works.

Second, the traveler may decide to stay before or after a meeting. A business trip to Denver in January may induce a traveler to arrive on the previous Friday for a weekend of skiing. People in managerial and professional positions account for seven out of ten business trips. Approximately 20 percent of these travelers tack on vacation days to business trips.

Third, the traveler attending a convention may decide to return, either alone or with family, for a pleasure trip at another time of the year. Fully one-third of business travelers revisit vacation sites where they had previously attended meetings or conventions.

As more and more spouses enter the business world, the opportunity for hybrid trips will increase. The major problem will be in meshing the two work schedules.

Pleasure Travel

A study by The Longwoods Research Group Ltd. for Tourism Canada broke the U.S. pleasure travel market into eight types, based on trip purpose.[2] Researchers found that approximately 130 million Americans, aged 16 or over, take nearly 500 million overnight pleasure trips a year and spend nearly 2 billion nights away from home. The study notes, however, that most travelers are in the market for more than one type of vacation trip and suggests segmenting the market on types of trips rather than types of markets.

Visiting Friends and Relatives.   Visiting friends and relatives accounts for 44 percent of total trip-nights (one trip-night is one trip that lasts one night; two trips that last four nights each would be eight trip-nights). These trips tend to be relatively unplanned, involve little use of travel agents or the media, and are of short duration.

Close-to-Home.   Close-to-home leisure trips account for 13 percent of all trip-nights and are also relatively unplanned and of short duration. Additionally, little use is made of the media for information on where to go. The average length of stay is between two and three days. Eighty-five percent of the travelers use their own cars. Just over one-third stay in motels while one-sixth use a hotel or stay with friends and relatives. Over 10 percent camp or take a trailer.

Touring Vacations.   Touring vacations make up 14 percent of all trip-nights. These trips have no single focus. They last an average of eight days, are planned one to two months in advance, and, while friends are the most used source of information, travel agents and the media are also important. One out of five trips involves a package deal. This type of tourist is interested in beautiful scenery with lots to see and do. Such individuals want to visit a well-known, popular area that offers familiar landmarks and is definitely not dull. In over one-quarter of the trips at least part of it is booked through a travel agent. These tourists tend to travel by car, although in one-quarter of the cases a plane is used. One out of eight travel by bus. Friends and relatives provide the accommodation 20 percent of the time; the remainder of the stays are split between motels and hotels.

Outdoor Trips.   Those taking outdoor trips represent 10 percent of all trip-nights. These people tend to plan their trip less than one month in advance and rely most on the advice of friends for places to go. The average length of the trip is between three and four days. These individuals are interested in beautiful scenery with lots to see and do. They want real adventure but not too wild; they want to travel not too distant, and most

Figure 2–4   Outdoor trips—Kaiteriteri Beach, Nelson, New Zealand.
(Courtesy New Zealand Tourist & Publicity Office.)

are interested in fishing and hunting. This tourist travels exclusively by car, truck, or van and, in two-thirds of the cases, stays in a campground or trailer park.

Resort Vacations.   Eight percent of the trip-nights are spent on resort vacations. Travel by plane accounts for almost 30 percent of the travel. Tourists stay either in a hotel (31 percent), motel (26 percent), lodge (14 percent), or condominium (13 percent). The average length of stay is five days, and in one out of five cases the trip is part of a package deal. This segment accounts for the greatest use of a rental car (15 percent). These tourists want to visit a place that is popular in a well-known area and that has beautiful scenery with lots to see and do. They want a place that is exciting yet still offers the opportunity for walking and strolling. Over one-third of these trips are planned more than three months in advance while another third are planned between one and two months ahead of time. Travel agents are used both for information and for booking the trip in one-fourth of the trips. The resort traveler is interested in relaxing, getting away, and being entertained. Less than 20 percent are interested in golf or tennis.

City Trips.   City trips make up 7 percent of all trip-nights. Half of these trips are booked less than one month in advance. They tend to be a short, impulsive getaway. The family car is the predominant (70 percent) mode of transportation while, at the destination, three-quarters of the travelers stay in a hotel or motel. Staying with friends and relatives makes up the remainder. For this tourist it is important that the city be famous with first-class hotels and elegant restaurants. It should be popular, definitely not dull, and should have well-known monuments. These tourists are less interested in nightclubs and bars.

Theme Parks/Special Events.   Visits to theme parks or special events make up only 3 percent of all trip-nights. Over 40 percent are planned less than one month ahead while just over a quarter are planned between one to two and over three months in advance. This traveler is interested in a well-known, even world-class, attraction, something that offers activities for all ages, that has lots to see and do, that is exciting, and that the children would enjoy. The average trip lasts just under four days. Three-fourths of the trips involve the use of a car; in one out of ten situations it is a rental car. Just under 20 percent of the trips involve staying with friends or relatives; the remainder of the stays are split between hotels and motels.

Cruise.   Lastly, there is the cruise. Accounting for 1 percent of total trip-nights, people who take cruises want to enjoy beautiful scenery, something different with lots to see and do. They want real adventure, do not want the trip to be dull, and are interested in all the comforts. Cruises average over six days, and almost two-thirds of such trips are packages. Most cruises are planned more than three months in advance. This segment of the market is the only one where the advice of a travel agent (67 percent) is sought more than a friend's (51 percent).

FACTORS INFLUENCING THE LOCATION OF TOURISM

Sun, Sea, and the Resort

The most important factors that explain the location of tourist attractions and facilities are physical. The growth of mass tourism in Europe is explained by the fact that there are large urban areas in the north of Europe that experience cool and cloudy weather and relatively underpopulated areas in the south with warm, sunny weather.

As a result, the summer months see major movements of Germans to Spain and Italy to bask in guaranteed sunshine at the beach. When the same attraction is sold—sunshine, beach, warm water—cost becomes important. As an example, tourist traffic has moved away from Italy and the south of France to Spain because that country was able to provide the same vacation experience while holding down the costs of accommodation and food. More recently the Eastern European countries of Yugoslavia, Romania, and Bulgaria have been competing successfully for the same business.

As more and more people have been able to afford both summer and winter travel, resorts in the north of Europe have experienced a decline. In Britain, Brighton served the population of London while Blackpool acted as the getaway by the sea for Britain's industrial north. In the United States, Atlantic City served the same function for the New York–Philadelphia area. With advances in transportation and economic growth of the population these resorts suffered greatly. Atlantic City looked to the legalization of gambling to revitalize itself. It could no longer compete on the basis of climate and beach.

A major part of the physical resource of resorts, in addition to the sunshine, is the quality of the beach. In general, a "good" beach is one that offers good-quality sand and a gentle slope into the sea without dangerous currents. The character and slope of the beach also create the conditions for surfing, so popular in California, Hawaii, and Australia.

For many resorts, boating and sailing are important. In these instances the beach is less important. What is important are a sheltered bay or channel, the lack of reefs and rocks, and a good harbor.

A major criticism of resorts is that they tend to isolate the tourist from the host population. This is probably the way the majority of tourists want it. When people travel to swim in clear water or lie on the beach they are thinking of pampering themselves, not understanding another culture. Yet this can create an "elitist" type of tourist and tourism where the economic benefits of tourism do not extend to many of the local people. It is argued that tourism can be a stimulant to peace because it encourages contact between different peoples. By keeping tourists physically separate from the host culture the benefits of that interaction are lost.

Winter Resorts.   The French Riviera originally debuted as a winter resort area. Because of its mild winter temperatures, the area appealed to a high-class clientele who could afford to take a winter break. There still is tourist traffic in the winter that seeks the sun and the warmth. In North America this movement is apparent in the winter when droves of northerners descend on Florida.

However, when we think of winter resorts we think of cold climate areas and winter sports. Most people take their annual vacation in the summer months. However, a growing number of people can afford a second vacation in the winter. The growing popularity of winter sports has meant significant business for winter resort areas.

Of all the winter sport activities skiing is the most popular. It is of relatively recent origin, having been introduced into the Swiss Alps in the 1890s from Norway. It took the invention of the ski lift in the 1930s

Figure 2–5 Winter resort fun—Turoa Skifield, New Zealand. (Courtesy New Zealand Tourist & Publicity Office.)

to spur the development of skiing and the introduction of the safety binding in the 1960s to start the mass appeal of the sport. Alpine skiing in the Alps has formed the model for downhill skiing.

Successful ski resorts require a good snow cover, hilly, if not mountainous, terrain, bearable temperatures, relatively long hours of daylight, and accessibility to the market. The success or failure of major resort areas depends on the presence or lack of these factors. Much of the southern Alps, for example, cannot guarantee sufficient snow for extended periods of time. Even in the northern Alps the combination of snow and sunshine is sometimes lacking. The mountains of Norway can offer the snow conditions, but the cold temperatures combined with the short daylight hours limit their popularity in the winter months. They manage to attract the spring skier in impressive numbers.

Scotland has attempted to develop its ski facilities. It has a west coast marine climate and the snow conditions are very variable. But Scotland attracts few skiers from outside Britain.

Some skiing is done in the Pyrenees between France and Spain. The areas on the French side, however, do not offer easy access to major centers of population. In the west the snow cover cannot be guaranteed. In Eastern Europe the best overall conditions are in the Carpathians.

In North America the Laurentians (outside Quebec) appeal to American tourists from the East and Midwest. In the Rockies, most tourists come from Texas and the Midwest. The major markets are regional and national.

In addition to the physical factors, the successful resort must invest heavily in a variety of facilities. Hotels must be built to house the skiers, ski lifts to transport them up the mountain, snow plows to keep the roads clear, grooming equipment to keep the slopes smooth, and *apres* ski bars and restaurants to allow for socializing.

Two types of development are apparent. The village that is self-contained—having a "life" of its own as well as a transportation system—is referred to as a resort development. A "center," on the other hand, is a much larger area with ski lift stations some distance apart and linked by public transportation. In some cases centers have been created from scratch, most notably in France and Italy. Vail, in Colorado, is an example of such a center.

A fairly recent move has been the construction of condominium complexes rather than the traditional hotel development. In a condominium each room or suite is owned by an individual or individuals. The common areas—walkways, reception areas, etc.—are owned jointly by the suites' owners. A maintenance fee is paid for the general upkeep of the facility. In some types of development the owners put their units into a pool and hire a management company to rent the facilities to others like a "regular" hotel.

For years cross-country skiing has been popular in Scandinavia. It did not grow in popularity in the United States and Alpine Europe until the 1970s. It is much cheaper than downhill skiing, is good exercise, is not dangerous, and can be done even on flat terrain. It is more important as a local type of recreation as distinct from an attraction that will bring tourists from afar.

A final note on mountainous resorts is the development of areas to appeal to tourists wishing to escape the summer heat. In the Himalayas, Darjeeling and Simla were developed as summer resorts for the British wishing to escape the heat of the plains. Resorts in the Catskills served the same purpose for those from New York City.

Scenery

Prior to the middle of the eighteenth century, nature was not regarded as an attraction. The Alps, for example, were to be avoided if at all possible during the Grand Tour. The Romantic movement changed this attitude. Now it became fashionable to enjoy the scenery rather than ignore it.

Scenery can be classified as landforms, water, and vegetation. Landforms are such things as mountains, canyons, or cliffs. The size of the Grand Canyon or of Mount Kilimanjaro cannot fail to impress. Water adds beauty to any scene. Water is important not only for its effect on the attractiveness of the area but also because of the recreational possibilities it opens up. Swimming, boating, and fishing are all activities enjoyed by many. The vegetation of the temperate forests of the Amazon, the moors of England, the fall colors in New England, and the tulip fields of Holland all attract the tourist.

Two important points can be made in regards to scenery. First, it does not cost the tourist anything to enjoy it. There is no "admission charge." Second, the variety of scenery is important. An area that offers a different type of landscape every few minutes can successfully compete with such giant landforms as the Rockies and the Grand Canyon.

Hunting and Fishing

While many people travel to view animals in captivity or in their natural surroundings, others travel to hunt them. Hunting is typically a local sport. However, a certain amount of travel is done to shoot wild game in Africa. Eastern European countries also advertise hunting vacations to Western tourists to shoot species of animal not found in the West.

Fishing tends also to attract from a local base. Countries like Scotland, Canada, Ireland, and Norway have successfully sold the idea of fishing in unspoiled surroundings to tourists from other countries. River and lake fishing tends to be done in northern areas. These areas make special efforts to breed sport fish such as salmon and trout. Deep-sea fishing, on the other hand, is found primarily in the tropics or subtropics. Fishing for swordfish and tuna is particularly popular. There have been some, largely unsuccessful, attempts to introduce shark fishing into northern waters. Spear fishing by divers with snorkels or breathing apparatus is also popular in the warmer waters of the Southern Hemisphere.

Spas and Health Resorts

The importance of spas as part of the historical development of tourism has been covered earlier. Advances in medicine and a lack of faith in the powers of mineral waters have combined to reduce the importance of spas. However, a great deal of faith in the curative properties of spa treatments still exist amongst the Germans. Some spas in Central and Eastern Europe remain popular. Rheumatism is treated in Slovakia through mud-bath treatments and attracts a large number of visitors from Arab countries.

The movement toward a greater health consciousness has given rise to so-called fat farms that offer a strict regimen of diet and exercise.

Figure 2-6   Fishing in Lake Brunner, New Zealand. (Courtesy New Zealand Tourist & Publicity Office.)

Urban Attractions

Many cities have a special character and atmosphere all to themselves. Paris, London, San Francisco, New York, and Amsterdam are obvious examples. This comes from a combination of distinctive architecture, pleasant streets or canals, good food and drink, and the lifestyles of the people who live there.

The two major groups of cities, as far as tourism is concerned, are *old* and *modern*. Rome, Athens, and Jerusalem attract the tourist seeking ruins, classical architecture, and museums. New York, West Berlin, and San Francisco offer modern architectural features, theaters, luxury hotels, and excellent cuisine. Some cities, such as London, Paris, and Rome, offer a combination of the two.

Some smaller cities are known for a particular feature and tend to be included as part of a tour. Examples are Stratford-Upon-Avon (Shakespeare), Edinburgh (the Castle), and Pisa in Italy (the Leaning Tower).

Cities of the non-Western world are known for their exotic appeal. Marrakesh, Istanbul, and Bangkok are cities that bring an image of excitement.

When young people travel they tend to make cities their destination. This was particularly true in the "hippie travel" of the 1960s. Many cities tried to prevent or restrict this type of travel because the visitors did not spend much and often created problems with drugs and thievery. Amsterdam, however, seemed to encourage it. This in itself was an attraction to the many "regular tourists" who came to stare at the young hippies.

Travel to towns for religious pilgrimages has been important throughout history. While this still generates some tourism, in the Christian world only travel to Rome and the Holy Land are of major significance. Shrines of more recent importance at Fatima in Portugal and Lourdes in France attract many believers annually. In the Moslem world the pilgrimage to Mecca is the most important of all religious reasons to travel.

Rural Attractions

Attractions of a rural nature tend to have a historical basis. It may be a castle, palace, or monastery. It may be a battlefield such as Waterloo in Belgium or Gettysburg in the United States.

In the developing countries such attractions are primarily the ruins of ancient civilizations. Examples are the Pyramids and the Sphinx in Egypt and the Mayan ruins in Mexico.

Sporting Events

Events like the Olympic Games, the Super Bowl, and the World Cup can bring many visitors to a destination. The event itself is usually short-lived but the publicity generated can increase the public's awareness of the area.

Developed Attractions

Developed attractions tend to capitalize on the location of an area. In the case of Disney World in Florida and Disneyland in California, the locational factor is climate. A good climate can be guaranteed year-round. In other cases, attractions are developed around the culture or history of the area. Opryland in Nashville is a prime example.

PATTERNS OF TRAVEL

From a study of where people travel, eight "principles" can be developed to explain travel movements. These principles can, in turn, be used to predict likely future movements and to discover potential markets for, as yet, undiscovered tourist destinations.

Distance

Distance is a combination of the time and money it costs to travel from origin to destination. Typically, distance would be seen as a negative to travel. The farther the distance between the destination and the market, the less travel we would expect between the two. Those marketing a destination would, therefore, concentrate on segments of the market that were accessible in time and cost from the destination. Reductions in travel time and cost will tend to increase travel between two points. The introduction of the jet plane cut travel time between California and Hawaii from 12 to 5 hours. The wide-bodied plane cut the cost of travel between the United States and Europe by almost 50 percent. In both cases a dramatic increase in travel between origin and destination resulted.

At some point, however, physical distance seems to become an attraction in itself. British tourists initially sought the sun on the French Riviera. As that became more popular (and more costly), the focus shifted to destinations farther afield in Spain and Italy. Now the "in" places are in Eastern Europe. These latter destinations were not a problem in terms of distance because of the transportation link. The fact that they are farther away seems to make them more glamorous.

International Connections

Certain countries have a strong foundation of economic, historic, or cultural ties. The presence of these ties strengthens the likelihood of tourist movements between the two. Obvious examples are the historic and cultural ties between the United States and Great Britain. There are also strong World War II ties between Great Britain and Holland that encourage travel.

In this regard it should be noted that, because there is a flow of tourists from country A to country B, there will not necessarily be a flow from country B to country A.

Attractiveness

The attractiveness of one destination to residents of another is based on the idea that opposites attract. People from the north are attracted to the sun; Americans are attracted to Europe because of the history and culture.

One key to finding suitable markets for a destination is to identify the features of the destinations and look for segments of the market that do not have these features.

Cost

The known or presumed cost of a visit to a particular destination will affect the likelihood of travel. Generally speaking the more expensive the trip the less will be the demand. Cost is both absolute and relative. It is absolute in that, if a vacation is priced at $1,000 and the traveler does not have $1,000, there is no way he or she can afford to go. Cost is relative in that people view the cost of something relative to the perceived value of it to them. Even if they have the $1,000 but do not believe that they will get $1,000 of value for their money, they will not travel.

In a small number of cases an inverse relationship exists between cost and demand. In these cases, the higher the cost, the higher the demand. Here, the trip has a certain snob appeal. An example might be the price of a luxury cabin on a cruise ship around the world.

Finally, there is a danger in pricing something too low. People may think that a correlation exists between price and quality. If a vacation is priced too low, in the minds of the customer that may denote low quality.

Intervening Opportunities

Intervening opportunity refers to the influence of attractions and facilities between origin and destination that influence travelers to make intermediate stops and even to forego the trip to the original destination.

Florida, which offers sun, is an intervening opportunity between the market in New York and the destinations of the Bahamas, which also offer sun. Everything else being equal, people will vacation in Florida. How, then, can we explain the "attraction" of distance in a quest for the sun mentioned above? In order to induce people to travel past Florida it is necessary to sell the glamour and the different culture of the Bahamas over Florida to the New York market.

Specific Events

As mentioned earlier, events like the World Cup and the Olympic Games offer destinations the opportunity of major publicity and recognition. This gives them exposure to potentially millions of people. It also means that the facilities built for the event are available for the future use of tourists. In fact, their presence may put increased pressure on the destination to market the area to fill the facilities.

National Character

Certain peoples have characteristics that influence tourist demand. The British simply must have an annual holiday. They will save and sacrifice all year for their two-week holiday. They also have a natural tendency to vacation near the sea. As a people, they have a long association with the sea. Additionally, they have ready accessibility to the seaside. Swedes and Finns, on the other hand, enjoy the seclusion of the forest that surrounds their summer cottages. This Scandinavian love for nature is combined with a desire for the southern sun. Italians and others of the Latin

Figure 2-7   Brisbane, Australia—site of many bicentennial celebrations in 1988. (Courtesy Australian Overseas Information Service.)

culture seek a measure of sophistication in their pleasures. "Roughing it" is not for them.

While it is dangerous to generalize about humans, the national character of a people can suggest the types of vacations important to them.

Image

Finally, people visit destinations based on the image they have of that destination. Through such media as TV programs, novels, news accounts, advertising, and the comments of our friends who have been there we develop a picture of how attractive the destination is. That picture may or may not be "the truth," but we nonetheless make our travel decision, in part, on that image.

Later chapters on marketing will address how an image can be developed and changed.

ENDNOTES

1. Fred R. Lawson, "Congresses, Conventions and Conferences: Facility Supply and Demand," *International Journal of Tourism Management*, September 1980, p. 188.

2. Travel & Leisure's *World Travel Overview 1986/1987*, American Express Publishing Corporation, pp. 116–119.

S T U D Y   QUESTIONS

1. List Maslow's Hierarchy of Needs.
2. What are the major characteristics of:
   (a) regular business travel?
   (b) meeting and convention travel?
   (c) incentive travel?
3. In order of importance, what are the major categories of pleasure travel?
4. What are the major factors that explain the location of summer resort areas?
5. Identify the factors necessary for the development of ski areas.
6. What are the two most important points regarding the development of tourism based on scenery?
7. On what basis are most rural attractions developed?
8. What are the eight principles that help explain travel movements and what effect do they have on travel?

D I S C U S S I O N   QUESTIONS

1. Identify the various needs that tourists seek to satisfy when they purchase a vacation and show how these differ in terms of the vacationer's choice of a holiday destination.
2. State the main characteristics of the following travel segments: regular business travel; meetings, conventions and congresses; incentive travel; hybrid travelers; visiting friends and relatives; close-to-home; touring vacations; outdoor trips; resort vacations; city trips; theme parks/special events; cruises.
3. Discuss how physical factors influence the location of tourism in: summer resorts; winter resorts; vacations to view the scenery; hunting and fishing; spas and health resorts; urban and rural attractions; sporting events; commercial attractions.
4. Identify and give examples of the eight principles identified as explaining patterns of travel movements.

3

HOW DO TOURISTS TRAVEL?

LEARNING
OBJECTIVES

At the end of this chapter the reader will be able to:

■ Describe the importance, ownership patterns, and market characteristics of airlines, rail, cruise and other ships, private cars, recreational vehicles, car rentals, and motor coaches.

■ Describe the characteristics of economic and physical regulation in the transportation industry.

■ Discuss the types of international air agreements common to the industry.

■ Outline the major effects of airline deregulation.

■ Show how the demand for and supply of transportation services leads to particular marketing strategies.

■ Define and correctly use the following terms:

Scheduled air carrier	Domestic trunk line
Passenger load factor	Domestic regional line
Charter air carrier	Public charter
Affinity charter	Single-entity charter
Deregulation	Hub and spoke
Rail support	Amtrak
Cruise freighter/cargoliner	Car rental
Motorcoach	Civil Aeronautics Board
Federal Aviation Authority	Bilateral agreement
International Air Traffic	Derived demand
Association	Frequent-flyer program
Primary demand	Income elasticity
Demand elasticity	Sunk costs
Capital intensity	Lineal route structure
Incremental cost	Indirect distribution
Direct distribution	Differential pricing
Vertical integration	Incremental concept
Contribution theory	

MODES OF TRANSPORTATION

Introduction

Tourists travel by a variety of means. This chapter will explore the characteristics of the various modes of transportation and focus on two areas of particular importance—regulation and the marketing of transportation.

Air Travel

Size and Importance. The airlines of the world carry over 900 million passengers a year. This represents a passenger load factor—the relationship between seats occupied and seats available—of 66 percent. That is, on average, passenger planes were two-thirds full. The U.S. scheduled airlines carry over 40 percent of total world passengers. Europe, on the other hand, accounts for 70 percent of the world's charter traffic. This is because of the well-developed package holiday business in Europe. Overall the percentage of kilometers flown on charters worldwide has been declining steadily and now represents just over 3 percent of total passenger kilometers flown. It is forecasted that air traffic will grow at an annual rate of over 6 percent in Europe and in the United States and 8 to 10 percent in Asia and the Pacific.

The largest IATAN-member airlines in terms of revenue passenger kilometers (number of passengers times number of kilometers flown) in 1986 were:

1. United Airlines
2. American Airlines
3. Eastern Air Lines
4. TWA
5. British Airways

   6. Japan Air Lines
   7. Pan American
   8. Continental Airlines
   9. Air France
  10. Lufthansa

In the United States over 70 percent of adult Americans have flown at least once in their lives. In any one year about one-third of American adults take an airline trip, just over half being for pleasure.

Ownership.   More and more government-owned airlines—British Airways, Japan Air Lines, KLM, and Singapore Airlines, for example—are being offered for sale to the public. However, most foreign airlines are totally or partially owned by the government. In the United States, airlines are privately owned, and airline management is responsible to a board of directors to produce a return on investment. Airlines must operate accordingly in the prices they charge and the services they provide as they compete with each other, with foreign (often subsidized) airlines, and with other modes of transportation.

   In the United States, eight major carriers account for approximately 90 percent of revenue passenger miles. Texas Air, which took over Eastern Airlines, Continental, People Express, Frontier, and New York Air, has 21 percent of the market; United has about 16 percent, and American has 13 percent.

Support.   The airways are federally owned. The federal government has also been actively involved in several areas that have encouraged development of the air transportation system. The government has been involved in the research and development of new aircraft, has helped provide terminals, has, through the payment of subsidies, helped defray some of the carriers' operating costs, and has taken a role in the training of personnel.

Market Characteristics

   Since 1981, U.S. airlines have been classified on the basis of annual revenues. *Majors* are those with annual operating revenues of more than $1 billion; *nationals* have between $75 million and $1 billion a year; *large regional* is the term for companies that have annual operating revenues of between $10 million and $75 million; *medium regionals* are those with less than $10 million in annual operating revenues. However, the industry still commonly thinks of airlines on the basis of whether they are scheduled air carriers or charter air carriers. We will discuss these differences next.

Scheduled Air Carriers. Scheduled air carriers are given a Certificate of Convenience and Necessity by the Civil Aeronautics Board (CAB) to provide service between various points on a regularly scheduled basis. They fall into one of several types. Domestic trunk lines operate the long-haul routes and serve large metropolitan areas and medium-sized cities. American, United, Eastern, TWA, Continental, and Western are thought of as falling into this category.

International airlines are those that operate between the United States and foreign countries in addition to those that operate over international waters and U.S. territories. While many airlines operate overseas, those regarded as international are Pan American, Northwest, and Trans World Airlines (TWA).

Aloha, Hawaiian, Alaska, and Wien Air Alaska are airlines operating primarily within Alaska and Hawaii.

Domestic regional or local airlines connect smaller cities with regional centers. The system is known as the "hub and spoke." Trunk airlines designate certain cities as "hub" cities for them. Regional airlines form the spokes to transport passengers to regional centers where they are fed into the trunk airlines. With the advent of deregulation many regional carriers have expanded to provide service to local communities and even to fly overseas. Republic and U.S. Air, for example, offer international flights.

Charter Air Carriers. Charter or supplemental airlines offer nonscheduled flights. They were originally started to provide lower air fares to people traveling as a group. As noted earlier, charters are more important in Europe than in North America. Within Europe, charter air services account for 60 percent of all air travel.

A variety of complex regulations developed in the United States to ensure that the flight was a bona fide charter. In the deregulation of 1978

Figure 3-1 *Concorde.*
(Courtesy Cunard.)

most of the categories were abolished and replaced with the term "public charter." A public charter is characterized as follows: There is no requirement to purchase a ticket in advance; there is no minimum stay requirement; no restrictions are placed on discount pricing; there is no minimum group size, and travelers are allowed to buy one-way charters. Two additional classification were kept. *Affinity* charters are for members of organizations with a common purpose, such as social, professional, or religious groups. *Single-entity* charters occur when a person, company, or organization hires an aircraft for a specific trip. Scheduled airlines may also offer charters.

Ever since deregulation, the charter share of the market has declined. Much of the reason is that, as competition intensified, ticket prices dropped. Because charters arose to provide lower prices, as regular air fares dropped, charters lost their reason for being. It is estimated, for example, that about 86 percent of revenue passenger miles are on discount fares with the average discount over 55 percent of the posted fare.

Charter airlines must be certificated by the CAB and meet Federal Aviation Administration (FAA) standards.

Other Carriers.   There are a variety of other carriers. Cargo air carriers carry freight rather than passengers. Commuter airlines operate small aircraft on a scheduled basis. They must meet FAA regulations but are noncertificated. Air taxi airlines operate only on a charter, contract, or demand basis. Helicopters have been used successfully to provide transfers between Kennedy International Airport in Queens and downtown Manhattan.

The Future.   The future of air transportation is dependent upon several factors. Designers are considering the development of *hypersonic* aircraft capable of traveling at up to 4,000 miles an hours. This would mean that a flight from New York to London would take 2 hours; a flight from Los Angeles to Tokyo, 2 hours 18 minutes. At present the supersonic planes (SSTs) operated by Air France and British Airways travel between New York and Europe in just over 3 hours. The airlines have found the SSTs uneconomical, however. If manufacturers can come up with a hypersonic plane that can be operated economically it will undoubtedly stimulate international long-haul travel.

Air transportation is heavily dependent on the price and availability of petroleum. Most experts expect oil prices to remain reasonable in the short-run. At any time, however, problems could occur because of the volatility of the world situation.

Deregulation, covered in detail later, has spawned more competition and fare wars. A shakeout phase ended in 1986, and the industry has moved into a period of consolidation. While price wars still occur in certain very competitive markets, it is expected that a period of stability will ensue.

Tourism is becoming more international in scope. As more attractions and facilities are developed there will be more attempts to lure the international traveler. Air transportation will benefit.

A final caution has to be given because of the safety and convenience factors. Deregulation has also brought more flights and carriers into the air. Concern has been expressed about the crowded skies. While flying is still the safest way to travel, more and more people are concerned about the safety of the skies. Terrorist bombings have caused great concern among airline passengers. There is also the inconvenience of crowded airports. In some cases the time spent on the ground from plane to downtown is greater than the time spent in the air.

Rail Travel

Size and Importance.   Travel by railroad steadily declined in the United States after World War II. This was due to several factors—construction of the interstate highway system; growth of the airline industry; the heavy fixed costs involved in developing and maintaining railroad equipment; disputes over the role of the private and public sectors in the railroad business; rising costs of operation because of union practices; a desire on the part of the public to travel faster in order to spend more time at the destination.

People often look to Europe and Japan and wonder why the United States cannot have a similar rail system. The population is more concentrated, distances shorter, and personal mobility less important than in the United States. In addition, the railroads are often heavily subsidized. A major problem as far as speed is concerned is the poor quality of the roadbed and rails. In the United States, heavy freight usage has slowed the speed of passenger trains using the same rails. Trains are available to travel faster; however, the roadbed cannot support faster trains.

Support.   Railroad development was aided by massive government grants, primarily in the form of land, in the late nineteenth century. In return, railroads agreed to haul government passengers and freight at reduced rates. This reimbursement did not end until 1945. While public assistance of the railroads was justified on the basis of carrying passengers—settling the West, drawing the nation together—railroads preferred to carry freight and often actively tried to dissuade passenger travel. Nevertheless, the system of rails in the United States is in great part the result of a desire to provide passenger transportation.

Figure 3-2   Traveling by train and barge. (Courtesy Britrail Travel International, Inc.)

Market Characteristics

Amtrak.   In 1981, Amtrak was formed to assume operation of all inter-city rail passenger service except for that of three railroads—The Southern Railway, Denver and Rio Grande Western, and the Rock Island and Pacific lines. These three, however, provide connections with Amtrak. Amtrak itself was organized by the government as a quasi-public corporation with the intent of cutting down on the number of routes and points served and upgrading the remainder of the system.

Service is provided to 525 communities covering 24,000 route miles in 44 states. Amtrak carries over 20 million passengers a year traveling over 5 billion passenger miles. Significant government subsidy is needed as revenue pays only 60 percent of the costs of operation.

International revenue from foreign visitors has been steadily increasing while the Florida Auto Train, which allows people from the Northeast to take their autos with them for a Florida vacation, has seen a large percentage increase in ridership.

The Official Railway Guide (ORG) lists fares, schedules, and routes. Amtrak offers the coach or basic fare with additional charges for such things as a bedroom, slumber room, or a drawing room; special fares for groups, families, travel agents, and the military, among others; and the USA Rail Pass, which gives unlimited train travel for a specified period of time.

In addition to carrying passengers, Amtrak has sold the right to lay fiber optic cables along the Northeast corridor to long-distance telephone companies. The line has also rescheduled east and westbound trains out of Chicago to compete with the trucking industry to carry second-class mail.

Charter Train Tours. It is possible for members of a group to charter a train. Tours include meals, bus excursions, accommodations, and the services of guides. Activities are also planned on board the train. Private operators operate tours to various places in the United States.

The Future. As the cost of owning and operating a car increases and the time required to go from downtown to downtown by plane expands, travel by train may be a viable alternative. It is likely, however, that rail transportation will play a relatively small part in pleasure travel.

Because of the subsidies given to Amtrak, other carriers, particularly the bus lines, have complained vigorously. Subsidies will probably continue to support what has been called "the world's largest train set."

Sea Travel

Size and Importance. There are about 130 cruise ships worldwide with a capacity of over 137,000 passengers and 57,700 cabins. About 80 ships serve the North American market. The Soviet Union operates 36 cruise ships in international waters. Although their rates are 20 percent below most Western ships, Soviet ships are banned from U.S. ports.

Over 2 million people a year take a cruise. Residents of the United States are the principal market segment, accounting for approximately 75 percent of all cruise passengers. West Germany, the United Kingdom, and Australia account for the majority of remaining passengers. Yet the surface has hardly been scratched. In the United States only one person in 20 has taken a cruise. California provides almost 20 percent of these passengers, followed closely by Florida. Substantial numbers of passengers also come from New York, Illinois, Pennsylvania, and Texas.

Support. Transportation by sea was the first major means of human travel. Countries with seacoasts were the explorers of the world. In the United States, waterways, harbors, and seaways have historically been owned and operated by the federal government. Federal involvement has continued with the building of canals, improvement of rivers and harbors, and the provision of navigational aids.

Market Characteristics

The late 1960s marked the end of regularly scheduled travel by ships between two points. Cunard's *QE2* is the only regularly scheduled passenger liner crossing the Atlantic today. Most all travel by sea today is in the form of a cruise.

Cruise Ships.   Cruises are sold on some combination of cost of the cruise, amount of time the cruise lasts, and the ports of call visited. The shape of the cruise business has changed over recent years. Cruises have become

Figure 3-3   (Courtesy Royal Caribbean.)

shorter, appealing to those who have the money but not the time to travel. Three- and four-day cruises are a growing segment of the market. The most favored destinations are cruises to the Caribbean from Florida and Puerto Rico. One item that resulted in a number of lines moving from the Mediterranean to the Caribbean was the hijacking of the *Achille Lauro* by terrorists in 1985. There is also a strong summer demand for cruises from the West Coast to Alaska.

The profile of the "typical" passenger is also changing. Passengers are getting younger. For U.S. passengers there is an equal proportion—about 37 percent—of people in the 15 to 34 age group and in the 55-and-over age group. For British passengers the respective figures are 40 and 34 percent. About 60 percent of cruise ship passengers are female, almost two-thirds of all passengers are married, and about one-quarter are single. The remainder are separated, widowed, or divorced. The average income is high. Over 50 percent of U.S. passengers have an annual income of over $25,000.

The major ports for U.S. ships are, in descending order, Miami, New York City, San Juan, Port Everglades, Los Angeles, San Francisco, and New Orleans.

Because of oversupply (or, as some prefer, underdemand) cruise lines have developed aggressive marketing strategies. Large price discounts were offered to passengers, and commissions far above normal were made available to travel agents, through whom most cruises are sold. On board as many as three different prices are charged, depending on the location of the cabin. Theme cruises with special celebrities are popular. Cruise lines have also teamed up with airlines to offer fly/cruise packages. In some cases the flight to the cruise port is "free" with purchase of the package. Stopover privileges have proved to be a successful sales strategy. Passengers can visit particular destinations either before or after the cruise. They may cruise some ports, stay a while, and fly back on a combination air/cruise/land package.

Freighter/Cargoliner. A freighter or cargoliner is a vessel that operates primarily for carrying goods. However, these ships are licensed to carry up to 12 passengers on board. Passengers bring added income while adding little to the operating costs. The cabins may be equivalent to first class on a cruise ship while the cost to the passenger is much lower.

The "price" the passenger pays is that there is no medical service or entertainment on board. Moreover, schedules are dependent on the freight carried. Itineraries can be changed because of delays in loading or unloading of the freight. It has also been the case that, en route to one destination, the goods on board were sold and the destination changed! For some daring people this might be an attraction!

Charter Yacht/Sailing Excursions. Some yacht owners charter their boats to help defray the high costs of ownership. A popular system in the Mediterranean and Caribbean is for people to buy yachts as an investment. A company controls a fleet of yachts, each individually owned. The company markets and maintains the yachts and shares the income generated with the yacht owners.

Riverboats. Riverboat travel is popular in Europe and, in North America, on such places as the Saint Lawrence Seaway and the Mississippi River. Boats may offer staterooms, restaurants, and entertainment.

Houseboat vacations are becoming more popular. They are rented by the week on various rivers and large lakes.

The Future. Annual growth of 12 to 15 percent is expected in the cruise industry. That growth will occur only if passengers will pay the rates necessitated by the high costs of construction and operation, which are steadily increasing. The *QE2* was built in 1969 at a cost of $94 million; to replace her today would cost over $300 million. The average age of the cruise fleet is over 20 years, and many replacements will be needed soon. Some lines are looking at modular ships capable of carrying 1,000 passengers. The hull would be built and an engine installed. The stateroom would be preconstructed and fastened into the hull in one piece. All staterooms would be the same size. As present, staterooms are built to fit the particular curvature of the ship, and first-class accommodations outsell the less expensive cabins. Can an all-first-class ship be built for which people will pay?

The cost of operating a ship is high. The principal costs are fuel and labor. A partial solution to the cost of fuel is to build longer ships. Long ships operate more efficiently than do shorter ones. Some lines have taken an existing ship, cut it in half, and added a new body section. This can result in the addition of up to 40 percent more space at a cost one-third less than the construction cost of a new vessel.

Road Travel

Size and Importance. Most travel in the world, domestic and international, is by the family car. In the United States over 80 percent of all intercity travel is by automobile. Over the years the growth of international traveler arrivals has paralleled, but at a slightly higher rate, the growth of passenger car registrations. For example, between 1960 and 1973 international traveler arrivals worldwide increased at an average of 7.8 percent a year while car registrations worldwide increased an average of 7 percent per annum; from 1974 to 1984 the respective figures were 4.8 percent and 4 percent.

In fact, a useful method of forecasting international tourism is to project the growth of passenger car registrations.

Support. Highways, streets, and bike paths are man-made and publicly owned. For pleasure travel the biggest boom has been the building of the interstate highway system. Properly titled the "National System of Interstate and Defense Highways," this network of roads has made much of the country more accessible to Americans. Typically, the federal government provides a portion of the funds to build and maintain the roads while state government owns, operates, and actually maintains the highways. User fees on such items as tires, gasoline, and vehicle-use pay much of the costs of building and maintaining the interstate system.

Market Characteristics

Private Cars. There are over 130 million private autos in the United States and over 145 million in Europe (both East and West). Domestic tourism in the United States is heavily dependent upon the desire of Americans to travel by auto. If the cost of owning and operating a car becomes prohibitive, tourism will suffer. There is no sign of that happening in the immediate future, but the one event that could dramatically change the situation is a shortage of gasoline, as occurred twice during the 1970s.

Recreational Vehicles. A recreational vehicle is one that has wheels and living quarters. There are over 8 million RVs in the United States used by over 25 million people. Owners spend an average of 23 days a year in their vehicles, traveling an average of 5,900 miles. A number of dealers rent recreational vehicles.

Car Rentals. Car rental companies operate over 700,000 cars in the United States. The major companies are Hertz, Avis, National, and Budget. American companies produce $4 billion a year in revenues in the United States, another $1 billion in foreign markets.

About 70 percent of car-rental customers rent at airports. The increase in air travel brought about by deregulation has helped stimulate the car-rental business.

Most customers are business travelers. Business customers are primarily concerned with how reliable the firm is and how convenient it is to rent the car. Most business occurs Monday through Friday. Because the industry operates on small profit margins, auto-rental firms have gone after the pleasure traveler, especially the weekend traveler. This makes use of cars that would otherwise stand idle over the weekend. Pleasure travelers also rent the cars for a longer period. This reduces the costs involved in selling and servicing the vehicles. Because pleasure travelers

Figure 3–4   Tourists with rental car. (Courtesy New Zealand Tourist & Publicity Office.)

put more miles on the car than do business travelers, companies are putting caps on their free mileage programs. This means that car mileage is reduced and the resale value of the car is increased.

There is room for creative marketing in the car-rental business. Less than 10 percent of the United States population has ever rented a car. Companies have teamed up with other sectors of the travel business to offer fly/drive and train/auto packages both domestically and internationally.

Motorcoach.   The motorcoach industry was deregulated in 1982. The immediate effect was to double the number of bus service companies from 1,500 to 3,000. Because of an increase in insurance rates ranging from $2,500 to $15,000 per vehicle, many of the smaller motorcoach companies ceased to operate. The major companies in the business are Greyhound Lines and Continental Trailways. Bus companies serve 14,600 communities, including 9,000 localities not served by any other public mode of transportation.

Lower-income groups, the young, the elderly, and minorities tend to use regularly scheduled bus transportation more than most.

Charters and Tours.   Slightly less than one-third of the motorcoach industry's revenue comes from charters and tours. Business growth has been slow but steady.

Most business is either a city package tour, an independent package tour, or an escorted tour. A city package tour includes accommodation and sightseeing in one city or its immediate area. An independent package tour consists of travel to a variety of places and includes accommodations and sightseeing. An escorted tour is scheduled during specific times of the year. Lasting from 5 to 30 days, this type of tour includes the services of an escort.

Ground Transportation.   Ground transportation is the term reserved for buses and limousines used for sightseeing at a destination and for carrying travelers between airports and hotels. In the United States, Gray Line and American Sightseeing International offer regularly scheduled sightseeing tours of most major cities. Other companies contract their buses for local services to a tour operator as part of a tour. Many hotels close to airports offer complimentary transfers between airport and hotel.

Figure 3–5   The Airbus connects downtown London and its airports. (Courtesy Britrail Travel International, Inc.)

REGULATION

The past decade has seen sweeping changes in the regulation of the American transportation system. In order to understand the present environment it is necessary to review the past.

Goals of Regulation

As the airline industry developed in the 1930s there was concern that unbridled growth could have negative consequences for industry and passengers alike. From this concern there developed a desire to control the growth of the airline industry through a variety of regulations.

The goals of regulation were twofold: to protect the public and to promote the best possible system of transportation. Because these goals can be contradictory, the result was a system that did neither one completely.

Types of Regulation

There were two types of regulations: economic and physical. The Civil Aeronautics Board or CAB was formed in 1938. The board consists of five members who are independent of the executive branch but appointed by the President with the consent of Congress. The CAB was primarily responsible for the economic aspects of regulation at the federal level.

Economic. Economically, control was exerted over rates, entry into and exit from the market, and the level of service provided. Economic regulations were intended to prevent a few airlines from controlling the market. The airlines were regarded as a public utility, and there was a fear that open competition might result in service to only the major markets; many communities would not receive airline service.

Control of the rates charged involved the concepts of "reasonableness" and "discrimination." Rates could be charged that would allow the carriers to earn a "reasonable" profit. The CAB ruled that airlines could earn a return of 10 to 12 percent on the fair value of the airline. The Interstate Commerce Commission (ICC), which regulated the railroads, ruled that railroads might earn 6 percent on fair value. In motor transportation, because of the difficulty of determining "fair value," commissions used the "operating ratio" approach to rates. The operating ratio is the operating expenses divided by the operating revenue multiplied by 100. A target of 92 would mean 92 cents out of every dollar of revenue would go for operating expenses.

"Discrimination" in economic terms refers to the idea of charging a different price that is not reflected in a difference in costs. Railroads, for example, had been using a system of differential pricing. Railroads low-

Figure 3-6   Hovercraft travel between England and France. (Courtesy Britrail Travel International, Inc.)

ered rates when they were in a market where they were in competition; they raised prices when they had a monopoly between two points. Transportation regulations prohibited "undue discrimination," and the board or commission defined "undue."

As a result of the ideas of "reasonableness" and "discrimination" the prices that carriers could charge had to be approved by the appropriate board or commission. The deregulation act of 1978, which affected the airline industry, established a "zone of reasonableness" around the standard fare level of the airline industry. Carriers could reduce fares by up to 50 percent or raise them up to 5 percent without formal approval. Now carriers can essentially charge whatever they like.

To enter the marketplace, carriers had to have a Certificate of Public Convenience and Necessity. They had to show that public convenience would be served and that a necessity for the service existed. Carriers also had to show that they were "fit, willing, and able" to offer the service. The principal concern in deciding whether or not to certify a new carrier was whether or not companies already doing business would be hurt economically.

Carriers were also required to apply for permission to add new routes. Today they can choose where to fly.

Regulations were developed to outline the services that carriers could offer. The goal was to ensure that the public was offered good service. Since prices were regulated, carriers might cut back on services to save money. In return for the right to operate, carriers had to assume certain duties. They had to serve all comers and could not abandon service between two points without permission. Carriers are now free to leave unprofitable routes.

On December 31, 1985, the authority of the CAB was eliminated.

Physical.   The second type of regulation relates to the physical aspects of safety and reliability. This was, and still is, the province of the Federal Aviation Authority (FAA). Established in 1958, the basic purpose of the FAA is to ensure air safety while promoting the growth of aviation. The agency is responsible for setting and enforcing safety standards; certifying the health and the skills of pilots; monitoring standards in developing, operating, and maintaining aircraft; investigating air accidents; and controlling air traffic while helping to develop a national system of airports.

Freedoms of the Air

The above aspects of regulation relate to domestic carriers. International travel requires the cooperation of nations. It has been accepted that it is not feasible to have an international system of air travel that is totally free. Some type of regulation is necessary. The foundation for such a system was laid down in the Chicago Convention of 1944 and the Bermuda Agreement of 1946. The notion of "Freedoms of the Air" was first discussed in Chicago, while the Bermuda Agreement focused on bilateral agreements to put into operation the various freedoms.

There are eight Freedoms of the Air, and they are illustrated in Figure 3–7. The first freedom refers to the right of an airline to fly over one country to get to another. The second freedom refers to the right of an airline to stop in another country for fuel or maintenance but not to pick up or drop off passengers. These first two freedoms are widely accepted. The next four freedoms are the subject of bilateral agreements. They are: the right of an airline to drop off, in a foreign country, traffic from the country in which it is registered to a separate country; the right of an airline to carry back passengers from a foreign country to the country in which it is registered; the right of an airline to carry passengers between two foreign countries as long as the flight originates or terminates in the country in which it is registered; the right of an airline to carry passengers to a gateway in the country in which it is registered then on to a foreign country, where neither the origin nor the ultimate destination is the country in which it is registered.

The final two freedoms, numbers seven and eight, are rarely allowed. These are the right of an airline to operate entirely outside of the country in which it is registered in carrying passengers between two other countries, and the right of an airline, registered in a foreign country, to carry passengers between two points in the same foreign country.

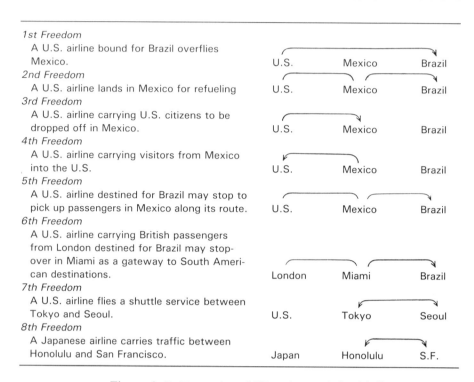

1st Freedom
  A U.S. airline bound for Brazil overflies
  Mexico.

2nd Freedom
  A U.S. airline lands in Mexico for refueling

3rd Freedom
  A U.S. airline carrying U.S. citizens to be
  dropped off in Mexico.

4th Freedom
  A U.S. airline carrying visitors from Mexico
  into the U.S.

5th Freedom
  A U.S. airline destined for Brazil may stop to
  pick up passengers in Mexico along its route.

6th Freedom
  A U.S. airline carrying British passengers
  from London destined for Brazil may stopover in Miami as a gateway to South American destinations.

7th Freedom
  A U.S. airline flies a shuttle service between
  Tokyo and Seoul.

8th Freedom
  A Japanese airline carries traffic between
  Honolulu and San Francisco.

Figure 3–7   Examples of "Freedoms of the Air."

Bilateral Agreements

A bilateral agreement refers to an agreement between two countries to offer airline service between them. Bilateral agreements are intended to protect the rights of both countries in three areas: to allow carriers of both nations to participate in the marketplace; to control the frequency of flights so that profitable load factors can be generated; to control prices to prevent discount fares in prime markets. This latter practice is referred to as *predatory pricing.* Many small nations felt they needed bilateral agreements to protect their national airline. A national airline of a small country may be subsidized by the government. The airline may be operated because of national pride or a fear of being dependent on foreign carriers for bringing in tourists or exporting other products. On the other hand, countries where the airlines must operate on a profit-making basis are concerned that a foreign subsidized airline could offer cut-rate prices, the losses being picked up by the government.

Because bilateral agreements were not sufficient to bring together the interests of for-profit and nonprofit airlines, the International Air Traffic Association (IATA) to bring about cooperation between international airlines was established. The functions of the IATA are covered in the next chapter. Both the IATA and the concept of bilateral agreements have come under increasing attack. Competition is greater; there is over-capacity on a number of routes, while the role of unscheduled airlines and the increasingly important part wholesalers—who are outside the regulatory framework—play in selling discount package tours have caused confusion and disagreement. Several countries have dropped the membership in the IATA. International travel will still require some type of agreement structure between nations, but at the moment the IATA and bilateral agreements seem to be it.

Deregulation

Although there is disagreement as to whether or not deregulation has been better for the airline industry and the air traveler, it appears that the following effects have occurred:

1. There are more carriers in the sky. Small commuter lines have moved into many of the smaller markets vacated by the majors. As more carriers offer more flights there have been concerns over safety.
2. There is a greater number of fares available to the public. As airlines practice free-market pricing they are able to adjust prices relative to market segment, time of day or week, and degree of competition. This has meant that there are bargain opportunities for certain people in certain geographic areas. It may, however, mean that two people flying on the same plane might be paying vastly different amounts for their tickets.
3. The consumer departing from major metropolitan airports probably has more flights to choose from and an increased opportunity for better prices; those who fly from small or medium-sized airports probably have less of each.

MARKETING OF PASSENGER TRANSPORTATION

Transportation marketing seeks to satisfy the needs and wants of the traveler by providing the right mix of services. To appreciate the difficulties involved it is necessary to consider the characteristics of supply of, and demand for, passenger transportation.

Characteristics of Demand

The demand for passenger transportation has a number of characteristics, all of which affect the way a company markets. First, demand is instantaneous. For carriers there is great uncertainty as to what the demand will be on a particular day at a particular time between two

Figure 3–8   Tourists with campervan. (Courtesy New Zealand Tourist & Publicity Office.)

points. While past trends are useful they cannot be totally reliable. When demand is greater than supply, travelers are unhappy. By the time adjustments are made to supply more capacity, customers may have changed carriers or found an alternate means of transportation. The tendency, then, would be to provide more capacity than is needed. Overcapacity shows up in the load factor. In a perfect match of supply and demand, load factor would be 100 percent. Anything less indicates the measure of overcapacity. The challenge in marketing is to create programs to fill each plane, train, ship, or bus on each trip.

Overcapacity is the result not only of instantaneous demand but also of the variability of demand. Demand for transportation is not the same each hour of each day of each month. It shows what is known as "peaks and valleys." At certain times of the day or week or month there is great demand; at other times the demand is light. Yet sufficient planes, boats, trains, buses, and terminal facilities have to be provided to cover peak demand. The result is that excess capital has to be invested, and this means that operating costs are increased. How should demand be priced? Should the peak traveler pay more than the off-peak traveler? Peak-load pricing states that those traveling at peak times should pay more for the extra capacity provided to meet peak demand. Some off-peak pricing is found in the airline industry and with passenger trains. Reduced midweek and night fares are an attempt at peak pricing.

Another characteristic of demand is that there is, in fact, more than one type or segment of demand for transportation. In its simplest terms, demand is either business demand or pleasure demand. The motivations, frequencies, and response to price are different. The motivation for the business traveler is *derived*—that is, the demand for travel exists because of the desire to do business in a particular territory. Demand for pleasure travel is *primary*—the motivation is to travel to a vacation spot. The distinction is important because derived demand tends to be affected more by factors external to the transportation industry. No matter how good the service between New York and Detroit, if business is bad in Detroit, travel demand may go down. A reduction in fares, for example, may affect primary demand but may not affect derived demand.

The business traveler travels more frequently than does the pleasure traveler. This makes this person very valuable to the airline. Frequent-flyer programs, which offer rewards based on miles traveled, have been targeted toward the business travel in an attempt to capture customer loyalty.

As mentioned above, derived demand may not be affected by changes in price. The company may absorb a fare increase as a cost of doing business. The business traveler may choose a more convenient, but more expensive, flight since the company and not the individual is paying for it.

In some situations people can substitute one mode of transportation for another—train for plane; bus for train, etc. This affects the way transportation is marketed. *Elasticity* is the economic term for the sensitivity of travelers to changes in price and service. An elastic demand is sensitive to substitution; an inelastic demand is not. The extent of elasticity is dependent upon the price of the other mode of transportation and the type of demand. Pleasure travel is more price-elastic than is business travel; primary demand is more price-elastic than is derived demand. When people choose how to travel, the decision is made on the basis of price, prestige, comfort, speed, and convenience. Amtrak could successfully compete with the plane on certain distances on the basis of several of these factors.

Competition also exists within one mode between carriers. Generally, prices and the speed of the journey are the same or similar amongst competing carriers. Carriers must then market on the basis of the factors mentioned above—prestige, comfort, and convenience. Often a small change in departure time can capture a significant number of passengers. This explains much of the congestion at airports at certain times; everyone wants to offer flights at what are believed to be the most convenient times for the traveler.

Still another aspect of demand is that some transportation modes offer more than one type of service. Passengers can fly economy, business class, or first class; trains also offer various classes of service. The different types of service are in competition with each other. Airlines, for example, have to decide the proportions of first-class, business-class, and economy- or tourist-class seats to offer on a plane. They then decide what additional services are necessary to justify the price differential—more leg room, better meals, free drinks, etc.

Demand for transportation is also affected by the relationship between the price charged and the income level of the traveler. Pleasure travel is income-elastic—that is, the demand for travel is affected by changes in the traveler's income. Economists say that demand is elastic when a reduction in price results in more demand that will result in more revenue. (Revenue equals price times number demanded.) The company gains revenue because the increased demand brought about by a drop in price makes up for the reduced price. Similarly, an inelastic demand is one where a reduction in price results in less revenue generated. More passengers may be attracted but not in sufficient numbers to offset the loss of revenue brought about by the reduction in price. Pleasure travel is discretionary—that is, the traveler has a choice of whether or not to travel. An increase in price may mean the traveler will postpone the vacation.

Business travel is also influenced by the income of the corporation. Much business travel is essential; but some is discretionary. Businesses may turn to teleconferencing as a way of reducing the travel bill if costs increase too much.

Finally, the demand for travel makes itself felt in a demand for non-price items. The frequency of departures, the condition of the equipment, the service of the employees, on-time performance—the entire package—is often more important than the price. Companies have to find out what is important to the different segments of the market they are going after (the list will be different for each) and seek to provide it.

Supply Characteristics

Just as the marketing of transportation is affected by the characteristics of demand, so too is it influenced by the supply characteristics.

The supply of transportation is unique in several distinct ways. First, the transportation industry is a capital-intensive industry. Terminals and equipment cost a great deal of money. The costs are also "indivisible"—airlines cannot put "half a plane" in the air if the plane is only half full. Because the industry is capital-intensive and because much of the capital is borrowed, most of the costs of running a transportation company are fixed; for example, interest on the debt must be paid in full regardless of the number of passengers and revenue. This puts a great deal of pressure on management to fill seats that would otherwise be empty. This may affect both promotional and pricing decisions.

Figure 3-9 Traveling by train in Great Britain. (Courtesy Britrail Travel International, Inc.)

Related to this previous point is the fact that transportation costs are "sunk" with few alternatives. This means that the cost of a plane is "sunk" in that the company has incurred the cost of buying it. It is up to the company to generate revenue to pay for the aircraft. It is not like a light that can be turned off, thereby saving money. The plane also has few alternative uses. It can fly; it might be possible to sell it as a unique type of restaurant, but essentially all a company can do with an airplane is fly it. This puts additional pressure on the company to use the resource (the plane) rather than have it sit idle. Hence, the large amounts of sunk costs also mean that there is a tendency to use old equipment rather than invest in more modern (and more expensive) equipment.

Another characteristic of transportation supply is that, although demand is instantaneous, supply is not. There is a long time between planning for a piece of equipment and placing the order for it; between placing the order and receiving it; and between putting it into service and scrapping it. Thus, while demand can shift very quickly, it takes a great deal of time to adjust supply. A company must live with its mistakes for a very long time.

Because of the high level of fixed costs, the incremental costs of operation are small. Incremental cost is the cost of adding one more unit. The running cost of adding another passenger car to a train, another bus to a route, or even a plane between two points is small compared to the cost of the actual piece of equipment. If a plane is scheduled to fly anyway, the cost of an additional passenger is incredibly small—an extra meal and some services. This means that, above a certain point, it makes economic sense to reduce the price charged in order to get some revenue coming in. This is the rationale behind discount fares. Airlines can predict, based on past records, how many seats on a particular flight will sell within a week before the flight. People who book within a week before a flight are usually business people. Assume, for example, that on a particular flight 80 percent of the seats will be bought at the regular fare in the last week before the flight. This means that the airline can sell up to 20 percent of the seats at a discount for people who will book and pay more than seven days before the flight departs.

Still another characteristic of transportation supply is that it cannot be stored for future use. A grocery store can sell a can of dog food today or tomorrow or next week. Every seat on a plane or train or bus must be sold only on that trip. The sale that is lost today is lost forever. This puts additional pressure on management to sell, sell, sell.

Transportation services must be available on a continuous basis. Travelers expect the same level of service whether it is day or night, summer or winter, whether the plane is full or almost empty. Because transportation is expected to be reliable on a continuous basis there is little opportunity to cut costs for inferior service at odd hours. This adds to the cost of providing the service.

Finally, there is the problem of labor. In transporting people the company takes on a great responsibility. Often the service—whether in operations or in maintenance—is offered 24 hours a day. Employees must be equally alert no matter what the time. Strict rules regulate the amount of time that pilots, drivers, or operators can be on duty at any one stretch. The FAA limits pilots to 30 hours of flying in any seven-day period. And airline pilots are paid well for their skills. Thus, although the operating costs are small compared to the sunk costs, they can still be considerable. A further complication is that there is little opportunity for the substitution of capital for labor. This is, after all, a service business.

Marketing has the task of ensuring that there is sufficient demand to utilize fully the supply of equipment and facilities. It must also ensure that there is enough of the right kind of supply to meet the demands of the passengers. Just as demand influences supply, so too does supply influence demand. The demand for vacations to Jamaica will influence a decision to operate flights to Jamaica; however, the existence of flights to Jamaica at times and prices appropriate to the market will stimulate demand. Marketing brings supply and demand together.

Marketing Strategies

In marketing, the offerings of the company are known as the four p's—product, promotion, place, and price. In tourism it is appropriate to change the "product" to "service" and "place" to "distribution."

Service.   Service refers to getting the ideal mix of services to satisfy existing or potential customers. This means offering transportation at the right times, in the right kinds of equipment, while giving a level of service before, during, and after the journey that will meet the needs of the customer—while making a profit.

Most carriers use a linear route structure; that is, the equipment travels from one point to another, turns around, and travels back. In the airline industry most fuel is used at takeoff and landing. Also, the speed of travel by plane is only appreciated on longer flights. Thus, for reasons of cost and customer benefit, jet aircraft operate in the most efficient manner when they fly on long hauls. A piece of equipment may, however, make an intermediate stop. While this increases the time and fuel costs, it can add significant additional revenue.

The airlines also operate what is known as a *hub-spoke* concept. Airlines have identified several major cities that serve as hubs (as in hub of a wheel) for them. Smaller towns serve as the spokes of a wheel connected to these hubs. Airlines attempt to have passengers fly into their hub city on a smaller or commuter plane for connection to a larger plane for travel to their ultimate destination. Colorado Springs is a spoke for the Denver hub (on Continental), which is itself a spoke city for St. Louis, which is a spoke (on TWA) for London.

Service must be provided on the right kind of equipment. Equipment has two facets that must be matched—identifying the operating costs of one piece of equipment over another while offering equipment that will attract the traveler. One example is the *Concorde.* While this supersonic aircraft could draw passengers because of its speed and unique shape, the operating costs are so high that the potential market is relatively small.

Scheduling is a major marketing weapon for carriers. Traveling from point A to point B leaves little opportunity for differentiating one company or carrier from another. Offering departures at times most convenient for the passenger is one way to do this. Unfortunately, everyone wants to do this. The result, certainly in the airline industry, is severe congestion at the most popular times. Generally speaking, the demand for business travel peaks on Monday mornings and Friday afternoons. It is also heavy during the morning and early evening hours during the week—Monday through Thursday. The demand for pleasure travel peaks on Friday evenings, Sunday afternoons, and early evenings.

Service can also be altered by such things as upgrading the quality of the interior of the vehicle. Tie-ins with other modes are possible—such as fly/cruise or rail/drive.

Promotion.   The subject of promotion will be dealt with in greater detail toward the end of the book. However, several points can be made now. Promotion can be seen as the communications link between carrier and

Figure 3-10   Street ferries as a form of transport in Tai O. (Courtesy Hong Kong Tourist Association.)

passenger. It is the responsibility of the carrier to communicate its message effectively. If the passenger has not understood the message, it is the fault of the carrier. To this end, it is important that clear promotional objectives be defined. These objectives should identify which target markets are to be reached, what tasks have to be done to reach the markets, who is to perform the tasks, and when they have to be completed. It is vital that the promotional theme be synchronized with the marketing plan, which, in turn, must be consistent with the overall objectives of the carrier. Carriers may, for example, feel that in order to meet their financial targets they must emphasize "quality" and "service." Thus, the way to reach the target is to stress quality and service. These concepts become the essence of the marketing campaign. As part of that plan, communicating the ideas of "service" and "quality" to the public becomes the promotional objective.

Distribution.   Distribution involves the mechanisms by which passengers can obtain the information they need to make a trip choice and, having made that choice, that they can make the necessary reservations. *Di-*

rect distribution occurs when passengers get in touch with the carriers directly. *Indirect* distribution is when the sale is made through an intermediary.

This latter procedure takes four forms. First is the emergence of independent companies to handle all aspects of travel. It might involve a wholesaler who arranges the specifics of a tour, for example; or it might be a retail travel agent who serves as an independent distributor for a wholesaler or carrier; it may even be a wholesaler-retailer who packages its own tours or who buys packages from other wholesalers for distribution.

A second method of distribution is the marketing of tourism either regionally or nationally. Countries, provinces, and states promote travel to their particular destination. This effort supplements the marketing plans of the carriers. In some cases the marketing effort of the carrier can dovetail with that of the destination.

A third method is the coordination of marketing plans by various private-sector companies. Tie-ins between airlines and hotels, or bus lines and various attractions, are becoming more prevalent.

Finally, there is the movement toward vertical integration. Airlines have moved in to take control of hotels and car-rental agencies. This has been an attempt to develop a "one-stop travel shop" experience for the traveler. The strategy recently backfired for United Airlines, which formed Allegis—an amalgamation of airline, hotel, and car-rental companies. Under stockholder pressure, United was forced to divest itself of the non-airline parts of the company. This subject will also be dealt with in greater depth later.

Price.   When the majority of airline passengers once consisted of people traveling on business and those who were rather wealthy, the airlines felt that the demand for travel was inelastic. That is, if prices were reduced, any increase in number of passengers would not produce more revenue. Because of this and a fear that open pricing would lead to price wars that might result in bankruptcy for smaller airlines, airline pricing was closely controlled. Pricing was a reflection of operating costs. The average costs of carriers serving particular markets were calculated and a reasonable return on investment added to come up with the price that could be charged. With deregulation a new era has come to pricing in transportation in general and in the airline industry in particular.

Three economic concepts are important when looking at pricing alternatives. These are the ideas of "differential pricing," the "contribution theory," and the "incremental concept." Differential pricing is the concept that there is not one but many demand curves. A separate demand exists for coach than does for first-class; separate demands exist for travel from Denver to New York than from New York to Denver. As such, carriers can calculate how price-sensitive demand is in one particular class or on one particular route and price accordingly. The demand for business travel, for example, is probably less sensitive to price changes than the demand for pleasure travel on that same route at that same time. A higher price can be charged where demand is inelastic.

The idea of contribution theory is that prices should be set at the level that contributes most to paying off fixed costs while still allowing traffic to move. The fare charged might be low on a route where the demand is elastic; higher where demand is inelastic. In effect, segments of the market that are price-inelastic are subsidizing others that are price-elastic. How low should the price be? Low enough to ensure the passenger travels while contributing as much as possible to paying off fixed costs.

Tied to the ideas above is the incremental concept. Incremental costs are those incurred by running an additional service. The operating costs of a particular plane or train are its incremental costs. Each fare should cover its incremental costs while contributing as much as possible to fixed costs and also ensuring that the traffic moves. It is up to management to analyze each route and each segment of the market and set prices accordingly.

S T U D Y   QUESTIONS

1. What are the major market characteristics of air travel?
2. How does government support travel by air, rail, sea, and road?
3. How did deregulation affect charters in the United States?
4. What factors affect the future of air travel?
5. Why did rail travel suffer a decline after World War II?
6. List the three factors on which cruises are sold.
7. What are the two goals of regulation?
8. What have been the effects of deregulation?
9. What are the characteristics of travel demand and supply?
10. In what ways do transportation companies compete in the marketing of their services?

D I S C U S S I O N   QUESTIONS

1. Discuss the importance to tourism of the following:
   airlines; rail; cruise and other ships; private cars; recreational vehicles; car rentals; motor coaches.

2. What actions have been taken to protect the traveling public while promoting the best possible system of transportation?

3. What have the effects of deregulation been on (a) the airline industry and (b) the traveling public?

4. In what ways do the characteristics of demand for, and supply of, transportation affect the way it is marketed?

4

WHERE DO TOURISTS GO?

At the end of this chapter the reader will be able to:
- ■ Describe for the countries of the world:
  - the major tourist attractions.
  - the major tourist destinations for the residents.
  - where visiting tourists come from.
- ■ Define and correctly use the following terms:

Balance of payments	Social tourism
Invisible export	Convertible/hard currency

TOURISM DESTINATIONS: ATTRACTIONS AND TOURIST FLOWS

Introduction

This section comprises a survey of the countries of the world from a tourism perspective. The focus will be on the flows of tourists to and from each country and the major tourist attractions within each country.

The study of tourist movements is important for several reasons. For those at a destination it is vital to know the origins of the visitors. By knowing *where* the market comes from, marketing plans can be drawn up to reach potential travelers. Also, by studying the geographic characteristics of existing tourists, it may be possible to identify additional untapped market areas. For example, we may note that visitors to a particular "sun and fun" destination tend to come from cold-weather cities within a 200-mile radius of the destination. Further analysis might show several large cold-weather centers of population within 200 miles where there is at present no marketing effort. These would be potential market areas for expansion of the marketing effort.

From a theoretical viewpoint the study of tourist flows is also important. By *analyzing* existing tourist flows, general principles can be developed to *explain* the movements of tourists. By *applying* these principles to other destinations we can *identify* areas of potential future tourist movements.

REGIONS OF THE WORLD

The vast majority of domestic tourism occurs in developed countries. Europe accounts for over half of all domestic tourism while tourism to the Americas (North America, Central and South America, and the Caribbean) adds an additional 37 percent; East Asia and the Pacific contribute less than 10 percent of the total; Africa, the Middle East, and South Asia combined only have 2 percent.

The same situation is true when international travel is considered. Europe receives over two-thirds of all international arrivals and well over half of all receipts. The Americas receive approximately 16 percent of all international arrivals and 25 percent of all receipts. East Asia and the Pacific, which account for 10 percent of arrivals and receipts, are the regions of the world showing the greatest rate of growth. The pattern of international arrivals and international travel receipts is shown in Figure 4-1.

The top two generators of tourism expenditures are the United States and West Germany. They are followed, at some distance, by the United Kingdom, Canada, Japan, and France.

The United States is also the major beneficiary of tourism receipts. It is followed by Italy, Spain, France, the United Kingdom, and West Germany. In terms of arrivals, however, the order is different. Italy receives most international tourists followed by Spain, France, the United States, and Czechoslovakia. Finally, the vast majority of international travel occurs between neighboring countries.

United States of America

Domestic Tourism. Because of the physical size of the United States and the large number of Americans who have the time, money, and desire to travel, it is difficult to summarize tourism in the United States.

There are three main areas where tourism is of particular importance. These regions are New England along with the Adirondack and Catskill mountains, Florida, and California.

The extensive population of the New York metropolitan area in combination with the population of New England makes for a sizable tourist potential. Added to that are the attractions of the region. New England combines a rich historical heritage with areas of outstanding natural beauty. The original colonists left a unique architectural style in addition to historical sites concerned with the American Revolution and early independence. Scenic resources run the gamut from the rocky shore to the forested mountains, the latter a particular favorite in the fall as the colors change. In the summer, coastal resorts offer tranquility and recreational opportunities. In the winter the 100-plus inches of snow attracts both downhill and cross-country skiers.

Florida benefits from an excellent year-round climate. In the winter it attracts tourists from the North. Because it is a peninsula, it combines sunshine with water-based recreational opportunities. Florida is also popular as a seasonal or year-round stay option for retirees. Summer is the traditional time for family vacations and the many commercial attrac-

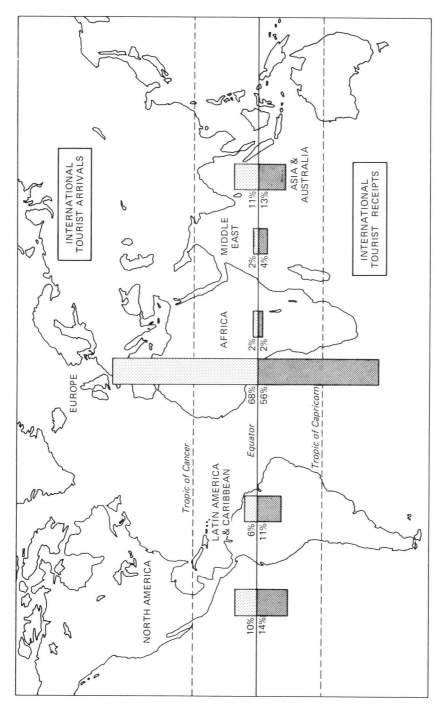

Figure 4-1 Pattern of International Arrivals and Receipts.

tions of the area offset the fact that humidity makes vacationing uncomfortable.

California's many tourist attractions revolve around the Sierra Nevada Mountains and national parks, the sunshine and the sea, and the inherent recreational opportunities afforded by them.

The importance of tourism in developing the West must be mentioned. Tourism has opened up areas that once were inaccessible and of questionable economic value. The region has relied upon scenery and recreational opportunities, and the result is that tourists are now exposed to such things as the diverse cultures of the Southwest, gambling opportunities in the middle of the desert at Las Vegas, and skiing in Colorado.

National parks have played a large part in this. The first national park, Yellowstone, was opened in 1872. In 1920 the various national parks attracted over 5 million visitors. Today that number is well over 100 million visitors annually.

International Tourism. On an international level, Americans account for over 20 percent of world tourist arrivals, and the United States is the major tourist-generating country in the world. However, on an index of foreign travel per 1,000 inhabitants, the United States rates very low. The reason has to do with distance. Outside of trips to Canada and Mexico, travel to a foreign country involves considerable distance and expense. A trip of 3,000 miles from New York to San Francisco is considered a domestic trip. If a tourist left London and traveled that same distance he or she would cross 10 frontiers. The impact of U.S. international travel has to be considered in this light.

On the other hand, the United States had only a 6.5 percent share of the world's international tourism market in 1986. The result of more Americans traveling abroad compared to the rest of world visiting the United States means that the United States has a travel budget deficit. In 1986 it was slightly less than $9 billion. The major destinations for traveling Americans are Canada, Mexico, the United Kingdom, West Germany, and France.

By far the major country of origin for foreign visitors is Canada followed by Mexico and Japan. Shared borders with Canada and Mexico account for the rankings. The major places visited by foreign tourists are, in order, California, New York, Florida, Hawaii, and Washington, D.C.

Traditionally, visitors to the United States have been relatives of recent immigrants; European artists, scholars, writers, and students who want to experience the American way of life; and business people who combine business with pleasure. Attempts to attract the pleasure travel have been moderately successful. The state of Florida was able, through package deals, to bring a number of British tourists over during the past few summers.

Regions.   For the purposes of tourism, the United States is divided into various regions. These are New England, New York/New Jersey, Mid-Atlantic, South, North-Central, Northwest, Southwest, and the Pacific.

New England, as mentioned earlier, is known for its rich variety of coasts, mountains, forests, and colonial history. In the winter it offers recreational opportunities in the ski resorts; in the summer, along the coast. Many of its historic sites have been preserved and renovated to their former glory. The fall colors bring visitors from great distances. Of particular note is Boston, Cape Cod, Salem, and the American village at Old Sturbridge.

New York City is a major business and trade center. It attracts numerous conventions, whose participants often stay afterwards for additional sightseeing. Attractions abound—museums, Broadway shows, the United Nations, Statue of Liberty, to name a few. Upstate New York has a number of areas of outstanding natural beauty. The Finger Lakes region is one that offers many recreational opportunities. Resorts in the Catskills continue to offer respite from summer in the city. Niagara Falls has lost its reputation as the honeymoon capital of the world, but it still attracts millions of tourists annually.

The Mid-Atlantic states have important business and convention destinations in addition to their attraction for pleasure visitors. The presence of the nation's capital, Washington, D.C., brings a great deal of business and convention travel. Nationally important monuments and museums add to the attraction.

The South boasts urban attractions, beautiful scenery and sun, and fun attractions of Florida. The city of New Orleans is renowned for the cuisine and jazz of its French Quarter. The scenery of the great Smoky Mountain National Park as well as the Everglades of Florida attract numerous visitors. With its combination of sun, beaches, and commercial attractions, Florida lures tourists on a year-round basis.

The North-central region is the heart of America's industrial belt. It offers many recreational opportunities including lakes and woods suitable for hunting, fishing, and water-related activities. Various European and Scandanavian ethnic groups are predominant in this region. The metropolitan areas of Detroit and, especially, Chicago offer fine museums and entertainment.

The Northwest region is made up of the Northern Rockies and the Plains states. Much of the area is rural and there is much travel for the purpose of visiting friends and relatives who have moved. Outdoor recreational opportunities abound. This region offers open space, mountains and lakes suitable for hiking, hunting, fishing, and winter sports. A number of National Parks, including Zion and Yellowstone, are major attractions. Mount Rushmore, the Badlands and the Black Hills evoke memories of the Old West.

The Southwest has an excellent climate which stimulates retirement living. It boasts a variety of man-made attractions such as Six Flags Over Texas, the coastal attractions of the gulf area and the deserts and mountains of Arizona and New Mexico. Particular mention should be made of the Grand Canyon and the Painted Desert.

The Pacific states are best known for sightseeing and entertainment. The casinos of Nevada and the entertainment and theme park industries of California are dominant. A number of National Parks—Sequoia and Yosemite to name but two—and the excellent climate offer outdoor recreation opportunities. The Sierra Nevadas offers facilities for both summer and winter sports. In addition we should note such urban attractions as Los Angeles and San Francisco and the wine regions of California.

Canada

International Tourism. Because of the socioeconomic status of its citizens, Canada is one of the top five tourist-generating countries of the world. Slightly more than half of all Canadians take an annual vacation. Canadians account for well over 50 percent of the visitors to the United States. The volume of travel is aided by several factors. Ninety percent of the Canadian population lives within a few hundred miles of the American border, and the border itself does not represent a major barrier. In addition, there are close business and communication ties between the two nations. A recent proposal allowing for free trade between the countries was approved and should act as a stimulant of both business and pleasure travel. The major beneficiary of Canadian tourism is the state of Florida, followed by the Western states. Significant travel also occurs to New England, New York/New Jersey, and the Great Lakes. Most vacation travel between Canada and these regions is by car and is of short duration.

Only about 10 percent of Canadians go overseas on vacation. The major destination is Western Europe, particularly the United Kingdom, Italy, and France. But there is also a well-defined (and growing) movement to the sun of Florida, Hawaii, Mexico, and the Caribbean. In recent years travel to the sun destinations has been growing at the expense of travel to Europe.

In-bound tourism is overwhelmingly from the United States. Almost 90 percent of international arrivals to Canada are from the United States. Significant numbers arrive from Europe, largely the United Kingdom, Germany, and France. Asia accounts for the next group of tourists, which are overwhelmingly from Japan. Europe has had the largest absolute increase in numbers of tourists to Canada while Asia has had the most significant percentage increase. Approximately four times as many tourists visit from Europe as do from Asia.

Domestic Tourism.   In Canada a trip involves a journey of more than 50 miles away from home. Most trips are taken to see friends and relatives. Travel to a vacation spot is followed in importance by outdoor recreation, city activities, and rural sightseeing as reasons for taking a trip. Almost three-quarters of all trips are taken by car, and about 60 percent of all trips occur between June and September. Quebec and Ontario, the two most populous provinces, account for most trips.

British Columbia, known for its natural beauty, offers the fjord-like coast of the Pacific Ocean, mountains, and a West Coast climate. There are numerous recreational resources including waters for rafting and salmon fishing, sandy beaches, and parks. Various seaside and hot springs resorts are to be found throughout the province.

Newfoundland has a number of fine parks and museums. Tuna and salmon fishing are popular. The Cabot Trail from Newfoundland to Sydney is regarded as one of the most scenic trips in Canada. Nova Scotia maintains its Scottish heritage in a variety of summer activities.

The scenery and natural phenomena of New Brunswick give it the title "Picture Province." Among the attractions are the river road from St. John, especially in the fall, Magnetic Hill and Hopewell Rocks near Moncton, the Bay of Fundy and Fundy National Park, and the Reversing Falls at St. John. At high tide the rising water in St. John Bay causes the St. John River to flow "backwards."

The scenic St. Lawrence River flows through Quebec for most of its 750 miles. Southern Quebec province offers easy getaway access to the wilderness for urban populations. In winter the Laurentides attract downhill skiers. The cities of Quebec and Montreal are well known—the former for its old city and excellent cuisine, the latter for its Olympic stadium and shopping facilities.

Ontario contains the country's largest city—Toronto—and its capital—Ottawa. Since the majority of the population is contained in the St. Lawrence Lowlands and the Lake Peninsula, southern Ontario, together with Quebec, is important as a getaway vacation spot.

Manitoba attracts tourists to its capital, Winnipeg. The Riding Mountain National Park is known for its buffalo while the many surrounding lakes offer excellent fishing.

Saskatchewan is best-known for its vast wheat fields, its Big Muddy Badlands, and its lakes and fishing.

The Canadian Rocky Mountains provide the backdrop for the spectacular scenery of Alberta. Banff and Jasper national parks, in addition to the scenery, are known for their hot springs and ice fields. The largest permanent body of ice between the Arctic and Antarctic is the Columbia ice field. While Banff and Jasper are known as headquarter resorts, the two main cities of Edmonton and Calgary are known, respectively, for Klondike Days and the Calgary Stampede.

Latin America

Mexico. The vast majority of Mexico's international tourism consists of trips of short duration from visitors from the United States. Canada is the second most important market followed by visitors from its neighbor to the south, Guatemala. The fact that Mexico takes in much more from foreign tourists than Mexican tourists spend abroad means that tourism surpluses make the difference between a balance of payments surplus or deficit. The balance of payments is an accounting of the transactions between countries. When country A exports more than it imports it has a balance of payments surplus. The reverse situation leads to a balance of payments deficit.

Tourism tends to be concentrated in a few tourist centers. Tourists are attracted to Mexico for three things—historic and archaeological sites, the culture, and the sun, sand, and sea.

Mexico City, the capital, is the oldest city in North America. Nearby are two outstanding attractions—the Floating Gardens of Xochimilco and the great pyramids of Teotihuacán. A variety of archaeological sites dealing with Mayan culture surround Mexico City.

Various Mexican towns offer a glimpse into part of the culture. Particularly noteworthy are the ancient city of Puebla, the art center of San Miguel de Allende, and the fishing center of Pátzcuaro.

Acapulco has long been known as the major resort community in Mexico. The town is located on the southwest coast in a series of bays extending 10 miles. It has recently been challenged by the eastern resort of Cancun, a totally planned community. The prime tourist season is from November through March.

Domestic and outbound tourism has increased in recent years. Growth is tempered by the fact that Mexico's wealth is unevenly distributed. Just over 10 percent of the population can afford to travel abroad for a vacation. However, foreign travel is considered a status symbol. In addition, a highly developed system of credit finance exists unlike any other in Latin America.

The vast majority of Mexican travel is to the United States. Increasing numbers of Mexicans, however, are traveling to Europe.

Central America

Tourism to Central America is, at present, limited by the political problems of the area and its lack of tourism infrastructure. However, the area boasts much of interest.

In Guatemala, immediately south of Mexico, tourism is second to coffee as a source of income. The country has a number of interesting market towns and archaeological sites. The United States is the principal source of tourists. The other Central American countries together account for about half of all tourists.

Honduras relies on visitors from Nicaragua, Guatemala, and the United States, but it lacks a well-developed tourism infrastructure. Copan is the site of a Mayan ruin while Comayagua is a well-preserved sixteenth-century town.

El Salvador gets most of its tourists from Guatemala. Visits peak in December although business is spread evenly throughout the year. It is known for its Indian culture, its pre-Columbian ruins, its scenery, and its Pacific beaches.

Nicaragua suffers from a poor location relative to other countries and some major physical and political problems, including internal strife. Tourism is not a major factor. It does have a large Indian culture, some Spanish-colonial cities, many lakes and volcanoes, and coastal resorts on both the Pacific and the Caribbean.

Costa Rica has a fairly well-developed tourist infrastructure, and promotion of its tourist attractions has resulted in significant tourist numbers. Central America, primarily Nicaragua, and the United States make up its major sources of tourists. Costa Rica is known for its volcanoes and its shoreline along the Pacific Ocean. Its political and economic stability have greatly helped its tourism development.

Panama's main claim to tourism fame is the Panama Canal. Cruise business accounts for much of Panama's receipts from tourism. Short excursions are also important. Panama's strategic location means that it attracts visitors from a wider variety of countries than any other Central American nation.

The West Indies

The Caribbean is commonly used as a synonym for the historically correct West Indies. The major islands that comprise the West Indies are the Bahamas, Bermuda, Barbados, British Virgin Islands, Jamaica, Trinidad, Cuba, the Dominican Republic, the French West Indies, Haiti, the Netherlands Antilles, Puerto Rico, and the U.S. Virgin Islands.

Tourism in the Caribbean dates back to the 1920s. Tremendous growth, however, is a post–World War II phenomenon. North American tourists account for approximately 75 percent of the arrivals although an increasing number of Europeans are being attracted to the islands. The success of the Caribbean is due, however, to its proximity to North America. On some of the islands such as the Bahamas and the U.S. Virgin Islands tourism is the major industry. On others—Jamaica and Puerto Rico—it ranks second or third in importance.

Tourists are attracted by the weather (tropical, cooled by ocean breezes, and offering almost constant sunshine), the varied scenery, the sandy beaches, the opportunities for water sports—swimming, sailing, and snorkeling—and the color and culture of the islands. The islands were originally colonized by first the Spanish and then the British, the French, the Dutch, and the Americans. The influence of each culture can still be found there.

The most important tourist centers are Puerto Rico, the U.S. Virgin Islands, Jamaica, and Barbados.

Puerto Rico.   Puerto Rico receives about half of all the visitors to the Caribbean. Puerto Ricans call their island *La Isla del Encanto,* or the Isle of Enchantment. The development of tourism there is the result of a number of factors. First, Puerto Rico possesses great natural beauty and a distinctive Spanish culture. Second, the government, beginning in the late 1940s, built a number of hotels at public expense. These facilities, in turn, attracted private capital and other hotel facilities. Third, the 1959 Cuban Revolution caused much of the tourist trade to divert from Cuba to Puerto Rico. Finally, air service between the U.S. mainland and the island was very inexpensive. Originally set up to help migrant Puerto Ricans, the low prices encouraged Caribbean travel from the United States.

Typically we think of demand stimulating supply. That is, when there is a demand for vacations, people are encouraged to develop facilities to meet the demand. From this it can be seen that the supply of tourist facilities—hotels and cheap air travel—can actually stimulate demand for vacations.

U.S. Virgin Islands.   St. Croix, St. Thomas, and St. John make up the U.S. Virgin Islands. Their free-port status means that goods, imported for resale, are exempt from duties and taxes. The result is that tourists can pick up many bargains. The largest island is St. Croix, which is also the most historic. St. Thomas, the liveliest, offers steel bands and limbo dancers. The most natural is St. John with its quiet beaches and wooded mountains.

A problem for the islands is that tourism may have developed too fast and too soon. There is some criticism that speculators, having made a quick profit, have left behind a contrived tourist environment and residents who are unhappy with the way the development has occurred. The future success of these islands will depend on recapturing the original roots of the islands. In addition, the locals will have to be educated to see tourism as a long-term process to be encouraged slowly rather than as a way to make as much money as quickly as possible.

Jamaica.   Jamaica receives approximately 85 percent of its visitors from North America. Originally tourists came primarily by cruise ship and banana boat. Now the vast majority arrive by air. In addition to its proximity to the market, tourism development in Jamaica was aided by the Cuban Revolution and the excellent efforts of the Jamaican Tourist Board, thought by some to be the best in the Caribbean. Tourism is the second largest foreign-exchange earner and the third most important economic activity after bauxite mining and sugar production.

Jamaica is best-known for its clean beaches of white and pink sand and its sheltered waters. Montego Bay is an international resort; Port Antonio offers fishing and yachting; Kingston is the capital while the North Coast has beautiful beaches and protected bays.

Barbados.   Barbados depends on North America for about 60 percent of its tourist visitors. It is also a traditional vacation center for West Indians from neighboring islands. Recent attempts have been made to tempt more Britons and Europeans to vacation there.

Other Tourist Centers.   There are numerous other islands in the West Indies that have great tourist potential. The British Virgin Islands offer facilities for sailing and other water sports. The attractions of Haiti—namely the culture, which includes voodoo, the Haitian Alps, and the beaches—are overshadowed by the unstable political system. The Dominican Republic—the burial place of Christopher Columbus—has gambling, free-port shopping, and water sports. Tourism is the major economic activity for Bermuda. It is known for its coral reefs, its beautiful flowers, and its settings for water activities.

The Netherland Antilles, originally controlled by the Dutch, consist of the islands of Aruba, Bonaire, Curacao, St. Eustatius, St. Maarten, and Saba. Because each island offers something different, island-hopping is popular. The various islands have elements of culture from France, the Netherlands, Great Britain, as well as their own independent histories. Aruba was named "Ora Uba" or "there is gold" by the Spanish. It is best-known for its beaches. Curacao has developed a reputation for inexpensive shopping. Bonaire has great natural greenery. St. Eustatius has stressed its history, while St. Maarten promotes its dual cultures—French and Dutch. Both cuisines can be found on the island. Saba has no beaches. The local airport is built atop a mountain. Both ends of the airstrip plunge steeply to the sea below. Saba's cool climate (the island rises 2,900 feet from the ocean) encourages the growth of many flowers and trees.

Cuba was once an important tourist industry because of its political, geographic, and economic ties to the United States. In Havana, the capital, tourists could gamble the night away. After the revolution, Fidel Castro wanted to rid the country of its dependence on the United States. For its part the U.S. government prohibited travel by American citizens to Cuba. As a result the tourist industry in Cuba collapsed.

The Bahamas.   The Bahamas share the same kind of tourist attractions and rely on the same market as the other islands mentioned above. Consisting of 3,000 islands, islets, and rocks, this independent nation offers a healthy climate, beautiful marine scenery, some elements of its British colonial background, and excellent bathing, boating, and fishing facilities. Because it is so reliant on the North American market its economy lives or dies with the economic conditions in North America. It is said that the Bahamas catches a cold six months after the United States sneezes. Because of this Bahamian officials are trying to diversify their tourism by developing lower cost facilities to appeal to the Europeans, who tend to stay twice as long as do North Americans. Attempts are also being made to rely less heavily on tourism, although tourism still accounts for about half of all government revenue and provides jobs for almost three-quarters of the population.

The Bahamas' reputation as a retirement haven came about because of the sunshine, inexpensive land, and lack of taxes. Tourism has of late caused land prices to rise and has taken the bloom off this source of business.

Cruising.   Caribbean cruising has undergone a remarkable growth in the past two decades. Several reasons account for this. With the introduction of the jet aircraft transatlantic crossing diminished sharply. The shipping companies were left with large ships and no passengers. Thus, they turned to cruising as a way of using their investment. The growing affluence of North Americans provided an impetus for the growth of cruises. Originally, most cruises left from New York, but now most leave from Florida ports. The reason was simple. Why sail through two days of cold, winter weather to reach the sun then leave that same sun early to sail back north?

Another factor that influenced cruising was the increasing cost of fuel. As fuel prices escalated dramatically in the 1970s it made economic sense to build ships specifically for cruising that were lighter than those necessary for a transatlantic crossing. It also made sense to visit a variety of ports rather than spend the entire cruise at sea. In port the ships were not burning up fuel. The variety of islands in the Caribbean offered ships the opportunity to sail from port to port, sometimes spending each day in a different island. Apart from the Greek islands, there is no other part of the world where this is possible.

Again we see an example of supply influencing demand. A combination of supply, transatlantic liners, and demand by affluent Americans led to the development of more cruises by the shipping companies. The price of fuel and the availability of numerous stopping places influenced the present shape of cruising.

South America

South America has outstanding and varied scenery, good beaches, more ski areas than Europe, an attractive climate, numerous wildlife, interesting cultures, and examples of important archaeological sites. Yet it is responsible for just over 1 percent of tourist arrivals worldwide. There are three reasons for this. First, South America is, by and large, undeveloped in terms of attractions and facilities. Second, it is a great distance from the major tourist-generating areas of the world. Brazil, for example, is 3,000 miles from both the United States and Europe. Third, there are many intervening opportunities—countries offering the same type of attractions—between South America and the tourist-generating countries.

Argentina. Argentina attracts the largest number of visitors to a South American country. Most come from the neighboring countries of Uruguay, Chile, and Paraguay. The largest numbers come in the winter months. When Argentinians travel abroad they go primarily to Uruguay, Brazil, and Chile. North America and Europe are the favored destinations of the relatively small number of Argentinians who travel overseas.

The country has a number of attractions. Its capital, Buenos Aires, is well known. The Iguassu Falls, on the river of the same name, is more spectacular than either Niagara or Victoria falls. The Lake District of western Argentina attracts visitors primarily to the northern lakes. Long coastal stretches offer excellent beaches, casinos, and resorts. Patagonia in the south marks the foothills of the Andes. The area offers recreational opportunities including hunting, fishing, and golf in the summer and skiing in the winter.

Uruguay. Tourism is the third most important of Uruguay's exports. Approximately 90 percent of its visitors come from Argentina and Brazil. Of the two, Argentina is more important. The tourists are primarily made up of those wealthy enough to escape from the summer heat. From Montevideo 200 miles north to La Paloma there are excellent beaches for sunning and swimming.

Brazil. Brazil is the largest country in South America, the fifth largest in the world. It runs a negative balance in its tourism account. Much less is brought in by tourism than is spent by Brazilians abroad. The United States is the principal source of visitors, followed by Argentina and Uruguay. Brazil's historical ties with Portugal result in a number of visitors annually from that country.

Brazil is seeking to develop tourism from a domestic base. Domestic tourism, however, is a fairly recent phenomenon. The popularity of water spa resorts in the 1930s led to the beginnings of domestic tourism. A small number of very rich and a growing middle class are stimulating the demand for vacations. The effort has also been helped by the setting up in the mid-1960s of Embratur and the National Tourism Council. Both have sought to assist in planning and financing the development of badly needed accommodation and other facilities such as roads.

There are three major areas of tourist potential. Amazonia has exotic wildlife and huge rain forests. Trips up the Amazon River appeal to a relatively small number of people.

The Northeast has magnificent natural resources including beaches and sunshine, wonderful churches, and towns brimming with what in tourism is called "local charm." The region is called the "Venice of America."

The South-Central region is the heartland of the country. It is the most densely populated port, the most economically developed, and the most urbanized. Rio de Janeiro is known worldwide for its Copacabana Beach. Sao Paulo is the commercial center of Brazil, and its capital, Brasilia, attracts much business traffic. The mountain resorts of the state of Rio de Janeiro serve as weekend retreats for office workers from the cities.

Other Countries.   Bolivia has a number of resources that have tourist potential such as archaeological and historic sites. However, little has been done to encourage tourism and thus it is of little importance to Bolivia.

The vast majority of tourists to Chile come from Argentina. They are drawn by the spectacular scenery of the Lake District. Portillo, in the Andes in central Chile, is the biggest center of skiing in South America. The ski season runs from June to October although the major months for tourism are January and February. (Remember, the seasons are reversed south of the equator.) There are a number of coastal resorts including the major port of Valparaiso. Four hundred miles west is the island of Juan Fernandez, the setting for Robinson Crusoe. The capital of Santiago is Chile's major tourist city.

Colombia attracts visitors from Venezuela, the United States, and, a distant third, Ecuador. Tourism is encouraged, and there are a number of resorts as well as scenic valleys and dense jungles. The tourist season is year-round and peaks in December.

Tourism is also encouraged in Ecuador. Tourism peaks in the summer months. The largest tourist-generating country is the United States. Visitors are attracted by the mountains, the volcanoes, and the local Indian culture.

Paraguay is known for its lakes, rivers, and waterfalls. Its capital and the main city to visit is Asuncion.

The United States is the leading generator of tourists to Peru. It accounts for more than twice as many visitors as the second-generating country, Argentina. Peru is known as the site of the lost city of the Incas at Machu Picchu. Extensive ruins are also found in Cuzco and on the plains. The capital, Lima, offers palaces, museums, and a colorful changing-of-the-guard ceremony.

WESTERN EUROPE

Western Europe is the single most important tourism-generating and tourism-receiving region in the world. Approximately 80 percent of all tourism in Europe is domestic. Yet foreign travel is gaining in importance. The most important generators of foreign traffic are West Germany, the United Kingdom, and France. The growth of travelers to Spain is the most significant trend in receiving countries. There is a marked seasonal effect with the vast majority of travel occurring during the summer. The automobile is used for about half the vacations taken, and hotels are the primary source of accommodation.

On a global basis Europe is the major tourist destination, accounting for about 75 percent of all international tourist movements. Tourists come primarily from Western Europe and North America. Tourists from outside of Europe mainly frequent Italy, France, the United Kingdom, and Spain.

When Europeans vacation outside of Europe they travel to North America and North Africa, the offshore Atlantic islands, and East Africa.

United Kingdom.   The United Kingdom is made up of England, Scotland, Wales, and Northern Ireland. The annual "holiday" is very important to the British, and the proportion of the population taking a vacation is over 60 percent. While an increasing percentage vacation abroad, most holidays are taken within Britain itself. Recent growth in the number of vacations has come from the growing numbers of people who are taking a second and even a third break, usually a short, off-season holiday. However, approximately two out of three vacations are taken in either July or August.

Traditionally the British have had a pattern of spending their vacations at the same seaside resorts year after year. Habits are changing as more and more people travel outside the country. However, the old pattern, particularly with manual workers, can still be observed. Almost three fourths of main holidays involve a stay by the seaside. Workers from the north of England make for Blackpool; in the south the favored places are Brighton, Margate, and Southend. The Southwest, because of increased accessibility to major population areas and its reliable climate, is the most important tourist region and has been ever since World War II. The major attraction is the coast. The Southwest is closely followed in importance by the Southeast and the South. The coast and the climate are, again, the major reasons.

Most tourists travel to one spot and stay. Only a small percentage take a touring holiday.

Outside of the Southwest, which attracts people from regions both near and far, the majority of visitors to other regions come from areas close by. Analysts have also noted a reluctance for people from the south to travel north on vacation, particularly on their main vacation.

There has been a tremendous growth in the numbers of British tourists traveling abroad. A major reason for the increase has been the growth of inclusive tours offering cut-rate holidays. The average length of stay abroad is two weeks in Europe although visits to North America average four to five weeks. About 90 percent of all visits abroad are to Europe. In the 1950s the most popular destinations were France and Switzerland; today it is Spain. Increasing numbers are traveling farther afield to Yugoslavia, Turkey, Tunisia, and Morocco.

The United States generates more visitors to Britain than any other country. Significant numbers also come from France, West Germany, the Netherlands, and Canada. Visits from North America are primarily because of ethnic, cultural, and historical ties. Geographic proximity together with the standard of living in the generating country probably accounts for the numbers from Western Europe.

The United Kingdom runs a surplus in its tourism account.

The so-called milk run for international visitors is London, Stonehenge, Stratford-Upon-Avon, and Edinburgh. Yet outside of these four places, there is a variety of things to see and do. London is known for its history, its museums, the pageantry of royal occasions, and its theater. A number of famous cathedrals—Canterbury, Winchester, and Salisbury—complement the monument of Stonehenge in the south. The Southwest has a mild climate with numerous small harbors. Plymouth was the departure point for the *Mayflower* Pilgrims. The Roman spas at Bath are spectacular enough without the magnificent eighteenth-century architecture of the buildings. Stratford-Upon-Avon is Shakespeare country and home to one of the loveliest gardens in England at the family cottage of his wife—Anne Hathaway. The Lake District in the northwest of England offers national park land in a lovely setting of lakes, hills, and moors.

Scotland is famed for its capital, Edinburgh, scene of the famous Edinburgh Arts and Music Festival every fall. Known as one of the most beautiful of capital cities, Edinburgh is famed for its spectacular castle.

The north of Scotland offers the Highlands, which attract hikers, cyclists, anglers, and those who want to marvel at its beauty. It is also home to Loch Ness of monster fame.

Wales offers the visitor the combined scenery of mountains and coast.

Eire. Eire is often referred to as the Republic of Ireland, or Southern Ireland. Compared to the rest of the world, Eire is not a major tourism country. Yet tourism is very important to Eire as a means of balancing its accounts with the rest of the world. Outside of Austria and Spain, no other European country is as dependent on tourism for this purpose.

The vast majority of tourists visiting the Republic of Ireland come from Great Britain. Despite a marked decline in numbers because of what the Irish call "the troubles," the violence that has occurred as supporters of the Irish Republican Army have attempted to unite the Republic of Ireland with Northern Ireland, Britain is still overwhelmingly the number-one market. Visitors from the United States comprise the second largest market, followed by travelers from Northern Ireland. These three markets account for essentially all tourist visits.

Tourists visit Eire for two reasons. First, they are attracted by the landscape—green rolling hills and undeveloped countryside that is quiet and restful. Second, they come to see and experience the Celtic culture, a distinctive and relaxed way of life. But this is a very difficult thing to "sell." As tourists are attracted, facilities must be developed for them. However, unless it is done very carefully, the development of modern hotels and restaurants can completely change the way of life that is being sold as an attraction. This is especially true in western Ireland, which has the greatest potential for tourism development. It is also the most rural area, which in itself is an attraction. Many of the locals speak Gaelic and rent out rooms as part of a bed-and-breakfast establishment. As more tourists are attracted there, the locals must speak English. Tourists create a demand for modern hotels. Yet both these factors can begin to break down the traditional way of life that tourists come to see. This is a problem, indeed a dilemma, not only in Eire but also in other lesser developed nations.

Scandinavia

Norway. Because there are no frontier restrictions among Norway, Sweden, and Denmark it is difficult to get accurate accounts of travel among these three Scandinavian countries.

Norway is called the "northern playground." The word "ski" is Norwegian and Norwegians have capitalized on their natural resources to provide some of Europe's best ski slopes. In addition to the many winter attractions, Norway offers spectacular scenery, particularly on the Atlantic coast. The Norwegians are also known for their hospitality, their crafts, and their quaint old towns.

Over 60 percent of Norwegians take a vacation of four or more nights away from home in any one year. This high percentage is aided by the fact that all workers are allowed four weeks' vacation annually. Most holidays in Norway are to summer huts or chalets. Slightly more than 10 percent of the population vacation abroad. Many visit Britain, about half traveling independently.

Of travelers to Norway, the major markets are Sweden, Germany, the United States, Great Britain, and Denmark.

Sweden.   Sweden runs a heavy tourism deficit on her balance of payments account. Nearly half of the tourists who annually visit Sweden come from Scandinavia, mainly Denmark and Finland. The British market is large, although many visits are on business.

Sweden has what is described as the least spoiled countryside in Europe. In addition to Stockholm with its royal palace and museums there is interesting folklore and crafts in the Dalarna region. A number of medieval cities and castles are to be found throughout the country.

Denmark.   Denmark has over three times as many visitors as does Sweden, although many are travelers from West Germany en route somewhere else who stay only a short period of time. Sweden, the United States, and Great Britain, in addition to Germany, make up over 90 percent of the travelers to Denmark.

Copenhagen's Tivoli Gardens are a major attraction. A variety of fishing villages and museums—including the famous open-air Maritime Museum—attest to the country's heritage.

Finland.   The number-one tourist market for Finland is Sweden, followed by West Germany, Norway, the United States, and Great Britain. About half the tourists are Scandinavian. Helsinki is a favorite starting point for travel to the Soviet Union. The old town of Turku and Lapland in the Arctic are popular attractions.

Iceland.   The United States accounts for almost 60 percent of the tourists to Iceland. The national airline—Icelandic Airlines—markets one- and two-day stopovers for travelers en route to Europe. Reykjavik, the capital, is heated by natural hot springs. Tourists are attracted by the solitude, the geysers, and the glaciers. In addition, there are day trips to the nearby Greenland ice cap. The amount spent by visitors to Iceland is overshadowed many times by that spent by tourists from Iceland.

The Benelux Countries

The Netherland, Belgium, and Luxembourg comprise what are known as the Benelux countries. Because of their location all three have a significant number of visitors who are in transit to somewhere else and might stay a day or two in the region.

Belgium is known for its coastal resorts, the rich history of Flanders, and its capital, Brussels. The 40-mile stretch of coast between France and Holland is essentially one long beach made up of firm sand up to a mile wide in some places. Ideal for family holidays, Belgium's prime tourist season is the summer. The major resort towns are Ostend and Blankenberghe.

Bruges (the city of bridges) is the best-known and most beautiful of the medieval towns in the Plains of Flanders. Brussels is the site of both the parliament of the Common Market and headquarters of the North Atlantic Treaty Organization (NATO). Its best attractions are the Grande Place—the ornate town square—which features a sound-and-light spectacular every night and the nearby Mannequin Pis, a famous statue of a small boy.

The Ardennes in the south offer spas, streams, parks, and woods. A number of designated parks and nature preserves attract the tourist. The town of Spar gave its name to the spa.

The major tourist markets attracted to Belgium are the Netherlands, West Germany, the United Kingdom, and France. Outside of Europe, the United States sends the most visitors to Belgium.

The Grand Duchy of Luxembourg offers lovely scenery, a restful atmosphere, and good fishing and boating. Luxembourg has a romantic quality about it.

The Netherlands attracts tourists to see the spring flower festivals and auctions in the fields around Haarlem. Picturesque villages such as Volendam, where traditional costumes are worn, show a slice of the culture. Dutch hospitality is understated but sincere. Amsterdam, the capital, is a vibrant city with outstanding museums such as the Rijksmuseum and the Van Gogh museum in addition to the very moving Anne Frank house.

West Germany is responsible for about three times as many tourists as the United Kingdom, the second source of visitors. The United States, third as a source of tourists, is responsible for approximately 10 percent of the visitors to Holland.

France

France, Spain, and Italy are the three major tourist countries in Europe. France is a large nation with a number of regions offering a variety of attractions. France has a moderate to ideal climate, is blessed with an excellent location and a rich cultural heritage, and enjoys a well-deserved reputation for fine cuisine.

France was an important destination back in the days of the Grand Tour when the country was thought of as the most advanced and civilized nation in Europe. Outside of the spas, the Riviera, on the Mediterranean, was the first tourist area. It began as a fashionable winter resort center catering largely to the British. After World War II the Riviera became more popular as a summer attraction to middle-class vacationers.

America sends more tourists to France than does any other non-European country. This is probably due to the image that France has as an ally of the United States, the importance of Paris to Americans, together with the other numerous attractions of the country.

There are also strong numbers from West Germany, the United Kingdom, Italy, and the Benelux countries. The majority of British tourists visit Normandy and Brittany.

Paris is the most popular attraction for foreigners. The city is beautifully laid out with many wide boulevards offering splendid vistas. As a center of culture, museums, history, and shopping, Paris is difficult to surpass. Close to Paris is the palace of Versailles. Built by Louis XIV it is regarded as one of the most outstanding structures in the world.

The rise in domestic tourism can be attributed to events in 1936. At that time all workers were given 15 days' vacation a year. The onslaught of World War II obviously halted any type of tourism. After the war, tourism accelerated because of two factors—increased prosperity of the working classes and the institution of four weeks of holiday with pay for workers. The prosperity led to increased car ownership, more mobility, and the development of vacations based on auto travel.

There are several features to domestic tourism in France. While the French worker has time off, long vacations are expensive. This has led to an increase in camping as a way to have inexpensive holidays. Many tourists use their own cars, sleep in tents or trailers, and fix their own meals. Camping tends to disperse the economic benefits of tourism to rural areas that would not otherwise benefit from visitors.

France is one of many countries offering what is known as *social tourism*. Social tourism involves a degree of subsidization to people of limited means to allow them to vacation. It often means that people who belong to a club or union can vacation inexpensively. In France this is seen in the *colonie de vacances*, which are hostels for young children located in the country. Opportunities are available for different kinds of outdoor recreation. On the other hand, many professional organizations own their own apartments and villas, which provide vacations to their members at rates far below that charged by companies in the marketplace.

Another feature of French domestic tourism is the relatively high percentage who stay with relatives while on vacation.

The vast majority of the French vacation in France. Provençe-Côte d'Azur is the most popular region. Most tourists travel south although Brittany is a popular regional destination. Spain and Italy are the most favored destinations outside the nation. July and August are the most popular months for holidays. The result, as elsewhere, is congestion and higher prices during the summer months.

In the northern part of France and Upper Normandy are a number of resorts that were very fashionable in the 1920s. A prime example is Le Touquet. These resorts now serve the industrial population of the north of France. Lower Normandy has a number of second homes on the coast owned by Parisiens. This area of the Channel coast contains the entry ports for tourists arriving by hovercraft and ferry from England.

Brittany offers a coast ideal for yachting and water sports because of its numerous coves and sandy bays. Small fishing villages show the Breton way of life. However, the region suffers from the moist air coming in off the Atlantic; the humidity is high and there are many cloudy and drizzly days. Winters are mild but not as pleasant as elsewhere in the south. Brittany is also physically remote from major centers of population. Because of the weather, the tourist season is very short.

The resorts of Aquitaine benefit from the southern location. The coast has a wide band of sand dunes. Several resorts, such as Biarritz, are popular in both summer and winter. The Trans-Aquitaine Canal runs parallel to the coast and provides opportunities for sailing and water sports.

Auvergne is the center of the Central Plateau region. Tourism began as an interest in the thermal springs and fresh mountain air as a treatment for various maladies. Winter sports have since developed in a region whose highest elevation is over 6,000 feet.

The Côte d'Azur or Riviera is probably the most famous tourist region of France. The coast is attractive; the climate is ideal; the sea is warm and deep blue; the resorts—St. Tropez, Cannes, Nice, Monte Carlo (in the Principality of Monaco)—are world famous. Originally a winter resort area, summer business in the Côte d'Azur is now three times as important as that in the winter months. Monte Carlo is best-known for its casino gambling.

The popularity of this region has led to a number of problems. Urban expansion has meant an almost continuous line of development the entire length of the coast. This has led to severe congestion. The growth of tourism has also made itself felt in inflated land prices. As a result, tourism has developed inland and swallowed up small agricultural villages. The high prices have also meant that industry cannot afford to develop in the area. While certain types of industry do not combine well with tourism, less industrialized development can offer employment in the off-season. A final problem is that of pollution. Certain beaches have been closed to the public because of this.

As tourism has changed—from tourists who would stay many weeks or even months to those requiring cheaper forms of accommodation for a shorter period of time—many resort areas have been unwilling or unable to respond. They also face increasing competition from the resorts of Spain and Italy.

Languedoc-Roussillon on the Mediterranean is the site of the most extensive tourism development operation in Europe. A narrow strip of coast 120 miles in length, it had few residents, was not well known, and was backed by land difficult to reclaim. It did have excellent sandy beaches and many lagoons capable of being developed for water sports. The result has been the development of several resorts—population 50,000 each—capitalizing on the beaches, the sunshine, and the recreational capabilities of the area.

France has 200 winter sports resorts. Most are in the Alps. The coming of the railway was responsible for the development of tourism in the Alps by opening up previously inaccessible areas. The seven-mile tunnel under Mount Blanc has opened up a route between France and Italy. Opinion is divided as to whether or not this will mean that tourists will continue to Italy instead of skiing in France. The popularity of winter sports has meant, amongst other things, that new areas have been developed from scratch. The result has been the repopulation of previously declining communities.

The Pyrennes region, between France and Spain, is a scenic mountain area populated by the Basques. In the foothills is the religious shrine at Lourdes.

The island of Corsica is best-known as the birthplace of Napoleon. Its rocky coastline offers yachting and water sports, while inland there are thermal springs. Corsica remains relatively undeveloped.

West Germany

West Germany and the United States are the world's largest generators of foreign tourists. This is, in great part, a reflection of the strength of the economies of the two countries. However, whereas almost half of the travelers from the United States visit another world region—predominantly Europe—most West Germans vacation within the same region. West Germany shares borders with nine other countries. Denmark is the recipient of most visitors from West Germany although they tend to be short-term excursionists. As a combination of number of tourists and amount of money spent in the destination country, the most important destinations for Germans are Austria, Italy, Spain, Switzerland, and France. German tourists spend more per capita than any other national outside of Americans.

Other European countries account for about 70 percent of the visitors to West Germany. This percentage is one of the smallest for European countries. West Germany ranks a distant fourth among European nations as a destination, behind Spain, Italy, and France. The two principal tourist-generating countries for West Germany are the Netherlands and the United States. The United Kingdom, France, and Belgium/Luxembourg follow distantly. The average length of stay tends to be short, an indication that much of the tourism is made up of people en route elsewhere. Visits tend to peak in June and July although tourism is strong throughout much of the year.

West Germany is known for her scenery and culture. The main tourist regions are the Rhine Gorge, the hill country of the Rift Valley, and Bavaria. On the middle Rhine in particular, between Bonn and Bingen, the scenery is spectacular. Romantic castles overlook the river every few hundred yards. Marksburg is the best-preserved of the castles. A number of towns feature curative mineral springs. The Rhine is also a major wine-producing region. Several villages have annual wine festivals. Rüdesheim features the *Drosselgasse,* an extremely narrow street that is wall-to-wall wine taverns. While Germany is best-known for white Rhine and Moselle wine, Assmannshausen is famous for its red wine.

The Rhine Rift Valley, farther south, is best-known for the Black Forest, a region that encourages outdoor recreation. Numerous youth hostels are available for the young traveler.

Bavaria is the end point of the 225-mile long *Romantische Strasse* (Romantic Highway) that runs south from Würzburg to Füssen. The capital of Bavaria is Munich, scene of the annual beer festival—*Oktoberfest.* South of Munich lie the German Alps. Garmisch-Partenkirchen is the most famous of the winter sports center. Apart from winter sports and magnificent mountains (the Alps extend 200 miles) Bavaria is also known for the castles of King LudwigII. His most famous castles are at Linderhof and the fairy tale Neuschwanstein, the "model" for Walt Disney's Disneyworld castle. Other important places are Oberammergau, site of the Easter Passion Play held every 10 years, the former concentration camp of Dachau, and Hitler's nest at Berchtesgaden.

Mention should be made of Berlin. The former capital of a unified Germany, Berlin today is divided into West Berlin and East Berlin, which is Communist controlled. A visit to the city makes for an interesting comparison.

Switzerland

The first visitors to Switzerland were in the Middle Ages when the attractions were the numerous mineral springs. The latter half of the nineteenth century saw the popularity of mountaineering in the country, predominantly by British climbers. Visitors who were attracted by the spectacular scenery or the possibilities of winter sports soon eclipsed the numbers of mountain climbers. Skiing was introduced from Norway in the 1870s and skating from Holland in the 1880s. The popularity of skiing increased dramatically after World War I and owes much of its success to the development of hydroelectric power and a transport system that allowed for the building of ski lifts and aerial cableways that opened up previously inaccessible areas.

Switzerland is blessed with almost year-round tourism. From Christmas to April winter sports are dominant in the Alpine areas in such famous resorts as Davos, Gstaad, St. Moritz, and Zermatt. Many of these resorts also attract the health conscious. Resorts on the lakes lure visitors, especially from West Germany, for their combination of healthy air and mineral springs. Centers at Montreaux, Lucerne, Lausanne, and Interlaken are among the best-known. The summer season runs from May to October.

The scenery of Switzerland is the best in Europe and offers abundant natural attractions—mountains, glaciers, rivers, lakes, along with a good climate.

The country has also gained a well-deserved reputation for standards of excellence in hotel management. The Swiss specialize in comfort, cleanliness, fine food, and special service.

Two other reasons for the success of tourism should be noted. First, Switzerland is located at the geographic center of Europe in a prime position to capture traffic across the Alps. Second, Switzerland has traditionally been a neutral country. It offers tourists a legacy of security and freedom.

Switzerland runs a large surplus on its tourism account, which makes up almost 10 percent of total income for the country.

West Germany accounts for almost one-third of all visitors to Switzerland. The United States is the second most important market.

Liechtenstein.   Located in the mountains between Switzerland and Austria, this tiny country is a place to buy stamps and send postcards from. Rumor has it that a Grand Duke put his nation on the tourist map by persuading tour operators in New York to stop in Liechtenstein for lunch. In this way they could advertise "Visit 9 countries in 15 days" rather than "Visit 8 countries in 15 days."

Austria.   Mountains cover 70 percent of Austria. It is not surprising, therefore, that the Alpine region or Tyrol is a major attraction. In the summer the resort center of Innsbruck offers access to glaciers, forests, green valleys, picturesque villages, and mountain peaks. In the winter it is a skier's dream.

To the east is the Austrian Lakeland. Salzburg is the center for this region. A medieval city, it is known for its international music festival. Salzburg is the birthplace of Mozart and, much more recently, the location for the movie *The Sound of Music.*

Vienna was the capital of the Hapsburg Empire, and it remains a beautiful city with fine churches, palaces, and museums. It is home to the Spanish Riding School, the Vienna Boys' Choir, and the Vienna Woods.

The peak tourist season is from June until the end of October. Tourism is very important to Austria, being the largest invisible (service) export. Few Austrians travel abroad. The result is a large tourism balance. Almost 60 percent of visitors to Austria come from West Germany. The Netherlands, the United Kingdom, and the United States make up the other most important markets.

SOUTHERN EUROPE

Spain

Tourism in Spain was relatively undeveloped until after World War II. Since then there has been a virtual explosion in visits to that country. Most tourists come from France. Portugal and the United Kingdom make up the other major markets. The growth of tourism can be explained by several factors. For the British the attraction is the sunshine. For the French and the Portuguese the difference is the cost. Because Spain entered the tourism business rather late, prices were lower than in France and Italy where tourism development had driven prices up. With the development of charter flights it became relatively inexpensive to vacation in Spain. Another factor dates back to the 1960s when it became very fashionable in Britain to holiday in Spain, especially on the Costa Brava. Tour operators followed the trend and their promotional efforts attracted even more tourists.

Tourism is the most important part of Spain's economy. Madrid, the capital, is a base for visiting the historic cities of Segovia, Salamanca, and Toledo. Some other towns attract tourists largely because they are on main routes to the coast. Tourism, however, is concentrated on the Mediterranean coast and the Balearic Islands, which account for about 70 percent of visitors to Spain. The Costa Brava (Rocky Coast), the Costa Blanca, and the Costa del Sol are the best-known areas although the Costa de la Luz has been promoted in an attempt to spread the benefits of tourism. The Balearic Islands of Mallorca (or Majorca), Menorca (or Minorca), Ibiza, and Formentera have about one-third of all the hotel beds in the country. Mallorca is the major tourist area, largely because of its direct air connections. Congestion is a problem, however.

The Spanish government has been aware of the need to spread the benefits of tourism further, and it has attempted, somewhat unsuccessfully, to promote other regions of the country. The Biscayan and Atlantic coasts offer fine beaches and excellent shelter for sailing. The northern resort of San Sebastián is regarded as the most elegant in the country.

It attracts a number of Spaniards, but tourism is limited to the summer months. The climate is pleasant but not as predictable as in the south. In the Pyrenees and Sierra Nevadas there are a number of ski areas. Spain also boasts various reservoirs as a result of the demand for hydro-electric power. These have potential as recreational resources.

Tourism is very seasonal, peaking in the summer months. There have been efforts—mostly successful—to attract winter tourists from Britain. The fact that most foreign visitors come when domestic demand is high means that a severe strain is placed on all tourist facilities.

The Canary Islands. The Canary Islands, off the coast of Spain, are administered by Spain and consist chiefly of Tenerife, Grand Canary, Palma, Hierro, and Gomera. The scenery is spectacular and the islands offer interesting geological formations. The lack of rainfall means that water can be scarce, and the islands lack the lush summer green of other areas.

The islands have easy access to Europe by air. Additionally, they are a favorite stopping point for cruise ships on their way to Africa and South America.

Portugal and Madeira

A large number of the trips to Portugal are made up of short visits by motorists from Spain, shore visits by cruise ship passengers, and short stopovers by air travelers. Spain accounts for most short- and long-term (over five days) visits. Short-term visits are to see friends and family and, as such, bring in little money. Cruise business is concentrated in Lisbon, the capital, and Funchal on the island of Madeira in the Atlantic. Tourists from the United Kingdom and the United States are important markets.

The Portuguese went after two segments of the market—the upscale tourist and the permanent foreign resident. By encouraging the development of second homes they hoped to encourage tourists who would return year after year and who would bring along friends. This type of tourist tends to spend more on local services. The result is that the economic benefits of tourism spread to many people. This type of investment also requires little government support.

Tourism is concentrated in three areas—Lisbon, the Algarve, and Madeira. Lisbon offers a variety of cultural attractions. The nearby resort of Estoril has casino gambling while the Tagus estuary coast is the major area for recreation and a favorite of the affluent, royalty, and the nobility.

The Algarve is the south-facing coastal strip that runs from Sagres to the Spanish border. Numerous fishing villages have developed into vacation resorts catering to tourists who stay for long durations. Because of the location the area relies heavily upon air transportation to bring in tourists.

Madeira lies 400 miles off the west coast of Morocco. The climate is magnificent and the scenery spectacular, especially from April to June when the island is ablaze with colorful flowers. A favorite place for affluent Britons, the island still retains that flavor, even as it attracts Swedes and Germans. Tourism is important year-round. Most visitors are short-stay passengers from cruise ships, who stop to buy embroidery, wickerwork, and, the chief export, Madeira wine.

Italy

In the days of the Grand Tour, Italy was the final destination of European travelers. Tourism still looms important for this country. Germany sends the most tourists to Italy, followed by Switzerland, France, and Austria. The United States, largely because of its strong Italian-American population, is also an important market.

Tourism exists on a year-round basis. Italy has a temperate climate, fine coasts, and a rich history and cultural heritage. Some of the most notable centers of culture are Venice, Florence, Siena, Rome, and Naples. Rome is the seat of Vatican City, center of the Roman Catholic Church. Italy also boasts over 150 hot springs that give life to spas and health-cure centers. Mountain resorts of the Italian Alps attract visitors in the summer and skiing enthusiasts in the winter.

Italy has 5,000 miles of coast. The Italian Riviera and western coasts have especially attractive winters and summers that are hot and sunny. The eastern coast is less attractive in the winter. The most popular resort areas are in the north in the region of Liguria (such as San Remo), farther south at Naples and Solerno (Capri and Sorrento), and just south of the Po delta (Rimini and Cattolica).

As a source of historic sites Italy knows no equal. Examples of Greek and Roman civilizations abound. A number of towns have their own individual personalities. Verona is built of rose-red brick; Ravenna is famed for its mosaics; Vicenza is known for its Palladian architecture while Pisa has its leaning tower.

In common with other countries, Italy faces the problem of overcrowding in the summer and underutilization the rest of the year. Despite government attempts to change the pattern of holiday-making, most Italians prefer to vacation in the summer, thereby adding to the problem. An additional problem is that most tourism takes place in the north of the country. Despite some success in developing facilities on the island of Sardinia most of the economic benefits of tourism accrue to the north.

Yugoslavia.   The completion of the Adriatic Highway from Rijeka in the north to Titograd in the south meant that fishing villages that once could be reached only from the sea were now easily accessible. This opened up Yugoslavia's major tourist resource—namely the long coastline of the Adriatic. The area offers sheltered lowlands, off-shore islands, long, sun-filled summers, and warm winters.

In the north is a national park, Plitvice Lakes, which features a staircase of 17 lakes in a gorge cut by the Korana River. In Slovenia, farther to the northwest, is an area of mountains and lakes suitable for relaxation and recreation.

Although Yugoslavia is a Communist country, tourism is encouraged because of the hard currency it brings in. The result is that most tourists are from the West. West Germany, Italy, and Austria are the most important tourist-generating countries. A significant number of British tourists have moved east in their search for the sun.

Greece.   Despite its many attractions, tourism to Greece has been a recent development. Distance from major tourist-generating countries, political uncertainty, and a lack of infrastructure have prevented the country from maximizing its potential.

Major attractions of Greece are its historic and architectural remains, attractive islands, unspoiled villages and ports, a sunny climate most of the year, and a people known for their hospitality.

West Germany, France, and the United States are the principal tourist-generating countries. The income from tourism is over 10 times as much as that spent by Greeks traveling abroad.

Recent concern has been expressed over whether or not the country can handle the number of tourists projected to travel there.

Malta.   Malta gained its independence from Britain in 1964. Up until that time the major economic activity was defense related. Tourism now provides substantial income for this Mediterranean island. Reflecting its past, the vast majority of tourists are British. A substantial number even retire to the island.

At one time or another Malta has been inhabited by the Phoenicians, Romans, Arabs, Normans, Knights of St. John, French, and the British. Each has added to the cultural heritage of the island. The climate is warm in summer, sometimes very hot or cool in winter. It tends to be windy in September. Water sports are available, including sailing regattas.

EASTERN EUROPE AND THE SOVIET UNION

Tourism in Eastern Europe is encouraged for two reasons—to publicize the political and economic achievements of the country and to bring in the hard currency required to purchase raw materials. Western travelers are shown the best features of the country in an attempt to impress on them that the political and economic system is working. The need for convertible or hard currency is also important. If the Soviet Union wishes to buy grain from the United States it must pay for that grain in U.S. dollars. To get the dollars it goes to the international money market and "buys" dollars. The greater the demand for dollars, the greater the price of dollars. If tourists can be encouraged to bring dollars into a particular country and spend the dollars in the country, there is less need to buy dollars on the international market. Socialist countries have very strict currency controls. They tend to specify that a minimum amount of foreign currency be brought into the country per day of the visit. Moreover, tourists may be allowed to take a limited amount of currency, whether foreign or domestic, out of the country when they return home.

All foreign tourism in Eastern Europe and the USSR tends to be under the control of the government. The government owns and manages the facilities. It also controls the movement of its own citizens. A national is allowed to visit a country if it is in the Soviet bloc. To travel outside of the Communist bloc requires a visa, which is very difficult to get.

Czechoslovakia.   Czechoslovakia has a well-deserved reputation for its spas, such as those at Carlsbad and Marienbad. The country also has winter sports facilities. Prague, the capital, is a major attraction.

This is the leading tourist-receiving country of the socialist countries. Most tourists come from East Germany, Hungary, and Poland.

Bulgaria.   Bulgaria has beautiful scenery, a number of coastal resorts along the Black Sea, recreational opportunities, and hot springs in the mountains. The towns, including the capital, Sofia, offer a glimpse into the culture of the old country. Most tourists come from Turkey. Eastern European countries account for the bulk of the remainder.

Romania.   Although the skiing in the Carpathians is excellent, Romania's tourist activity is concentrated in the coastal resorts of the Black Sea. Visitors are also attracted to the capital, Bucharest. Eastern Europe accounts for almost 80 percent of the tourists to the country. They come from Czechoslovakia, Poland, and Hungary.

Poland.   When tourists visit Poland they go to the historic and cultural attractions of Warsaw (the capital), the resorts on the Baltic coast, the many spas, the ski resorts of the Tara Mountains, and the recreational opportunities afforded in the Masurian Lake district. Poland is second to Czechoslovakia in Eastern Europe in attracting tourists. They come from East Germany, Czechoslovakia, and the USSR.

Hungary.   In Hungary the attractions are the capital city of Budapest, the lake resort of Lake Catalon, and the folk culture of the small towns. Cruise ships from the Soviet Union come up the Danube. About 70 percent of visitors are from neighboring countries.

East Germany.   Travelers to the German Democratic Republic—East Germany—visit East Berlin, most entering from West Berlin and staying for less than a day, and also Dresden and Leipzig. Tourism is not important to East Germany.

The Soviet Union

Tourists to the Soviet Union are interested in the people—the country encompasses over a hundred different nationalities—the way of life under a Communist system, and the art and architecture of the nation.

The major tourist areas are Moscow, Leningrad, and Kiev, in the central region. In Moscow the principal features are the Kremlin, Red Square, and Lenin's Tomb. Along the Baltic coast, Tallinn and the ancient city of Riga are much visited. The Crimea and Black Sea regions are the Soviet Union's "Riviera." Major resorts include Odessa and Yalta. Resorts are varied, ranging from coastal towns and spas, founded originally on warm sulphur springs, to the skiing and climbing resorts of the high central Caucasus region. Further east is the Central Asian region. While Tashkent is a modern city, other towns in the region offer memories from past civilizations.

The average Soviet worker receives three to four weeks' annual paid vacation. Leisure time is considered an opportunity to recharge the body and soul. Official Soviet policy encourages health resorts and spas for this purpose. Spaces at these places are allocated through the trade unions to workers as a reward for their labor. This type of vacation is another example of social tourism.

The development of tourism from the West is hampered by a general suspicion of foreigners, generally lower standards of food and accommodation, tight controls on tourist movements, a lack of nighttime entertainment, and problems with communication.

AFRICA AND THE MIDDLE EAST

Tourism to Africa and the Middle East is heavily dependent on long-haul traffic. Development of speedy air transportation and inclusive tours has given tourism a boost. Its development, however, is hampered by a lack of infrastructure and political instability. Five distinct regions exist—North Africa, the Middle Eastern countries, West Africa, East Africa, and South Africa.

North Africa

From the viewpoint of tourism, North Africa is best described as the countries of Morocco, Tunisia, Algeria, Libya, and Egypt. The development of the region is an extension south of people's desire for the sun.

Tourism in Morocco has several elements. A number of cruise ships call at Casablanca and Tangier; because of its proximity to Spain by ferry—a two- to three-hour ride—there are many visitors from the northern Spanish coastal resorts who stay from one to three days. Moroccan nationals returning home for visits represent another source of tourists. Then there are the Europeans, primarily the French, who come primarily for the sun, sand, and sea of the Mediterranean.

The major coastal resorts of Morocco are Mohammedia in the north and Agadir in the south. Skiing is possible in the Atlas Mountains, which rise to a height of 13,000 feet. Visitors are also attracted to the culture of the country. It is a place where two worlds meet—the old and the new. An image of romance and mystery is conjured up by such places as Casablanca and the old walled city of Marrakesh, which was popularized by Sir Winston Churchill.

Most tourism occurs in the summer months, although the climate allows for year-round swimming and sunning.

Tourism is the major foreign-exchange earner for Tunisia. Lacking the diversity of attractions of its neighbors, tourism consists primarily of the attractions of its 750 miles of Mediterranean coast. It relies on package tours arriving by air from Europe, the most important markets being France and West Germany. The country boasts some of the best hotels in Africa. There is a semi-official law that prevents any building being higher than the tallest palm tree.

Tourism in Algeria is under the control of the government. The country is using tourism to bring in foreign exchange and jobs, to encourage balanced economic development to the various regions of the nation, and to revive the old Moorish culture. This latter development is evident in the architecture of the buildings and the revitalization of craft industries to furnish the hotels. Thus, in addition to the typical beach vacation, Algeria is interested in promoting the history and culture of the country. Initiatives have been taken to open up the Sahara to visitors. At various oases, facilities have been built—namely "caravanserai" or small hotels to cater to the short-stay visitor, luxury hotels to appeal to the longer-stay tourist.

Because of Algeria's colonial ties with France, this country sends most of the tourists to Algeria.

Libya's tourist industry is small and is dominated by visits from other Arab countries. The peak season is in the winter. Political instability hampers tourism development.

Although Egypt has both a Mediterranean and Red Sea coast, both coasts are not well developed as far as tourism is concerned. The prime attractions are the archaeological treasures—the Pyramids, the Sphinx, the Temple of Karnak, Ramses II, the City of the Dead. The mosques of Cairo are magnificent, as is the city of Alexandria. Most visitors come from Arab countries. The summer months are the peak tourist season.

Middle East

The Middle Eastern countries are Israel, Jordan, Syria, Lebanon, Turkey, Iran, and Iraq. The major attraction of Israel is religious. The country contains places that are considered holy to three religions—Judaism, Islam, and Christianity. Visitors come on pilgrimages, to visit families who have settled there and to see their Jewish ancestral homeland. The United States is the major tourist-generating country. Since the 1960s the proportion of visitors from North America has decreased while that from Europe has increased.

Almost all visitors go to the Holy City—Jerusalem. Bethlehem, the Dead Sea, and the Negev are also major centers of attraction associated with religion.

A growing number of Europeans travel to Israeli resort areas. Tiberias, on the shore of the Sea of Galilee, is a winter resort that features hot springs; Safed is a summer resort. Most tourists arrive in July and August, although there are peaks in March and April (Easter) and December (Christmas).

The Arab-Israeli war in 1967 resulted in Jordan losing land on the West Bank of the Jordan River to Israel, which recovered part of Jerusalem as well as Bethlehem and Jericho. Over 80 percent of Jordan's hotel accommodations were on the West Bank. Tourism essentially collapsed overnight. Since then attention has been turned to the East Bank. Jordan, called by some "an open-air museum," has a number of outstanding archaeological and historical sites. Chief among these are the ancient "lost" city of Petra, Jarash (a preserved Roman city), Madaba (extensive mosiacs), and the Ommayad castles around Amman. Tourism peaks in the winter months.

The majority of visitors to Syria are from the neighboring countries of Jordan, Lebanon, and Turkey. There are a number of desert palaces and Roman ruins. Damascus features a bazaar with over 3,000 shops.

Tourists from other Arab countries have long visited Lebanon. It is a country that possesses a wonderful climate, pleasant scenery, beaches, and mountain resorts offering relief from the heat in the summer and skiing in the winter. There are many historic sites and a tradition of hospitality. Beirut alone once had 120 nightclubs and 14,000 restaurants. But the present political situation and civil war has, obviously, had a negative impact on attempts to encourage tourism, particularly from the

West. The central government is not strong. Apart from the political ramifications, from a tourism viewpoint this means that overdevelopment of some prime areas has taken place with corresponding problems of visual and waste pollution.

Turkey is a blend of the cultures of the East and the West. It is a Mediterranean, Middle Eastern, and Balkan country. Despite its archaeological treasures, tourism development, to date, has concentrated on the coastal regions of Marmara, the Aegean, and Levantine seas. Cruise ships account for a large percentage of the visits. If tourism is to develop in a major way it will take the efforts of tour operators. At present Turkey suffers from its distance from major tourist-generating areas and a general lack of knowledge about the country. The leading generators of tourists are West Germany and France. There are a large number of Turkish nationals who work in West Germany. This may well have stimulated interest in Turkey as a vacation destination.

Pilgrimages to the Iranian holy cities of Isfahan and Qom account for a large number of visitors. Additionally, there are numerous sites and museums relating to the Persian Empire to attract the tourist. Iraq also has remnants of former civilizations including the ruins of Babylon, which feature the Hanging Gardens, one of the seven wonders of the ancient world. Recent hostilities between Iran and Iraq and an anti-Western bias in Iran have put a strain of tourism development.

Much of the flow of tourism in the countries mentioned above is a flow of Arabs to Arab countries. In attempting to revive Muslim traditions there has, in many places, been a desire to discourage visits from the West. Some Arab countries fear the effect that Western tourists will have on their traditional views toward alcohol and women.

Islamic tourism is centered around several themes. There is an attraction to cities. For the traditionalist, there are the mosques, the baths, and the bazaars, while the modern Islamic person travels to cities for business. Second, burial pilgrimages for the dead to such holy places as Najaf, Kadhimain, Hebron, and Medina are an important travel motivation. To people who live in or by the desert, water is an attraction. To escape the summer heat many travel to the mountains. Finally, family travel is important—visits to family members abroad or family members returning home.

West Africa.   The Ivory Coast offers the best tourism infrastructure of all the areas in West Africa. The most popular months for visitors are March and December. France is the major tourist-generating country. Tourists are attracted to the beaches set amid fishing villages.

Tourism is less important to the other West African countries. Ghana, Nigeria, and Zaire can all capitalize on their coastal beaches, bright scenery, and local color and culture.

East Africa.   Kenya, Uganda, and Tanzania offer essentially the same type of tourist attractions. Of the three, tourism is most widely developed in Kenya. Over 40 percent of the tourists to Kenya come from Europe, principally the United Kingdom, West Germany, Switzerland, and Italy. The United States accounts for about 10 percent of the visitors to Kenya. They come to visit the game parks, the wildlife reserves, and the coast. The vast majority of tourists visit the capital, Nairobi. From here the attractions are easily accessible. Photo safaris are popular in Nairobi National Park. A variety of other national parks combine magnificent scenery with animals and birds. Some of these are the Aberdare National Park with the Treetops Hotel set amidst mountain scenery; the Meru Game Reserve, and the Tsavo National Park, the largest national park in the world, which lies midway between the coast and Nairobi. The main road and railway line between Mombasa and the capital cross through it. Over one-fourth of the tourists to Kenya spend some time at the coast. The two principal resorts are Mombasa and Malindi.

While Uganda and Tanzania have beautiful scenery and game parks, tourism has not developed. Lake Victoria is a major resource for sailing and fishing although the major attraction is the Murchison Falls in the national park. The political situation in Uganda and the lack of facilities had a great deal to do with the lack of development there.

Tanzania is the largest East African country. Tourist resources exist in the coastal resorts around Dar-es-Salaam, the northern parks near the Kenyan border, and in the parks and game reserves in the southern part of the country. These resources have not, however, been developed to attract tourists.

The Republic of South Africa.   Political problems have tempered the development of tourism in South Africa, even though the country possesses some magnificent resources. The Kruger National Park and the Umfolozi Game Preserve are well known. The country shows its ties to the Afrikaner culture. People on the coast move inland for their vacations; those inland travel to the coast. Spas and country centers exist inland. Mineral waters and hot springs are the source of the spas. Other centers rely on mountains, camping, and fishing.

South Africa has 2,000 miles of coastal beaches. The chief resort areas are those of the Cape region, particularly those of the Hibiscus Coast.

ASIA AND THE PACIFIC

Distance and cost have meant that tourism in Asia and the Pacific has been slow to develop. It is expected that, as the focus of the world economy increasingly turns to this area, tourism will become more important, both inbound and outbound. The four areas that have had a long history of tourism are Hong Kong, Malaysia, Thailand, and Singapore.

Hong Kong.   The British lease on Hong Kong runs out in 1997. After that time the territory reverts to China.

The major generator of tourists to Hong Kong is Japan followed by the United States. Approximately two-thirds of the visitors to Hong Kong are from Pacific-area countries. They come to experience the Chinese culture and the free-port shopping. However, on the nearby islands there are good beaches. Visits tend to be short-term, an average of less than three days. Tourists often stop en route to somewhere else. Despite this, tourism is a major export for the island.

Malaysia.   As with Hong Kong, most tourists visiting Malaysia come from within the Pacific region, primarily Thailand. The influence of its membership in the British Commonwealth, however, is felt in the number of visitors from Australia and the United Kingdom. Tourists are attracted to picturesque towns (such as the thatched houses on stilts in the old part of Kuala Lumpur), the Buddhist temples, black sand beaches, jungles, and culture of the locals.

Thailand.   Thailand attracts visitors from the Pacific region and Europe. The United States accounts for about 10 percent of tourists to the country. The months of April, May, and June are the slowest months. Visitors come to see the temples, ancient cities, religious sites, jungles, and to enjoy the beach resorts. In addition, there are six hill tribes in the country, each with their own culture, who can be visited by tourists.

Singapore.   Singapore benefits from its location at a crossroads for both ships and airplanes. It is on the air routes to the Far East and Australasia and has what is regarded as the finest airport in Southeast Asia. However, tourists are usually en route to somewhere else. About half of tourist expenditure is on shopping. Singapore does have beautiful natural attractions including beaches and coral reefs. Government attempts to improve tourism have focused on developing Singapore as the convention capital of Southeast Asia. Conventions bring a captive group and can attract visitors in the off-season. Many festivals have also been developed, focusing on a blend of culture, food, and music.

The Indian Ocean Islands.   The white sand beaches, palm trees, high temperatures, clear skies, and warm seas give this area its "island paradise" image. The largest island by far is Madagascar. In fact, its size and limited means of communication pose problems. Tourism is concentrated in the capital of Tananarive, the volcanic "paradise" island of Nosy-Be and at Diégo-Suarez, a bay fringed by coral reef.

Tourism is fairly well established in Mauritius, which offers a variety of scenery in addition to coral reefs and beaches. Reunion, which is French, the Comoros, and the Seychelles, offer the tourist the opportunity to get away from it all. Facilities are lacking but the features of these islands will bring tourists and facilities to meet their needs. The problem will be to ensure that development does not harm the natural beauty of the islands.

India.   The chief tourists to India come from the United Kingdom and the United States. The attractions are the wildlife, ancient monuments, and, perhaps more importantly, the culture. The country offers a blend of Hindu, Moslem, and European influences. The dominant religions are Hinduism and Islam and many of the attractions relate to these. Temples and mosques, holy cities, and religious festivals abound. The most famous attraction is, of course, the Taj Mahal. A major problem for tourists is the large size of the country. The package circuit is recommended for many tourists—Bombay, Udaipur, Agra, Benares, and Dehli.

Sri Lanka.   Europe sends about two out of every three tourists to Sri Lanka (formerly Ceylon). The country has beaches comparable to those in the Caribbean—all 1,000 miles of them. There are also a variety of ancient monuments and temples. The peak months for tourism are between December and April, while the monsoons discourage tourists in June and July.

Taiwan.   Most visitors to Taiwan are from the Pacific region, notably Japan. North America accounts for a large number of tourists. The area has great natural beauty. The Taroko Gorge is reputed to be one of the wonders of the world while the vertical cliffs along the east coast are said to be the world's highest. Additionally, Taiwan offers a combination of old and modern China.

South Korea.   As with Taiwan, Japan is the major source of tourists to South Korea. Approximately 80 percent of visitors come from the Pacific region. The main attractions are Seoul, the capital, with its palaces and museums, and Kyongju, known for its temple and museums.

Japan.   Because of the strength of its economy, Japan has a heavy tourism deficit on its tourism account. Japanese travel to Southeast Asia (largely Hong Kong and Taiwan), the United States, and the United Kingdom. Travel abroad has been aided by the development of inclusive tours. Despite the distance separating the two, the United States is the major tourist-generating country for Japan.

There are many tourist regions in Japan. Hokkaido, the northernmost island, offers winter sports and mountain scenery. Tohoku, the northeastern section of the main island, is known for its national parks, hot springs, and local festivals. Kanto includes Tokyo in addition to shrines and temples; in the center of the main island of Honshu is Chubu, which features seven national parks, outstanding natural resources, and ski resorts. Kansai, which contains the cities of Kyoto and Osaku, has beautiful scenery and seascapes as well as the ancient capitals of Japan. Hiroshima, site of the first atomic bomb dropped on Japan, is in Chugoku. Located on the western end of the main island, it has beaches, coastal plateaus, and the Inland Sea National Park. Finally, Kyushu is an island with a subtropical climate, six national parks, and a variety of historic sites.

Australia.   New Zealand is the principal tourist-generating country for Australia, followed by the countries of North America. Tourism peaks in December, February, and August.

Tourists come for three reasons. About one in four visitors—mainly those from New Zealand and Great Britain—travel to visit relatives. Large numbers from neighboring islands visit for a change of physical environment and for recreation. Third, many travelers come for business reasons but stay for pleasure.

Australia does possess various natural attractions—the Great Barrier Reef, Ayers Rock—and superb beaches. There is a fairly well-developed domestic tourism business. The Australians greatly enjoy outdoor recreation.

New Zealand.   The tourist season in New Zealand runs from November to March. Most visitors come from Australia. The attractions are both natural and cultural. The scenery is spectacular; the country offers opportunities for sport and recreation such as sailing, skiing, hunting, and fishing; Maori settlements show the life and culture of the native people.

South Pacific.   Tourism in the South Pacific islands varies from the well-developed Fiji Islands to the less important (from a tourism perspective) Solomon Islands and Cook Islands. Tourism to these islands accounts for a very small percentage of Pacific tourism. Australia, followed by the United States, sends most tourists to these places. Visitors come for the natural beauty—mountains, lagoons, and vegetation—and the beaches. The various island cultures can also be experienced.

Oceania Islands.   Tourism to the islands of Oceania is a little greater because of Guam, an American island that has an extensive infrastructure. Japan and the United States send most tourists to Guam and to the other islands of Oceania, namely American Samoa, Tahiti, Trust Territory, and Western Samoa. The islands are known for their climate, spectacular sunsets, clean beaches, and friendly people.

S T U D Y   QUESTIONS

1. In which regions of the world does most domestic and international tourism occur?
2. List the three regions in the United States where tourism is of prime importance.
3. Canadians account for well over 50 percent of the visitors to the United States. Why is this?
4. Caribbean cruises have undergone a remarkable growth in the past 20 years. Why is this?
5. What attracts tourists to Mexico?
6. What two factors are presently limiting the growth of tourism in Central America?
7. What factors account for the large numbers of North Americans who visit Great Britain?
8. List the three major tourist countries of Europe together with their major attractions.
9. Why does Eastern Europe encourage tourism?
10. Why do people visit the Soviet Union and what factors limit the development of tourism from the West?

D I S C U S S I O N   QUESTIONS

1. Select five countries and, for them, describe:
   a. the major tourist attractions;
   b. where their residents travel to on vacation;
   c. where visiting tourists come from.

5

HOW IS TOURISM ORGANIZED?

LEARNING
OBJECTIVES

At the end of this chapter the reader will be able to:

- Describe the major types of agreements among countries that affect tourism.
- Discuss the functions of international, regional, national, and state organizations involved in tourism.
- Compare and contrast the organizational structure and functions of the national tourism organizations of the United States, Canada, and Mexico.
- Define and correctly use the following terms:

Diplomatic recognition	Bilateral tourism
Consular office	agreement
Bermuda agreement	Visa
International Airlines Travel	World Tourism
Agent Network	Organization
Organization for Economic	International Civil Aviation
Cooperation and	Organization
Development	Pacific Area Travel
National Tourism	Association
Organization	U.S. Travel and Tourism
Heritage Conservation and	Administration
Recreation Service	Corps of Engineers
U.S. Forest Service	National Park Service
Tourism Canada	FONATUR

INTERNATIONAL

Tourism involves the movement of people across county, state, and national borders. In order for *international* movement to occur there must be agreements among countries to ensure the rights of travelers.

International Agreements

Diplomatic Recognition.   When one country offers diplomatic recognition to another it acknowledges the legal right of that country to exist. Two-way tourism cannot exist between two countries that do not recognize each other. Without diplomatic recognition treaties cannot be negotiated regarding such things as the reciprocal issuing of visas and the safety of visitors. A government will generally refuse to allow visits from citizens of countries it does not recognize. Travel by its own nationals to the unrecognized country is also restricted.

Commercial Agreements.   One way in which countries formalize their cooperation in the area of tourism is to negotiate a formal treaty. These treaties spell out the rights and privileges of travelers to the two countries. Since 1978 the United States, through the Travel and Tourism Administration, has signed bilateral tourism agreements with Mexico, Philippines, China, and Egypt. These agreements state a commitment to promote tourism by exchanging such things as statistical information and vocational training techniques.

Consular Offices.   Consular offices carry out a variety of activities essential to tourism. For example, they are responsible for such things as the protection of, and providing services for, their nationals in a foreign country and the documentation of tourists who wish to visit that country.

Visa Agreements. Holding a valid passport may not be sufficient to obtain entry into a country. Travel between two countries is seen as a privilege rather than a right. Nations can require that a visa be obtained for entry into and/or exit from their country. This is usually done to discourage undesirables. At the present time, France requires that visitors obtain a visa to enter that country. The French government, concerned about terrorist bombings in France, wishes to have additional control over who it allows into the country.

It is also necessary for an overseas tourist to the United States to receive a visa. It is up to the tourist to prove that he or she is worthy of nonimmigrant status. To obtain a visa to enter the United States the applicant must be able to prove that he or she will leave the United States at the end of the visit, that permission has been obtained from another nation to enter that country at the end of the U.S. stay, and that he or she has enough money to finance the purpose of the visit to the United States. The United States currently has visa agreements with more than 80 nations.

Air Agreements. The first bilateral agreement between countries concerning air travel was signed by the United States and Great Britain in 1946. Known as the Bermuda Agreement, it provided the model for later bilateral agreements. It basically stated that:

1. The exchange of routes was to be negotiated between governments.
2. There would be no restrictions on the number or frequency of flights on the routes agreed upon.
3. Fifth-freedom traffic (see Chapter 3) would be negotiated between the governments.
4. Rates would be controlled.

In the late 1970s the United States began to negotiate "procompetitive" bilateral agreements. These agreements sought to make international air travel more accessible to the population by encouraging low fares through price competition. Such agreements allowed each country to name as many airlines as it wished to be part of any negotiated agreement, disallowed unilateral limits on the frequency of flights of the other country, and stated that price of flights should be determined by the marketplace.

Recent agreements have included nonscheduled services also.

International Organizations

World Tourism Organization. Headquartered in Spain, the World Tourism Organization (WTO) is recognized as the world's most important tourism organization. Among other things, it serves as a consultant to the United Nations. The WTO seeks to promote tourism throughout the world, particularly in the developing countries. It collects information and issues publications dealing with such things as world tourism trends, approaches to marketing, and the protection of natural and cultural resources. Its affiliates conduct training and education programs. The WTO also works to ease foreign travel in a variety of ways: by reducing the number of passport and visa requirements and by standardizing travel signs.

International Airlines Travel Agent Network. The IATAN is an international organization open to any airline that holds a certificate for scheduled air service from a government eligible for membership in the International Civil Aviation Organization. It exists to ease the movement of people and goods throughout the world by air. Dues to support its operation are paid by the 100-plus member and associate member airlines.

The IATAN is principally involved in two areas. First, it standardizes documentation between international airlines. In this way, for example, it is possible to travel anywhere in the world, even using several different airlines, on one ticket bought at one price and paid for in one currency. The network acts as a clearinghouse for monies due the various airlines. If, for example, a tourist were to travel from Chicago to London on United Airlines and continue on to Amsterdam on KLM, the tourist could travel on one ticket and pay for it in U.S. dollars. Part of the money would go to United, part to KLM.

The IATAN is also involved in setting rates. Once governments have concluded a bilateral agreement on air travel between the two countries, IATAN convenes a traffic conference to negotiate the rates to be charged. These rates must then be accepted by the governments involved.

International Civil Aviation Organization. Formed in 1944, the ICAO membership is composed of 80 governments. A specialized agency of the United Nations, it works to promote worldwide civil aviation and is also concerned with the safe design and operation of aircraft and facilities to be used for peaceful purposes. It also seeks to promote efficient and economical air transport.

Developmental Organizations

A number of international organizations have shown a willingness to finance the development of tourism. The World Bank, in Washington, D.C., has been a supporter of tourism development in developing countries in the past. More recently, however, it has cut down significantly on its interest in tourism.

Regional International Organizations

Organization for Economic Cooperation and Development.   The members of OECD are Australia, Austria, Belgium, Canada, Denmark, Finland, France, the Federal Republic of Germany, Greece, Iceland, Ireland, Italy, Japan, Luxembourg, The Netherlands, New Zealand, Norway, Portugal, Spain, Sweden, Switzerland, Turkey, the United Kingdom, and the United States. Yugoslavia is an associate member. The OECD was formed in 1960 to encourage economic growth among member countries.

Through its tourism committee, the OECD studies problems concerning tourism and makes recommendations to the member countries. In addition to publishing an annual report on tourism in the member countries, the organization takes an active role in collecting tourism statistics and encouraging the use of standard definitions.

Figure 5-1   The Opera House at Sidney, Australia: A member country of PATA. (Courtesy the Australian Tourist Commission.)

Pacific Area Travel Association.   The 2,000-plus members of PATA represent 34 countries in the Pacific region and Asia. The goal is to encourage the growth of tourism in the Pacific area. This is achieved through joint marketing efforts (marketing representatives have offices in London, Frankfurt, and Paris) and through development and research. An annual conference is held, along with several Pacific travel marts that bring together buyers and sellers of travel.

Other Organizations.   A variety of regional organizations exist, similar to the ones mentioned above. The Caribbean Tourism Association and the European Travel Commission have been set up to promote tourism in the Caribbean islands and Europe, respectively.

NATIONAL ORGANIZATIONS

The tourism policies of a nation are developed by and implemented through a national tourism organization (NTO).

Objectives

The major objectives of an NTO are economic. They seek to improve the export earnings of the country by attracting more tourists. In this way it is hoped that the economy will expand, increasing the number of jobs, income, and taxes while promoting regionally balanced economic growth.

Tourism has also proven to be useful in protecting a nation's heritage—its buildings and its traditions. In some situations, buildings or customs have been protected on the economic grounds that they are important to the visitor as attractions. For the locals, their heritage is maintained. Some countries use tourism as a political tool to show the world how successful they have been.

Structure

The way in which tourism is represented at the national level is a function of the political philosophy of the country and the importance it places on tourism.

Ministry.   National tourism organizations tend to take one of three forms. First, they may be an independent ministry or part of a larger ministry. The State Secretariat for Tourism in Mexico is an independent ministry, whereas in France the responsibility for tourism comes under the Ministry of Free Time. Fifteen countries have autonomous ministries of tourism, while others place the responsibility for tourism under any of

Figure 5-2   Sevilla (Seville), Spain, a country with a Minister of State for Tourism. (Courtesy National Tourist Office of Spain.)

the following ministries: Commerce (or Commerce and Industry), Development, Economic Affairs, Education, Finance, Information (or Culture and Information), State or Transport (or Transport and Aviation, Transport and Power, Transport, Telecommunications and Tourism or Transportation).

Department.   Second, tourism may be represented by a government agency or within a bureau that is part of a larger department. Tourism Canada is part of the Department of Regional and Industrial Expansion, while the Japanese Department of Tourism finds itself in the Department of Transportation. Tourism bodies that have government status have the broadest range of functions of the NTOs.

Quasi-Public.   A third type of national tourism organization is where the official agency is a quasi-public government-funded corporation, board, or authority, such as the Hong Kong Tourist Association, the Irish Tourist Board, or the British Tourist Authority. A major advantage of this form of organization is the greater flexibility in dealing with the private sector in the areas of development and promotion. People from the private sector are often asked to serve on the board as directors.

A planned economy in which tourism is highly regarded would tend to place tourism in the first type of organization (ministry), whereas a market economy in which tourism is not regarded as very important will tend to see tourism found in one of the latter organizations (department or quasi-public corporation).

One of the problems for tourism in its attempt to be recognized is in knowing where to place it. Tourism, as we have seen, is a diverse activity, being represented in the United States in 30 sub-industries. It is difficult to get all industries and all trade associations to speak with one voice.

It is also a fact that other and more powerful agencies of government may see the encouragement of tourism as working against their own stated purposes. Attempts to ease entry restrictions into the United States, for example, have been viewed with alarm by those who have the responsibility to keep out drugs and undesirable characters.

Functions

What the NTO does is a reflection of how it is organized. In a free market economy the functions revolve around the encouragement of tourism; in a planned economy the state may get into developing and managing tourist attractions and facilities.

Most all organizations are involved in the promotion of tourism to the country; many operate offices abroad. The vast majority of NTOs collect tourism statistics while most also conduct some type of market research. To a lesser extent, organizations get involved in the areas of regulation and licensing for hotels, travel agencies, tour guides, and interpreters. In Mexico, the NTO regulates the prices of hotels, restaurants, tourist guides, and travel agencies, while in Japan it licenses travel agents and examines guides and interpreters.

Many NTOs are responsible for drafting national and regional tourism development plans. This is true in such countries as Canada, Mexico, England, and Spain.

Moreover, NTOs may also get involved in operating hotel schools or offering vocational training for guides and interpreters. A lesser number are actually involved in operating resort facilities.

In order to function effectively, a national tourism organization must have

1. the authority to initiate the changes that are needed to expand tourism in the future;

2. the full support of the government together with the ability to influence the various government departments that affect tourism;

3. the support of the private businesses that make up tourism;

4. a budget large enough to carry out properly the duties assigned to it and appropriate to the income generated by tourism;

5. experienced staff.

United States

The organization of tourism at the national level in the United States has been, and continues to be, hampered by the fact that so many of the prerequisites for effective function have, and are, missing.

U.S. Travel and Tourism Administration. The prime government agency involved in tourism in the United States is the U.S. Travel and Tourism Administration (USTTA). Authority for tourism development and promotion has changed from one agency to another.

In 1940 Congress passed the Domestic Travel Act authorizing the National Park Service, through the Department of the Interior, to promote travel within the United States and her territories and possessions as long as such activities did not interfere with those of the private sector. The entry of the United States into World War II in 1941 halted any plans for encouraging domestic travel. Gasoline was rationed and passenger traffic across the Atlantic curtailed. After the war the National Park Service had little budget. In addition, its priority was the expansion of park facilities to meet the numbers of visitors. No attention was given to encouraging domestic travel, and funding for this program was not renewed.

At the same time, Americans were encouraged to travel to Europe as a means of helping the European economies. It was felt that the inflow of U.S. dollars would stimulate demand on the part of Europeans for American goods. Many European countries were restricting foreign travel by their own nationals because of the need for American dollars. The result was a tourism balance of payments deficit for the United States.

In 1958 the Office of International Travel was formed in the Commerce Department to act as a government *spokesperson* for tourism and act as *liaison* between private industry and the various government agencies whose activities affected tourism. Information about the United States was distributed through consular and diplomatic offices. As a rule this is an unsatisfactory method of promoting tourism. Such offices are primarily concerned with matters other than encouraging travel. Tourism promotion is given little, if any, attention. Diplomatic offices tend to be located in areas that are not readily accessible to potential travelers.

In 1960 President Eisenhower proclaimed a "Visit U.S.A. Year" but felt that government should not promote and advertise travel.

The International Travel Act of 1961 made the United States Travel Service part of the Department of Commerce. The agency was authorized to set up offices overseas to promote the United States. Its goals were to:

- Contribute to the maximum extent possible to the balance of payments position of the United States.
- Contribute to the maximum extent possible to the health and well-being of the American People.
- Contribute to the maximum extent possible to international goodwill and understanding.

The agency was to promote travel to the United States; to encourage the provision of facilities for visitors; to coordinate travel facilitation among the various government agencies indirectly involved in tourism with a view to reducing the barriers to travel, and to collect and publish tourism statistics.

In 1970 Congress authorized matching funds to states or nonprofit organizations for projects aimed at attracting foreign travel to the United States. At the same time the director of the agency was given the rank of Assistant Secretary of Commerce for Tourism.

The authority for domestic tourism, which had been given to the Secretary of the Interior in 1940, was given to the United States Travel Service in 1975.

After an eight-year-long lobbying effort the government accepted, in principle, the need for a national tourism policy but rejected the recommendation for an independent agency to carry it out. The National Tourism Policy Act of 1981 resulted in the creation of the U.S. Travel and Tourism Administration (USTTA), headed by an Under Secretary of Commerce for Tourism (an elevation from assistant secretary). The act stated that

1. tourism and recreation industries are important to the United States;
2. tourism and recreation will become even more important to our daily lives;
3. there needs to be better coordination of government activities that impact on tourism.

A Travel and Tourism Advisory Board, made up of representatives of private industry, organized labor, academics, and the public sector, was set up. The Secretary of Commerce was to chair a Tourism Policy Council comprised of representatives of the Office of Management and Budget, the Commerce Department's International Trade Administration, and the Departments of Transportation, Interior, State, Labor, and Energy. All these agencies impact on tourism. The council was given the task of coordinating federal programs and policies that affect tourism, recreation, and heritage resources.

The under secretary oversees four offices—policy and planning, research, management and administration, and marketing. These offices reflect the programs of the USTTA.

Controversy still exists over the role of the government in tourism in the United States. Opponents of government intervention argue that only a few businesses involved in tourism are affected by an increase in tourism. As such, it is inappropriate for the government to spend public funds for an activity that will benefit relatively few people. The private sector should spend the money for tourism development, research, and marketing. On the other side of the issue are those who argue that the balance of trade is a federal issue and that the travel deficit is a public and a federal concern. The encouragement of tourism will have ramifications greater than some private businesses making a profit.

Over the years the responsibility for tourism has been given to government officials whose authority has gradually been increased. The top tourism government person went from director to assistant secretary to under secretary. This reflects a growing realization of the importance of tourism. However, the agency involved in tourism has had constant battles over funding to do the job assigned to it. It has consistently been underfunded. As a result, the agency has not been able to achieve many of its goals. Thus, it remains to be seen whether future administrations will give tourism affairs sufficient funds to accomplish its purpose.

Other Agencies.   There are over 150 different programs in approximately 50 different agencies or departments that affect tourism, travel, or recreation. The effect is felt primarily in two areas—natural resources and facilitation.

Of the 760 million acres of land owned by the federal government, 447 million acres have been set aside for recreational use by tourists. Federal lands represent approximately 85 percent of the recreation space in the United States. The natural resources of the United States are the responsibility of the Department of the Interior, the Department of Agriculture, and the Department of Defense in addition to several other independent agencies.

The Heritage Conservation and Recreation Service (HCRS)—formerly the Bureau of Outdoor Recreation—is responsible for research, development, planning, and maintaining a comprehensive nationwide outdoor recreation plan. The HCRS can only make recommendations on recreation policy, planning, and research and has no authority to manage land, water, and recreation areas. That authority lies primarily with the Corps of Engineers, the U.S. Forest Service, and the National Park Service.

The Corps of Engineers, part of the Department of Defense, is responsible for navigation, control of beach erosion, hurricane flood protection, major drainage, flood control, and water resources on both federal land waterways and improved inland and intercoastal waterways. Recreation is taken into account in cost-benefit analyses to determine whether or not to undertake a project. While recreation areas at project sites are operated by the Corps of Engineers, it prefers to turn operation over to nonfederal units.

The U.S. Forest Service, which is part of the Department of Agriculture, controls both national forests and national grasslands areas. About half of the nation's ski areas operate under permit and on lands managed by the U.S. Forest Service.

Lands managed by the National Park Service (NPS) in the Department of the Interior are an attraction for millions of visitors each year. While the original purpose of the NPS was the preservation of the unique natural wonders of the country, subsequent legislation added historic preservation, intensive outdoor recreation, and cultural activities to the list.

Within the area of natural resources the debate continues to be the extent to which resources should be preserved or developed. Tourism is heavily dependent on the natural resources of an area. A certain amount of development is, however, necessary to cater to the needs of the traveler. The debate focuses on the balance between the two.

The Departments of State, Transportation, Treasury, and Justice are concerned with the facilitation or movement of tourists. The U.S. Travel and Tourism Administration has worked with these federal departments in an attempt to reduce the barriers to travel. It is possible, for example, to go through U.S. customs in Toronto before boarding a flight to the United States. A 1986 bill passed by Congress includes a section that permits waiver of visa requirements for tourists from as many as eight countries that provide reciprocal waiver rights. In general, however, the interests of national security have come before the interests of travelers, and the principal concern remains making sure that people do not enter the country illegally or bring illegal items in with them.

Tourism Canada

Tourism Canada is the government agency responsible for tourism in Canada. It is part of the Department of Regional Industrial Expansion (DRIE), which encourages development in manufacturing, resource processing, tourism, and small businesses. Overseas activities involving tourism are handled through the Department of External Affairs. The DRIE, however, remains responsible to the Canadian government for the overall tourism program.

Based in Ottawa, Tourism Canada is charged with formulating national policy in the areas of development and marketing. These are translated at the local level by Regional Executive Directors, one to each province, in a fairly decentralized way.

There are three main activities of Tourism Canada—marketing, corporate affairs, and general development.

Within the area of marketing there are directors of development marketing, development U.S., development overseas, and development Canada. The director of development marketing is responsible for strategic planning in the area of marketing—identifying future potential markets with high potential.

The U.S. market is responsible for over 90 percent of all foreign visitors to Canada. Because of this, a director is assigned to coordinate activities relating to American visitors. Advertising is aimed at auto travelers within 400 miles of Canada, bus travelers up to 600 miles away, and air travelers and convention groups at longer distances.

Overseas offices are maintained in seven countries. Advertising is aimed at the tourist and the travel trade, both wholesalers and tour operators.

Domestically, Tourism Canada seeks to encourage Canadians to vacation in their own country.

In the area of development, Tourism Canada is concerned with the overall tourism product. Whereas in marketing the concern is demand, in development the concern is supply. A number of agreements have been worked out on a 50–50 to a 90–10 cost-sharing basis between the central government and the provinces to encourage various tourism projects. These show promise of stimulating the economy and generating jobs. Efforts are also underway for the stimulation of development by the private sector in tourism.

The corporate affairs group is responsible for guiding the overall direction of Tourism Canada. This group advises senior management on the future direction of the program, what policy issues should be considered, and how to respond to the various concerns of the industry. Members get involved in research, maintain an inventory of package tours to Canada, and coordinate with tourism organizations in the provinces of Canada as well as with international tourism groups.

Mexico

The public sector is more involved in tourism in Mexico than in any of the other countries discussed thus far.

Since 1974 the principal national tourism organization of Mexico has been the Secretariat of Tourism, which is responsible for overall tourism policy and for the regulation of both prices and the quality of services of the various industries that are part of tourism. Planning and developmental assistance are given to the private and public sectors in addition to operating the Green Angel program. The Green Angels are tow trucks, painted green, that offer emergency help to stranded motorists.

There are two branches of the Secretariat of Tourism—one for planning and one for operations. The Subsecretariat for Planning is primarily responsible for the development of a national tourism plan. Such plans consider, amongst other things, the role of tourism in the Mexican economy, the appropriate role of the public sector, and the setting of objectives for tourism.

The Subsecretariat for Operations regulates hotels, travel agencies, tourist guides, coffee shops, and equipment-rental firms and also supervises tourist services and the Green Angels.

In 1961 a National Tourism Council was established to offer advice on tourism studies and promotion. Made up of five members appointed by the president of Mexico, the council has, since 1977, been responsible for overseas promotion. Only one of the members is from the private sector.

The National Fund for the Promotion of Tourism—FONATUR— provides funding for government-approved tourism projects. Members are involved in buying real estate, in developing new areas, in promotion, and in giving credit to those involved in approved tourism projects.

The final agency of the organization is *Nacional Hotelera*—a government-owned hotel company—that receives its funding from FONATUR.

As can be seen from this section, the degree of government involvement in tourism depends upon how tourism is recognized and organized at the national level.

STATE ORGANIZATIONS

Structure

As at the national level, there are different forms of state involvement in tourism. Three types of organization are found.

1. A public or quasi-public travel commission or bureau.
2. An independent or semi-independent travel or development bureau.
3. Travel development within another department.

Travel Commission.   Hawaii is an example of the first type of structure. The Hawaii Visitors Bureau is operated by a president who is responsible to a board of directors. Separate officers are concerned with conventions, special events and promotions, information services, sales and services, visitor satisfaction, research, and membership. The bureau also operates sales offices in major American metropolitan areas.

Figure 5-3   Lanai City, Hawaii, where tourism is promoted through the Hawaii Visitors Bureau. (Courtesy Hawaii Visitors Bureau.)

Independent Bureau.   The state of Tennessee has a Department of Tourism Development with an independent cabinet-level status. This is an example of the second type of structure mentioned above. The commissioner of tourism development has access to the governor as a member of the governor's cabinet. This can ease problems of communication. It is also particularly useful at budget time as the commissioner can approach the legislature as a full department.

The three main functions of the department are travel promotion, information and media services, and support services. The travel promotion division has the responsibility to promote the tourist attractions of the state. Programs are aimed at the tourist and the other industry-related organizations such as travel agents and tour brokers. The information and media services division has the responsibility of developing feature articles and new items for placement in magazines, newspapers, and trade publications to promote the state as a tourist destination. The division works with Memphis State University to develop a research program for statistical data relative to the economic impact of tourism in Tennessee. The support services division has the responsibility for coordinating the effort to upgrade hotels and restaurants within the state. In addition, division staff members operate the welcome centers across the state.

Within Another Department.   The third type of structure is represented by the state of Montana. The travel promotion unit is part of the Department of Highways. Within travel promotion there are three functions—film location, tour and photo, and publicity. From the viewpoint of tourism, the concern in this type of structure is that tourism would be regarded as secondary to the major function of the department.

State Functions

All 50 states have some kind of official government agency responsible for tourism although, at various times in recent years, California and Maine have not had a state travel office.

The major activity of the states is in marketing. Most states use an advertising agency to handle their promotion. About 60 percent offer a matching formula, usually on a 50–50 basis, to both private and public groups engaged in state-approved promotional campaigns. Most state advertising is done in newspapers and magazines. Radio is used by about 10 percent of the states, television by even less. Most states exhibit in travel shows, while approximately one in four operates information centers outside the state. All states have their own themes, but less than one in six have different themes for separate segments of the market.

About 90 percent of state travel offices help develop package tours to their respective states. Two-thirds operate familiarization tours for tour operators and travel agents while about three-fourths of the states conduct press or travel-writer tours.

Over half the states assign a staff member, usually on a part-time basis, to travel research. In approximately 40 percent of the states, research is done by university faculty members; in about one-quarter of the states this function is handled by employees of other government agencies. About 30 percent of the states hire private research organizations to conduct research on a continuous basis.

States that have the most active travel and tourism programs possess the following characteristics:

1. They have the personal interest and active support of either the governor or lieutenant governor and the legislature.
2. A committee of the legislature deals specifically with travel and tourism.
3. A program of research and evaluation is carried out to indicate the effectiveness of the marketing effort and the impact of tourism on the state.
4. The economic development aspects of tourism are emphasized.
5. Active advisory councils or commissioners are present, and liaison between the private and the public sector is strong.
6. State travel/tourism plans are part of the planning/budgeting process.
7. Spending of promotional dollars has shifted from promoting the

Figure 5-4   Spouting Horn, Kauai. (Courtesy Hawaii Visitors Bureau; William Waterfall, photographer.)

natural resources to promoting urban, convention, and commercial attractions.[1]

Finally, the organization of tourism at the local level will be dealt with in the chapters dealing with the development and management of tourism.

PRIVATE BUSINESS FIRMS AND ORGANIZATIONS

In most countries the private sector plays an important role in the development, marketing, and management of tourism.

The primary industries involved in tourism are the transportation companies—air, bus, rail, automobile, and cruise lines; the lodging industry; the food service industry; attractions, shopping, tour wholesalers, and travel agents. The role of the various transportation industries has been covered in Chapter 3. Lodging, food service, shopping, and attractions will be dealt with in Chapter 9, "The Management of Tourism." The importance of tour wholesalers and retail travel agents is covered in Chapters 11 and 12, respectively.

ENDNOTES

1. Robert Christie Mill and Alastair M. Morrison, *The Tourism System: An Introductory Text* (Englewood Cliffs, N.J.: Prentice-Hall, 1985), pp. 260–261.

S T U D Y   QUESTIONS

1. What were the four major provisions of the Bermuda Agreement?
2. What are the principal functions of:
   • World Tourism Organization?
   • International Airlines Travel Agent Network?
   • International Civil Aviation Organization?
3. National tourism organizations (NTOs) tend to take one of three forms. What are they?
4. What are the major functions of a national tourism organization?
5. What five factors must be present for a national tourism organization to function effectively?
6. What are the major functions of the United States Travel and Tourism Administration?

7. What are the three common forms of state involvement in tourism? Give an example of each.
8. List the characteristics of states with the most active travel and tourism programs.

D I S C U S S I O N   QUESTIONS

1. What kinds of agreements between countries are needed to ensure the rights of international travelers?
2. What accounts for the different ways in which a national tourism organization is organized?
3. Compare the development of tourism administration at the national level in the United States, Canada, and Mexico.
4. What are the major functions of state tourism offices in the United States?

6 | WHY DEVELOP TOURISM?

At the end of this chapter the reader will be able to:

- Identify the distinguishing economic characteristics of tourism.
- Compare and contrast the direct and indirect or multiplier effects of tourism.
- Identify the factors that influence the extent to which a destination will benefit economically from tourism.
- Identify the social, cultural, and environmental impacts that tourism has on a destination.
- Define and correctly use the following terms:

Price elastic	Income elastic
Income multiplier	Sales multiplier
Employment multiplier	Payroll multiplier
Marginal propensity to consume	Balance of payments
	Backward linkages
Propensity to import	Demonstration effect
Opportunity costs	Cultural involution
Acculturation	

GOALS OF TOURISM DEVELOPMENT

Properly developed, tourism can provide benefits for both tourist and the host community. Tourism can help raise the living standards of the host people through the economic benefits it can bring to an area. In addition, by developing an infrastructure and providing recreation facilities, both tourist and local people benefit. Ideally, tourism should be developed that is appropriate to the destination. It should take the culture, history, and stage of economic development of the destination into account. For the tourist the result will be an experience that is unique to the destination.

At the same time there are costs involved in the development of tourism. Properly handled, the development of tourism can maximize the advantages of tourism while minimizing the problems.

ECONOMIC IMPACTS OF TOURISM

The economic characteristics of tourism explain the types of impact that tourism has on a community. There are five distinguishing characteristics. First, the tourist product cannot be stored; second, demand is highly seasonal. This means that in some months there is great activity while in other months there is little in the way of business. Pressure is put on businesses to make sufficient income during the season to sustain the business during the off-season. Businesses can attempt one of two strategies:

1. Alter supply to meet demand. This might mean meeting peak demand by reducing the quality of services provided or cutting off supply at a level lower than peak. For example, a restaurant might add tables during the peak season. More people could be served but customers would be cramped. Alternatively, service could be maintained but fewer customers served.

153

2. Modify demand to meet supply. The supply of facilities is constant year-round. This strategy involves offering such things as cheaper prices in order to induce demand in the off-season to fill up places.

Third, demand is influenced by outside and unpredictable influences. Changes in currency exchange rates, political unrest, even changes in the weather can affect demand.

Demand is, fourthly, a function of many complex motivations. Tourists travel for more than one reason. There is also little brand loyalty on the part of most tourists. That is, most tourists are inclined to visit a different spot each year rather than return to the same place every vacation. This puts great pressure on the destination to select carefully the segments of the market it is going after.

Finally, tourism is price and income elastic. Demand will be greatly influenced by relatively small changes in price and income. Price elasticity refers to the relationship between the price charged and the amount demanded. When demand is price elastic it means that a small change in the price will result in a larger amount demanded and that total revenue generated will increase. The same is true for a demand that is income elastic—changes in demand are linked to changes in income.

Direct and Indirect Economic Impact

The economic impact of tourism is both direct and indirect. The direct effect comes from the actual money spent by tourists at a destination. When a tourist pays a motel owner $100 for two nights' stay, the $100 has a direct economic impact.

Indirect effects occur as the impact of the original $100 is felt on the economy. The motel owner might take the $100 and use some of it to pay for food for the restaurant and some of it to pay the wages of the motel's employees. The food supplier, in turn, will pay the farmer for the crops while the employee might buy a pair of shoes. The impact of the original $100 is increased.

The money will continue to be spent and respent until one of two things happen: The money is saved instead of spent or the money is spent outside the community. In both cases "leakage" occurs. When money is saved it is taken out of circulation as far as the generation of income is concerned. Similarly, when a hotel in the Bahamas pays for steaks imported from the United States, the economic impact is felt in the United States and not in the Bahamas. The more that a community can cut down on imports resulting from tourism, the greater will be the economic impact of tourism on that community. The $100 spent by the original tourist is respent by the motel owner, the employee, and the farmer to generate income in the local economy of more than $100. Conversely, money spent on imports or money that is saved is removed from the local economy.

Income Multiplier.   The direct and indirect effects of an infusion of income into an area is termed the "multiplier." Multipliers can be generated in terms of sales, income, employment, or payroll.

We have seen that the initial spending of money by a tourist will generate more than that in income to the community. In order to know how much more, it is necessary to know something about what happens to money in the community. As noted above, the motel owner can do several things with the income brought in by tourists. First, money can be either saved or spent. And it can be spent locally or spent outside the community. As far as the community is concerned, saving the money is similar to spending it outside the community. The effect is the same—the income-producing potential is lost. The extent to which someone spends part of an extra dollar of income is termed the *marginal propensity to consume* (MPC). The extent to which an individual will save part of extra income is termed the *marginal propensity to save* (MPS). The more self-sufficient the community, the less will be the imports and the more the MPC.

The income multiplier is 1/MPS. If, in the above example, the motel owner saved $60, the income multiplier would be 1/0.6 or 1.67. If this effect was the same throughout the community it would mean that every $100 spent by tourists would generate $167 of income for the community.

Multipliers vary greatly by country. Most island economies have income multipliers between 0.6 and 1.2, whereas developed economies have a range between 1.7 and 2.0. The income multiplier for the Cayman Islands, for example, is 0.650, and that for the United Kingdom anywhere

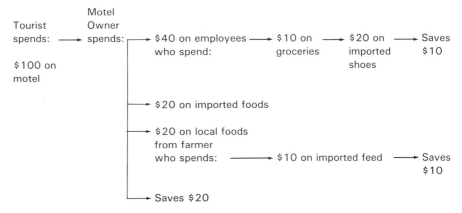

Figure 6–1   Multiplier Effect of Tourism.

from 1.7 to 1.8. The output or sales multiplier for the United States is 2.96.

Employment Multiplier. Increased spending as a result of tourist spending creates jobs. This results in an *employment multiplier.* The employment multiplier for the United States is 2.23. This means that, for every person directly involved in a tourism job—hotel receptionist, tour guide, etc.—an additional 1.23 jobs are created in other industries.

Payroll Multiplier. This results in another multiplier—the *payroll multiplier.* The payroll multiplier is the wages generated by these additional jobs. Again, for the United States, it is estimated that the payroll multiplier is 3.4. This is higher than the employment multiplier because, while many tourism jobs are low paying, tourism generates other jobs in higher-paying industries.

Economic Benefits

Tourism contributes to foreign-exchange earnings, generates income and jobs, can improve economic structures, and encourages small-business development.

Foreign-Exchange Earnings

The balance of payments for a country is the relationship between its payments to the rest of the world and the money received from the rest of the world. When one country buys something from another country it is an import; when one country sells something to another country it is an export. Countries strive to achieve a positive balance of payments. Because most have trouble doing this, attracting tourists—who are regarded as "exports"—is encouraged as a way of helping the balance of payments. On the other hand, when residents of a country vacation abroad, that is regarded as an import (because money leaves the home country). Some countries work to attract foreign tourists while keeping their own. For example, in 1969 the British government would allow people to take a maximum of only £50 spending money out of Great Britain.

Effects on the economy are either direct or indirect. The direct effect is the actual expenditure by the tourists. Indirect, or secondary, impact is what happens as the money flows through the economy. Tourist spending creates such things as spending on marketing overseas, the paying of commissions to travel agents, purchases of goods and services by the original recipient of the tourist's payment, and the wages paid to the employees of these goods and service companies.

Figure 6–2   Agrodome, Rotorua, New Zealand. Sheepskin rug sales help New Zealand's foreign-exchange earnings. (Courtesy New Zealand Tourist & Publicity Office.)

Propensity to Import.   Several factors determine the extent to which a destination benefits from an infusion of foreign tourist money. These are the difference between the gross income—the money brought in—and the net income—the money kept. The factors are the extent to which the country imports, the amount of foreign labor used, and the type of capital investment.

When tourists from, say, the United States are attracted to a destination they bring with them not only their dollars but also a demand for items that they are used to. They may want steaks, for example, for dinner. If the destination does not have beef of a suitable quantity or quality, it must import the beef to satisfy the tourist. The result is that some of the money spent by the tourist on the steak is used to pay a supplier outside the country for it. The steak is imported and the payment for it reduces the economic benefit of tourism to the destination.

Developing countries are less self-sufficient than are developed economies and are more liable to have to import such things as foodstuffs, beverages, construction materials, and supplies. Developed countries have backward linkages—economic links between the sectors of the economy such that the domestic economy provides the grain to make the buns and the beef to make the hamburgers to sell to the tourist.

The propensity to import is the amount of each additional unit of tourist expenditure that is used to buy imports. It is estimated, for example, that the import propensity for Hawaii is 45 percent. This means that, for every dollar spent in Hawaii by tourists, 45 cents is used to import goods and services to serve these tourists. The more a country can have the tourist buy souvenirs made locally, eat food grown locally, and stay in hotels constructed of local materials, the more the tourist money will stay in the country.

Foreign Labor.   Many countries use foreign labor in serving the tourist. The hotel industry in England, for example, uses many Spaniards and Portuguese. In some cases it is because the locals will not do the work; in other situations it is because the locals do not have the skills. It was learned, for example, that almost two-thirds of employees in managerial and administrative positions in the Cayman Islands were expatriates. The result is that money paid in wages to the employee is spent not in the destination but in the employee's home country. The hotel employee from Portugal sends money home each week, lives on very little, and returns to Portugal at the end of the season with his or her co-workers from Portugal. A number of countries are now requiring that, after a certain period of time, most managers of foreign-owned properties should be locals. They encourage the company to develop local people for managerial positions.

Capital Investment.   In the initial stages of tourism development a great deal of money is required for infrastructure and facilities. Most lesser-developed countries cannot afford to finance construction internally and must turn to foreign countries and corporations for assistance. The foreign companies come in, build the facilities, attract the tourists, and send the profits out of the country. The destination needs the influx of foreign money to develop the tourism potential; it loses control (and profits) from the venture.

Because of these factors, leakage from the local economy can be high. For developing countries, tourism has not brought the foreign-exchange benefits once thought possible.

Income Generation

The income from tourism contributes to the gross national product of a country. The tourism contribution is the money spent by tourists minus the purchases by the tourism sector to service these tourists. In most developed and many lesser-developed countries the percentage share of international tourist receipts in the gross national product is

Figure 6-3   Sheraton Hotel, Auckland. Hotels require substantial capital investment. (Courtesy New Zealand Tourist & Publicity Office.)

low—typically between 0.3 and 7 percent. Adding in the effects of domestic tourism increases the percentage significantly because domestic tourism is usually much more extensive than foreign tourism.

The total income generated depends on the multiplier effect noted above. Different sectors of the industry produce more income than others. Income generated is a reflection of the total amount spent and the amount of leakage within that sector. It has been found, for example, that bed-and-breakfast places have relatively low leakage because of their ability to buy what they need locally. However, they produce much less revenue initially compared to a large hotel, which will have a smaller multiplier effect because of its need to purchase goods and services outside the destination.

Certain sectors of the economy benefit from tourism more than others. The primary industry beneficiaries of tourist spending are food and beverage, lodging, transportation, and retailing. A strong secondary effect is felt in real estate, auto services, and repair and trucking.

Government Revenues.   Tourism income accrues to the government in three ways: from direct taxation on employees as well as goods and services; from indirect taxation such as customs duties; and from revenue generated by government-owned businesses. The Bahamian government, for example, estimates tourist revenue from the following sources:

- customs duties
- excise duties
- real property tax
- motor vehicle tax
- gaming taxes
- stamp tax
- services of a commercial nature
- fees and service charges
- revenue from government property
- interest
- reimbursement and loan repayment

Employment

It is estimated that over 60 million jobs worldwide are generated both directly and indirectly by foreign visitors and domestic travelers journeying to places 25 miles or more from home. Thirty-three thousand jobs are created for every $1 billion of spending in OECD countries, while the same amount generates 50,000 jobs in the rest of the world.

Several points can be made. First, there is a close, though not perfect, relationship between employment and income. There is both a direct and an indirect effect for both. Direct employment would be for jobs that directly result form tourist expenditures. Indirect employment is generated from jobs resulting from the effects of the tourist expenditures. Trinidad and Tobago, for example, estimates that three jobs are generated by the creation of every two hotel rooms. Multiplier effects are not identical, however.

Second, it can be noted that the type of tourist activity affects the type and number of jobs generated. Accommodation facilities, for example, tend to be more labor-intensive than other tourism businesses. They are also highly capital-intensive; large amounts of capital are required to create a job.

Third, the type of skills available locally affects employment generated. Most tourism jobs require little skill. The number of managerial positions are relatively small and, as mentioned earlier, are often occupied by nonlocals. Tourism industries also rely heavily on females. There is, thus, great demand for unskilled workers who are often female. Critics have argued that tourism offers low-paying jobs that are seasonal in nature. There is limited opportunity to increase productivity because of the service nature of the positions. Because of this, it is argued that tourism can have a depressing effect on economic growth.

Others argue that the employment benefits of tourism are disguised.

Tourism, they say, takes people from other sectors of the economy, especially rural people, or those not normally considered part of the available work force, such as married mothers, the retired, or those outside the national economy. The question then arises, does tourism generate new jobs or merely shuffle jobs around?

Finally, the seasonal nature of tourism should be stressed. While seasonal jobs are attractive to students and some teachers, they can discourage people from year-round, more productive work.

Small-Business Development

Many tourism businesses are small, family-owned concerns. It might be a taxi service, a souvenir shop, or a small restaurant. The extent to which the direct employers such as hotels and transportation companies can develop links to other sectors of the economy will determine how many jobs and how much income tourism can generate. Too often, when massive development of tourism occurs in developing countries, local suppliers cannot supply the quantity or quality of goods desired. As a result, good are imported, leakage occurs, and potential income and jobs are lost.

The extent to which tourism can establish ties with local businesses depends upon the following factors:

Figure 6–4   Aborigine bark painting. Tourism can help the establishment of local small businesses. (Courtesy Australian Tourist Commission.)

1. The types of supplies and producers with which the industry's demands are linked.
2. The capacity of local suppliers to meet these demands.
3. The historical development of tourism in the destination area.
4. The type of tourism development.[1]

More and more tourists seek authenticity as they travel. If this can be translated into buying locally produced souvenirs and eating locally produced food and staying in rooms furnished with local artifacts, then tourism will have generated the backward linkages necessary to contribute to the economy.

Economic Structure. Tourism alters the economic structure of destinations. There is no agreement, however, as to how positive the alterations might be. A major change when tourism is developed is the change in jobs of rural people. There is a tendency for farmers to leave the land to pursue what are, for them, better jobs in tourism. This can put rural lands in jeopardy. Changes in land use are also common. Often less-developed areas have only two things on which to build an economy—agriculture and tourism. As tourism develops, competition for the land occurs. The price of land increases; people sell. While a few benefit, it is difficult for locals to buy their own piece of land.

On the other hand, tourism can help reverse the depopulation of rural areas. In the Scottish Highlands, for example, the woman who takes in bed-and-breakfast guests may be married to the local postmaster. If tourism were to falter, the community might lose not only a bed-and-breakfast establishment, but also the postmaster.

Economic Costs

There are a number of economic concerns about tourism.

Inflation and Land Values. As noted above, tourism development raises both the price of land and the prices of other goods and services. Even if a local resident does not sell, his or her costs increase as property taxes rise. In the five years following the acquisition of land in Florida for Disney World land values surrounding the attraction increased significantly. The land was originally purchased under assumed names for $350 and acre. Five years later the surrounding land brought upwards of $150,000 an acre!

Seasonality. Most tourism destinations are seasonal; many hospitality facilities close down during the off-season. However, large amounts of capital are necessary to build these facilities. Interest costs are high on the capital needed for construction. Interest costs are also fixed; they must be paid irrespective of the amount of business generated. As a result of high fixed costs and seasonal demand, there is constant pressure to produce a profit in what some call "the hundred-day season." As a result of underutilization of the investment on a year-round basis, the return on investment is often less than that generated in other industries.

Often financial incentives from the public sector are necessary to get tourist facilities built.

Public Services. Tourism is touted as a "smokeless industry" that requires few public services. Schools do not have to be built for the children of tourists, whereas they must be constructed for the children of workers brought in to work full time in other industries.

However, an increase in tourism tends to increase the costs for residents in such areas as garbage collection and police and fire protection.

Opportunity Costs. When governments invest scarce resources in encouraging the development of tourism they forego the opportunity to invest that money in other, perhaps more productive, ways. This is known as *opportunity cost*. It does appear that investments in tourism yield returns comparable to returns in other industries. Both the private and public sectors, however, should be aware that an investment in tourism facilities may be made at the expense of other sectors of the economy.

Overdependence on Tourism. It is generally agreed that it is unwise to base an economy on tourism. Tourism growth is affected by changes both internal—price increases and changes in fashion—and external—political problems, energy availability, and currency fluctuations. Just as an individual property can rely too heavily on one segment of the market, so too a destination can rely too heavily on tourism. The key is to develop a balanced economy.

In a "traditional" development, a country's economy shifts from the primary sector—farming, mining, fishing, etc.—to the manufacturing or secondary sector to the service sector. For destinations that have only agriculture and tourism, the economy "misses" the middle stage of development. It is as if there is the lack of a foundation on which to build a strong service sector. This is the danger of an overdependence on tourism.

SOCIAL IMPACTS

In addition to the many economic impacts that tourism has on a destination, there are impacts on people—the effect of the interaction between host and guest.

Tourist Density

For numerous events a large number of tourists congregate at one time. Additionally, the seasonal aspect of tourism means that, for most destinations, tourists are concentrated at the destination during a relatively few months. There are two approaches to dealing with the problem of tourist density. One approach is to spread the tourists geographically or over time throughout the destination. Off-season rates can attract tourists away from the major tourist season. Development of trips and packages to other parts of the country may spread the economic benefits of tourism while minimizing the negative social impacts.

The second approach is to develop "tourist ghettos"—areas that are built specifically for tourists. In this way, contact between host and guest is kept to a minimum.

Demonstration Effects

The demonstration effect is the term given to the notion of local people seeking to emulate the ways of their visitors. Foreigners bring with them different ways of behaving and an exposure to different standards of living. When the demonstration effect encourages locals to work and strive for the things they lack it may be regarded as "good." However, most of the time the result is that for most of the people what they see is not what they can ever expect to get. The result is discontent among the local residents.

Tourists behave differently on vacation from how they behave at home. To the locals, however, all they see is the vacation behavior. This can lead to the creation of stereotypes on both sides. It has been reported, for example, that young Spaniards were convinced that all unattached female tourists had rather loose morals. This stereotype induces certain behavior on the part of the locals that, in turn, develops into a stereotype of locals on the part of the tourist.

Migration

Economically, in an attempt to share in the economic advantages of the tourist, local people in many lesser-developed destinations have moved off the land and into service jobs. This may lead to problems for the nation in keeping enough people on the farms to harvest the crops. Migration of workers from rural to urban areas, and even from one country to another, is one impact of tourism.

Part of the movement of workers into tourism industries is undoubtedly the entrance of women and younger people into the work force. While this is readily accepted in Western societies it is not so apparent in other regions of the world. In many countries the structure of society is very rigid; there is great respect for the elderly and for the male. As a result of jobs in tourism, youngsters may leave home and immediately begin earning more than their parents or grandparents. The same is true for women who may be earning more than their husbands. Opinion is divided as to whether this is harmful or not. Studies have indicated that such a situation can lead to a lack of self-respect and an increase of jealousy on the part of the husbands and increased stress on the part of their wives. Others point to the opportunities for women to feel better about themselves as they contribute more income to the family. The result certainly is a feeling of greater independence on the part of both women and youngsters. In Tunisia, on the other hand, employers used to pay the girls' wages to their fathers rather than to the employee.

Figure 6–5   Ackee fruit vendor. In some areas people have moved from farms into service jobs. (Courtesy Jamaica Tourist Board.)

Consumption Behavior

As tourism increases, local businesses import goods to appeal to the tourist. Locals may see that the imported goods are superior to their own local items. As the local workers earn more money they begin to demand imported goods also. Some people call this "progress." The fact is, however, that such exposure increases imports, thereby increasing leakage, and diminishing the economic impact of tourism.

Sense of Identity

In marketing we are taught to identify the needs and wants of the tourists and to develop goods and services to satisfy these needs and wants. For a community the task is to do so while still maintaining its own sense of identity. British tourists are notorious for wanting "chips (french fries) with everything," cups of tea, and British ale. American tourists are reluctant to speak any language other than English and must have iced water. In an attempt to adopt a marketing orientation, locals can lose sight of their own unique culture. If we end up with a series of similar destinations then where is the incentive to travel?

Moral Conduct

It has been suggested that tourism brings prostitution, crime, and gambling to the destination. However, no demonstrated link exists between tourism and prostitution. It must be admitted, though, that a number of destinations sell the four S's—sun, sand, sea, and sex. Residents of the Seychelles, for example, have been described as "happily amoral." Appealing to the vacationer's hedonistic tastes encourages a certain frame of mind prior to the visit.

Crime.   A relationship does exist between tourism and crime. The existence of large numbers of people with lots of money to spend attracts criminal elements. The main effects seem to be in the areas of robbery, larceny, burglary, vandalism, drug abuse and alcohol-related disorderly behavior.

Gambling.   While many destination areas—Las Vegas, Atlantic City, Monte Carlo, Tijuana—owe their existence to gambling, no link has been established between tourism and gambling. However, while the economic advantages to a destination of gambling have been identified, less work has been done on the potentially negative effects on the residents of the destination such as the effect on the value system and whether or not there has been an increase in prostitution, crime, and violence.

Measuring Social Impact

It has been suggested that an "index of tourist irritation" exists.[2] By identifying where a destination is on the index it is possible to "measure" the social impact of tourism. If the process of tourism development is left unchecked, the social impact of tourism is felt at five levels.

Euphoria.   In this first stage of social impact the local people are excited about the development of tourism in their community. Tourists are welcomed and locals have a certain satisfaction and pride in knowing that someone wants to visit "their community." It appears that there will be opportunities for local people to profit from the attraction of tourists.

Apathy.   As tourism grows, the visitors are taken for granted. The accent is on making as much money as possible. Host-guest contacts are limited to those where purchases are made.

Irritation.   At some point tourism grows to where, in the opinion of the locals, the destination cannot handle the numbers. Streets become clogged; restaurants and bars are crowded. At this point, the mood turns to one of irritation.

Antagonism.   When locals begin to feel that the problem of the community—pollution, crime, rising taxes—are the fault of the growing numbers of tourists, they turn openly antagonistic to the tourist. The result is often that tourists are cheated.

Final Level.   At this fifth and final level those in the community have forgotten that the tourist was attracted to their community initially for some physical or cultural reason. Development has changed the community, perhaps forever. The type of tourist who comes is different now, and the realization for the locals is that the destination will never be the same again. The question arises: "Can it adapt to the new tourist types?"

The point at which locals move from one stage to another varies from one destination to another. It depends, first, on the distance—both culturally and economically—between host and guest. The greater the distances, the greater the social impact and the greater the likelihood of movement through the stages. Second, it is a function of the destination's ability to physically and psychologically absorb the growing numbers of tourists. The key is in the ratio of visitors to residents. Thus, a major city can absorb more tourists than can a small island community. The third criterion is the speed and amount of tourism development. The faster and the more intense the level of development, the greater will be the tendency for social impacts to occur.

It is wrong to say that tourism alone causes any or all of these changes. When people are exposed to magazines, newspapers, or films about other countries, change can occur. Tourism, however, accelerates this change by bringing host and guest into contact. Neither can we say that the change is "good" or "bad." When traditional societies become Westernized some people will be hurt while others will benefit. Tourism also accelerates this change.

CULTURAL IMPACT

The culture of a people consists of the beliefs, values, attitudes, and behaviors that are shared by a society and which are passed on from one generation to another. Culture finds expression in such things as the work, dress, architecture, handicrafts, history, language, religion, education, traditions, leisure activities, art, music, and gastronomy of a people. Tourism impacts the culture of a country in a number of ways.

Cultural Change

Cultures evolve and change naturally as the host culture adapts to a changing world. Tourism accelerates that process because it introduces contact between two societies with different cultures. In the process both societies change. Visitors to a country may enjoy the local food and, upon returning home, prepare the same foods they had on vacation. The locals, on the other hand, may acquire a desire for fashions they have seen the tourists wear. The process by which cultures borrow from each other when they come into contact is called *acculturation*. It is generally accepted that, when a "strong" culture comes into contact with a "weak" culture, it is the weaker culture that is likely to borrow from the stronger. Much of tourism involves tourists from strong, Westernized countries visiting poorer, less-developed countries. The culture of the latter is the one that will change.

Arts and Crafts.   One major way in which the impact of tourism can be seen on a culture is in the area of arts and crafts. Typically, the process of change goes through three stages. In the first stage traditional artistic designs and forms of art, especially those with deep religious meaning, disappear into the souvenir market. This is followed by the growth, in the second stage, of mass-produced replacements, often imported. In response to the decline in meaning of the traditional arts, there may be a growing interest (third stage) on the part of the local community to resurrect their artifacts through the development of distinctive styles and skilled work.

Tourism has worked both to encourage and discourage traditional

Figure 6-6   Tourism can help bring different cultures together. (Courtesy Jamaica Tourist Board.)

art forms. In a number of cases traditional arts have been revived to sell to the tourist. This is true of the Aaraya women of Cuna, Panama, who had to be taught to make the traditional mola or blouse. It is also true of the Canadian Inuit or Eskimos who began to carve soapstone only in response to demands by Europeans. In the first case, a traditional art form was kept alive through tourism; in the second, tourism encouraged the development of another art form. Many of the theaters in London stay open (and available to the locals) because of the business brought by tourists.

On the other hand, tourism has given rise to what some call "airport art." These mass-produced, often imported souvenirs give the tourist something that is inexpensive, durable, and easily portable as a memento of the trip. In the process, part of the culture has been debased if not lost.

Events. Every culture has a number of festivals or events that might have a meaning that is historic or religious. When the event is changed for the sake of the tourist, the meaning behind the event is lost. The result is that part of the culture is lost. A good example is the Alarde, which we will examine here in detail.

Fuenterrabia is a village in the Basque region between France and Spain. During the many battles between the two countries the town was besieged several times. The most famous was the siege of 1638, by the French, which lasted 69 days. But the town held and the French were defeated. The Spanish crown honored the villagers in a number of ways, and today this tradition continues in the form of the annual festival that brings the townspeople together.

Fuenterrabia consists of a walled citadel, a fisherman's ward, and five local wards, each with its own identity. Each ward sends to the annual parade youngsters who play flutes and drums and men who carry shotguns. Each ward also selects its loveliest young woman to be a water carrier; she is dressed in a military uniform. There is also a group of nonlocal occupations represented in the parade, which is led by town council members who wear military uniforms and ride on horseback.

The festival has many symbolic aspects to it. During the siege the rich and the poor stood together against the enemy. This is symbolized by having all groups involved. Also, the men stop at the town hall and fire their shotguns in unison. The idea is to fire as if only one gun had gone off. At the end of the parade, all groups fire together with the same objective—all symbolic of the coming together. The entire town takes part in one way or another, and the festival is for the townspeople and by the townspeople.

With the increase in Spanish tourism the Alarde became an attraction to the point that the municipal government declared in 1969 that the festival should be performed twice a day so that all who wanted to see it could do so. Although the festival only occurs once a day—the proposal for two festivals was dropped—it is difficult to get the volunteers necessary to put it on. Many people dropped out because the spirit and meaning were taken out of it as it became a commodity to be sold. There is talk today of paying people to perform.

This same situation is true in the United States with many of our own holidays. Anniversaries commemorating various historical events and birthdays of presidents have been moved from the true anniversary to the closest Monday in order to provide three-day weekends. This has

Figure 6–7   Sevilla (Seville), Spain. Festivals are a major tourist attraction. (Courtesy National Tourist Office of Spain.)

increased opportunities for weekend trips; however, any meaning behind the holiday has been lost.

Tourism has also been accused of encouraging cultural *involution*. The development of an area can be halted because of the tourist's demand for the "old ways." This is the other side of the coin. Does tourism "force" people to remain artisans at the expense of attempts to achieve economic growth and independence?

It does appear that tourism acts as a medium for social change because it involves contact between host and guest. The change that occurs is usually on the host culture rather than on the tourist, and the change is often negative. It is not suggested that tourists must be scholars in order to visit a foreign country. However, one of the reasons that tourists visit a foreign country is to experience the different culture. If all cultures begin to look alike, there will be no reason to leave home. To the extent that tourism debases a host culture, the locals can be expected to react negatively to tourists and tourism. Visitors will not be welcome. The key is to present the culture of an area to the visitor in a way that is attractive to the tourist and in a way that the locals can be proud of.

ENVIRONMENTAL IMPACT

Tourism development, like any kind of development, has an impact upon the environment. The impact can be positive or negative. In the case of less-developed areas, tourism development can improve the environment for tourists and locals alike through improvements in sanitation, sewage, and housing. In developed areas tourism development is more likely to be thought of in negative terms such as pollution and congestion.

The natural environment is a major attraction for tourists. Visitors tend to be attracted to areas that are scenic, offer a pleasant climate, and have distinctive landscapes. However, in order to cater to tourists, a certain amount of development is necessary. Roads must be built to make the area accessible; lodging to house tourists, and restaurants to feed them, must be available.

In the best of all possible relationships the distinctive features of the environment would be left as natural as possible while still providing benefits to the tourists who see and experience it. In most cases, however, tourism is in conflict with the environment.

Impact on Conservation

Tourism has undoubtedly had a positive impact on the conservation of the environment.[3] Tourism has stimulated the rehabilitation of historic sites, buildings and monuments. In Cape Cod, small villages, the area's major tourist resource, have been maintained and local lighthouses and harbors refurbished to attract tourists. The same is true in many other areas including Williamsburg, which has been completely restored to its eighteenth-century glory because of tourism.

A second positive impact is the way that tourism has provided the impetus for developing old buildings into new tourist facilities. In Savannah, Georgia, the waterfront area consisted of old, decaying warehouses that were important in the cotton trade. Retaining the original structure, the buildings have been turned into shops and restaurants. The same is true in Larimer Square in Denver where a rather seedy red-light district is now an attractive area for shops, restaurants, and festivals.

Moreover, tourism has provided the push for the conservation of natural resources. National parks in Africa have increased in number because of the desire not only to protect the wildlife but also to offer areas that would appeal to tourists. By adding an economic incentive to the preservation of wildlife, it becomes more attractive. More than 80,000 square mile of national parks have been set aside in eastern and southern Africa alone.

Finally, the pursuit of tourism has resulted in controls on the destination that are designed to protect the environment. Unfortunately, in

Figure 6-8   Powerscourt, County Wicklow, Ireland. Tourism can assist in preserving the environment. (Courtesy Irish Tourist Board.)

many cases, these controls have taken effect after the negative ramifications of too many tourists have been felt. Such controls can take the form of eliminating access to a particular site, as is the case at Stonehenge where tourists must view the stones from about 10 yards away. Previously, tourists could walk among and touch the standing ruins. Similar restrictions are in place at the Parthenon in Greece. In other cases, traffic has been eliminated in many historic areas in Europe.

While some argue that tourism has served to encourage an appreciation for nature and history, others say that the pressure of tourism on the environment has led to conflict.

Conflicts with the Environment

Use of a destination will have an impact on the environment, and the more the area is used, the greater will be the impact. There comes a point when more people use the area than can be supported by it. The result is a spoiling of the environment.

The effect can be seen in the following ways:

- Increased levels of generalized congestion and pollution.
- Alterations to the natural landscape and changes in the ecological balance of living things.
- Costs of preventing localized congestion and pollution.
- Costs of the loss of wilderness areas or inevitable degree of lessening of the natural attraction.
- Costs of creating conservation areas on resort lands.
- Costs of undertaking enhancement projects.
- Costs of undertaking historical or cultural preservation.[4]

When a previously undeveloped destination becomes a tourist attraction, development can offer benefits to the area and to the residents of the area. Land may be protected for the enjoyment of locals and tourists; basic infrastructure may be added that improves the quality of life for locals. Without careful planning, however, the destination may develop much too quickly. As a result, there is a danger that both the natural and cultural environment may deteriorate. The local environment may be destroyed and the quality of life of the locals adversely affected. If the destination is allowed to deteriorate, tourists may well be turned off, for the very thing that attracted them in the first place (the environment) is no longer attractive. The key is for a well-planned program of tourism development.

ENDNOTES

1. Alister Mathieson and Geoffrey Wall, *Tourism: Economic, Physical, and Social Impacts* (London: Longman Group Limited, 1982), p. 82.

2. G.V. Doxey, "When Enough's Enough: The Natives Are Restless in Old Niagara," *Heritage Canada*, Vol. 2, No. 2, 1976, pp. 26–27.

3. Mathieson and Wall, *Tourism*, pp.98–100.

4. Chuck Y. Gee, Dexter J.L. Choy, and James C. Makens, *The Travel Industry*, (Westport, Conn: The AVI Publishing Company, Inc., 1984), p. 119.

S T U D Y   QUESTIONS

1. What are the five distinguishing economic characteristics of tourism?

2. When a tourist pays a motel bill, the money can be "spent" in three ways. What are they and what is the impact on the community?

3. List the major economic benefits of tourism to a destination.

4. What factors determine the extent to which a destination will benefit from an infusion of foreign tourist dollars?

5. How does the government raise revenue from tourism?

6. Identify the major economic costs of tourism.

7. What are the social impacts of tourism?

8. List the five stages of the "index of tourist irritation." What factors are present when a destination moves from one stage to another?

9. How can tourism affect the local culture?

10. How has tourism development positively impacted the environment?

D I S C U S S I O N   QUESTIONS

1. Tourism has a number of economic characteristics. Discuss their effect on tourism.

2. Identify the direct and indirect effects of tourist dollars spent at a destination.

3. How does tourism benefit a destination economically? What can a destination do to maximize tourism's economic impact?

4. In what ways can tourism be "bad" for a destination socially, culturally, and environmentally? Discuss what a destination can do to minimize tourism's negative effects.

7

THE PLANNING OF TOURISM

At the end of this chapter the reader will be able to:

- Understand why a tourism destination should have a development plan
- Identify the components of a tourism development plan.
- Realize the importance of basing a plan on objective data and identify how that data can be collected.
- Define and correctly use the following terms:

Allocentrics	Midcentrics
Psychocentrics	Product life cycle curve
Integrated planning	Secondary research
Primary research	Representative sample

WHY PLAN?

The impacts of a lack of planning on a destination have been documented in the literature. They include the following:[1]

Physical Impacts

- Damage or permanent alteration of the physical environment.
- Damage or permanent alteration of historical/cultural landmarks and resources.
- Overcrowding and congestion.
- Pollution.
- Traffic problems.

Human Impacts

- Less accessibility to services and tourist attractions for local residents that result in local resentment.
- Dislike of tourists on the part of local residents.
- Loss of cultural identity.
- Lack of education of tourism employees in skills and hospitality.
- Lack of awareness of the benefits of tourism to the destination area.

Organizational Impacts

- Fragmented approach to the marketing and development of tourism.
- Lack of cooperation among individual operators.

- Inadequate representation of tourism's interests.
- Lack of support from local public authorities.
- Failure to act upon important issues, problems, and opportunities of common interest to the community.

Other Impacts

- Inadequate signs.
- Lack of sufficient attractions and events.
- High seasonality and short lengths of stay.
- Poor or deteriorating quality of facilities and services.
- Poor or inadequate travel information services.

Consequences of Unplanned Growth

Allocentrics.   Stanley Plog offered a widely used model of what can happen to a destination without adequate plans for the future. The model is shown in Figure 7–1. Plog believes that destination areas have a life cycle

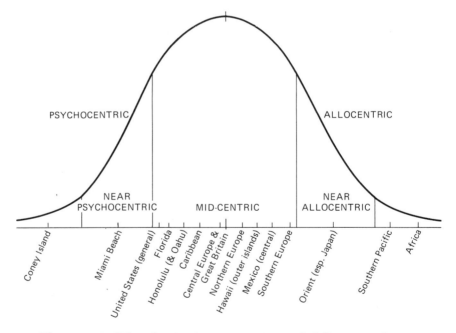

Figure 7–1 Why destination areas rise and fall in popularity. (*Source:* Stanley G. Plog, "Why Destination Areas Rise and Fall in Popularity," *Cornell Hotel and Restaurant Administration Quarterly,* February 1974, p. 14.)

as they go through a process of appealing to different segments of the market. As a new destination is discovered it appeals to what Plog calls the *allocentrics*. Allocentrics are self-confident, frequent travelers who prefer to fly. They also prefer destinations that are uncrowded and where they can seek out experiences that are novel. They are very interested in meeting people and exploring new cultures. This is similar to innovators—people who are the first to buy a new product just because it is new. Africa would be an example of a destination appealing to the allocentric.

As word of the destination gets out, more tourists are attracted. However, these early adopters are not as pioneering as the allocentrics. Called the *near allocentrics,* they remain interested in the culture but demand more services. The Orient might be in this category.

Mid-Centrics.   As more and more people visit the area, the allocentrics move on to discover new destinations. Those who do come exhibit *mid-centric* characteristics. More and more of the familiar is desired. At the same time, however, there are more mid-centrics in the population than near-allocentrics or allocentrics. Most of Europe falls into this category.

At this point the destination has gone through several stages of what in marketing is called the "product life cycle curve." It has been *introduced* into the marketplace, has *established* a place for itself, and has gone through a period of *growth.* Plog warns that destination areas carry the seeds of their own destruction.

Psychocentrics.   Left unchecked, destination areas can begin to appeal to *psychocentrics.* Psychocentrics are unsure of themselves and have relatively low socioeconomic status. They do not travel much, preferring to go by car when they do and seek the familiar in the destinations they choose. They prefer tours and types of restaurants that they are accustomed to at home. Miami Beach is an example of a destination appealing to this group. As more development occurs the destination begins to resemble the area the tourist lives in. At the same time the size of the market declines. The rate and extent of development has turned off even the mid-centrics. The destination is into the *maturity* stage of the product life cycle. Businesses and destinations can tell when this is occurring. In the growth stage of the life cycle, sales rise at an increasing rate each year—5 percent one year, 7 percent the next, 8 percent the next, etc. In the maturity stage of the life cycle, sales are increasing but at a *decreasing* rate—5 percent one year, 4 percent the next, 2 percent the next, etc.

Without drastic action, the destination moves into *decline.* Overdeveloped, it appeals to the relatively small number of pure psychocentrics. Coney Island might be in this category. This is an example of a destination that has gone through all of the stages. Once appealing to sophisticated visitors, its former glory days are gone.

Such changes are probably inevitable if development is allowed to occur without any thought as to the future. However, life cycles can be extended if the changes are anticipated and steps taken to adapt to the changes. One destination that has gone through many of these stages is Atlantic City. Once a proud resort town, it had become run down. The city is hoping that the legalization of gambling there will help reverse the process that began many years ago. One of the functions of planning is to provide the framework that will allow the destination to cope with change.

WHAT IS PLANNING?

Role of Planning

Much tourism development has occurred without a comprehensive tourism plan. We have seen in the previous chapter that, left to chance, tourism can have negative economic, social, cultural, and environmental effects on the destination. Additionally, investing in tourism without a plan to guide one's actions can be disastrous for private companies and public agencies. The answer is an integrated plan.

Integrated Planning.   An integrated plan for tourism destination development is important for several reasons. First, tourism is interdependent. Facilities cannot be viable unless there are attractions to pull tourists into the region. Yet we have also seen that, just as the demand for lodging can create supply (hotel rooms), so the opposite is true. Having hotel rooms for tourists to stay in is necessary before visitors will come. A comprehensive approach taking all of the elements of tourism into account is necessary to ensure that all the pieces fit together.

An integrated planning approach will help ensure that the type of development that results will be one suited to the community. The needs and wishes of the community should be taken into account as part of the planning process. The result will be a type of tourism that is unique to the region (and to the tourist) and one that will tend to be supported by the locals.

As noted earlier, one of the economic benefits of tourism is that it encourages the development of small family businesses. Yet these types of businesses are most likely to have high rates of failure because they lack the management and financial skills of larger concerns. By themselves they have neither the time, money, nor expertise necessary to plan effectively. They can, however become part of a larger umbrella approach to planning.

When banks or government agencies are approached for funding they will want to see some evidence that the proposed project will be

Figure 7-2 Avila, Spain. Planning is necessary to protect a country's attractions. (Courtesy National Tourist Office of Spain.)

successful. The process of planning and the resulting analysis might be the documentation necessary to obtain such funds. Certainly it will be impossible to get financing without evidence of a plan.

Components of Planning

While the process and the output of tourism plans vary, they do tend to have certain components.

Definition of Needs. When a destination decides to develop tourism it is generally for a reason. It may be to bring in jobs, obtain foreign-exchange earnings, help stabilize population declines, or to improve local amenities and the quality of life. It is important that the needs of the destination be the focal point for any plan, for this will determine the type of tourism that should be developed. Identifying the needs of the area will not only determine the type and intensity of tourism to develop but also which market segments to go after. When a course of action is in doubt, the ultimate question should be, "Will doing this help solve the needs of the destination?"

Assessment of Potential.   It is all very well to identify the problems that we wish tourism to solve. However, we must next identify whether or not the community has the potential to attract, keep, and satisfy tourists. Such an assessment should begin with a determination of the extent of existing tourism. This provides a point of reference for growth potential. Assessment of a region's potential should include an identification of the area's tourism resources and their quality. It should include such factors as:

- Man-made resources: rooms, restaurants.
- Natural resources: lakes, mountains, beaches, historic sites, etc.
- Infrastructure: roads, airports.
- Transportation.
- General resources: human, technological, cultural, leadership potential.

Community Support.   Successful long-term development of a community requires the support of the people in that community. It is very important to take the feelings of the locals into account before enbarking on a major project. Often the negative aspects of tourism—noise, congestion, rising prices—are more visible than are the benefits. Gauging community support will serve to identify potential problems later on.

Legal Environment.   Laws can either ease development, as in the case of grants, or constrain it, as in the case of zoning. The laws and regulations particular to a destination must be known.

Scheduling.   Destination development requires many separate activities, some happening at the same time, some which must proceed or follow others. They are organized by means of a schedule. There may be a short-term and a long-term phase. Generally speaking, short-term activities take place over a year; long-term phase activities are those that occur over a longer period of time.

Short-term plans seek to maximize the productivity of existing facilities. Funds are needed for operations while the marketing strategy emphasizes advertising and public relations. The marketing objective is to increase use by the present market, whereas within the local community there is an emphasis on gaining community support and increasing local awareness of the benefits of tourism.

Long-term plans are more concerned with developing new potential facilities. The need is for investment funds while the marketing stategy is on product development. The marketing objective is to attract new markets, whereas in the community the emphasis is on encouraging local entrepreneurs and investors and providing training to upgrade employee skills.

Experience. Ultimate leadership will likely fall to people in the community. Thus, it is vital that they be identified early on in the planning process and heavily involved in the process. Not only will they be able to offer sound advice but they will also be more committed to achieving the objectives of the plan because they have been involved with it.

Measurement. It is not enough to do a good job. People have to know that a good job has been done. The way this can be achieved is through some measurement of the various effects of tourism. By measuring, before and after, such factors as the economic impact of tourism, the number of tourists, and the amount of investments attracted as well as community attitudes, the results of the effort can be determined.

Flexibility. The objective in planning is not to end up with a plan—a finished, bound book that planners can proudly point to. The objective is to set a course for a community. Plans are not static. As situations change, so must the plan. Planning is a continuous process. It may be, in fact, that the major benefit of planning comes from going through the process rather than preparing a written document.

Barriers to Planning

A number of problems are associated with planning for tourism. Many people, especially those in free-enterprise economies, are against planning in principle. They feel that tourism planning is an encroachment on individual businesses. A second concern is cost. Properly executed plans depend upon extensive research that must be funded. The public sector is usually called upon to fund extensive projects. A third difficulty relates to the extent of business activities associated with tourism. Because of the many businesses and activities involved in both the private and the public sector, it is difficult to get a unified approach to tourism planning.

IMPORTANCE OF DATA COLLECTION

In planning something as important as the development of tourism within a region or destination, it is vital that decisions be based on scientific data rather than guesses or hunches.

Types of Data Collection

Secondary Research.   In collecting data we can collect it ourselves or collect it from previously published sources. *Primary research* is the term used for collecting data firsthand; *secondary research* or *literature review* are the terms used when identifying data already collected. A variety of organizations collect and publish data on tourism. The major sources of such information are given in Appendix 1. The United States Travel Data Center can provide, for example, the following tourist-impact information by county:

- Level of expenditure
- Business receipts
- Employment
- Payroll
- Federal, state, and local taxes
- Receipts by Standard Industrial Classification code for the following industries, which account for 90 percent of tourist expenditures:

Classification Number	Industry
581	Eating and Drinking
701	Hotels, Tourist Courts, Motels
554	Gasoline Service Stations
794	Sports Promotion, Amusements, Recreation Services
599	Retail Stores Not Classified Elsewhere
783	Motion Picture Theaters
793	Theatrical Producers, Bands, Entertainers
702	Rooming and Boarding Houses
721	Laundries
703	Trailer Parks and Camps

Secondary research is relatively easy to collect, both in terms of time and money. However, it is generally not as specific as that required for a particular project.

Primary Research

Although more costly than is secondary research, primary research enables the planner to collect data specific to the project at hand. It can take several forms.

Direct Observation.   This method consists of observing people to determine what they like or dislike. It may involve the use of observers at a site or television or photographic recordings. People communicate more with nonverbal gestures than with the words they actually speak. This can be picked up by direct observation. This method will tell what people do but will not identify the reasons for the behavior.

Counting.   An accurate count of facility usage can be obtained by counting the visitors. Gate receipts, turnstile readings, counters on roadways, and the number of parking spaces used can give numbers of patrons. One limitation is that roads and facilities may be used by both tourists and locals, and thus it may be difficult to adjust the numbers accordingly. Ideally, counting should be done on a regular basis to give accurate data.

Surveys.   The most important aspect of conducting survey research is the statement of the problem. Too often data is collected because it seems "good to know this" and an attempt to make sense of it comes later.

Figure 7–3   Collecting data in Rotorua, New Zealand. (Courtesy New Zealand Tourist & Publicity Office.)

The objective of the project—namely, what we need to know—should be carefully outlined first. The following guidelines are suggested for developing a survey:

1. Review what other researchers have done. If the objectives are similar it may be possible to use or adapt the previous questionnaire.

2. If a new questionnaire has to be constructed, write down, on 3-by-5-inch cards, the information desired. Because the order of asking questions is often important, putting the questions on separate cards allows easy substitution of the order.

3. Think in advance of how the data will be presented in final form. Draw up the tables the way they will be presented; fill in hypothetical data. Ask yourself, "Does this format tell me what I want to know?" The final format of tables will help decide how questions should be worded.

4. Begin with exploratory research on a sample group of people. By asking several representative people general questions about why they visit an area, what is important and unimportant to them, it is possible to develop appropriate categories of items for more widespread data collection later.

5. It is not necessary to interview everyone. Researchers survey a representative sample of the target market. This might involve surveying every tenth person, for example. Another technique is to use random samples. A statistics book generally can provide a list of numbers generated randomly by a computer. These numbers indicate the people who should be interviewed—the second, seventh, twenty-third, etc., person to pass the interviewer, for example.

6. Make sure to take *bias* into account. Bias may occur in several ways. Interviewers may survey more male than female tourists; they may ask biased questions that are ambiguous to the tourist (testing the survey on a small group of people can help eliminate this); bias can also occur when people are interviewed—if different types of tourists visit each season, the results will be biased if the answers from one season are expanded to give a picture of the entire year.

7. Consider the various forms of surveying—registration methods (such as hotels do), suggestion boxes, informal surveys by mingling and talking with people, or using questionnaires.

8. Questionnaires may be self-administered, done by telephone, or face-to-face encounters. Self-administered questionnaires are

either given out, filled in, and collected on site or handed out to
be mailed back later. On-site questionnaires are easy to adminis-
ter and are inexpensive. Participation rate is usually high. Mail-
return questionnaires have lower response rates and have higher
costs associated with having to provide postage. Using the telephone allow the researcher to cover a wide geographic area at a
relatively low cost. If the tourist had just returned from a satisfying trip the response rate will probably be good. Face-to-face interviews are relatively expensive. It is important that a place be
selected that is conducive to the tourist. Few people will stop for
an interview if they are on their way somewhere else; on the other
hand, tourists waiting in line may be glad of the opportunity to
answer some questions as a way of helping pass the time.

The various characteristics of these methods are contrasted in Figure 7–4.

In summary, a solid plan, based on data appropriate to the destination, is necessary before the development of tourism can occur.

Figure 7–4   Methods of Collecting Tourism Data.

Type of Method	Design			Usefulness			Cost			Administration		
	E	M	D	L	M	H	L	M	H	E	M	D
Informal Surveys	X				X		X			X		
Suggestion Boxes	X			X			X			X		
Direct Observation		X			X				X			X
Counting Methods	X				X		X			X		
Registration	X				X		X			X		
Questionnaires												
Telephone			X		X				X			X
Self-administered			X		X			X			X	
Face-to-face			X			X			X			X

E = Easy; M = Medium; D = Difficult; L = Low; H = High.

Source: The University of Missouri, *Assessing Your Product and the Market, Tourism U.S.A.,
Volume II: Development* (Washington, D.C.: United States Department of Commerce,
1978), p. 9.

ENDNOTES

1. Robert Christie Mill and Alastair M. Morrison, *The Tourism System:
An Introductory Text* (Englewood Cliffs, N.J.: Prentice Hall, 1985), p. 288.

S T U D Y   QUESTIONS

1. Describe Plog's life cycle of a destination.
2. What are the stages of the product life cycle curve?
3. Why is integrated planning important to a destination?
4. What are the components of an integrated tourism plan?
5. What are the characteristics of a short-term plan?
6. What are the characteristics of a long-term plan?
7. List the barriers to planning.
8. What are the common forms of primary research?
9. Identify some guidelines to improve survey research.
10. List the various methods of survey research.

D I S C U S S I O N   QUESTIONS

1. Discuss why a plan is necessary for the development of tourism.
2. What are the components of a tourism plan for a destination? Why are they important?
3. Compare and contrast secondary and primary tourism research.
4. Evaluate the design, usefulness, cost, and administration of the various methods of collecting tourism data.

8

DEVELOPING TOURISM

LEARNING OBJECTIVES

At the end of this chapter the reader will be able to:

- Identify the relationship between the private and public sectors in the development of tourism.
- Identify the information that must be collected in order to prepare a tourism development plan.
- Develop statements from the collected data reflecting present and desired positions.
- Describe the important elements of an areawide master plan.
- Understand how the principles of tourism planning act as guidelines in tourism development.
- Be able to define and correctly use the following terms:

Core attraction	Supporting attraction
Market segmentation	Demographic segmentation
Geographic segmentation	Attracting power
Competing destination	Environmental impact statement
Loan guarantee	
Sole proprietor	Zoning
Corporation	Partnership
Attraction-service linkage	Clustering
Capacity	Natural/cultural resource dependency
Touring	
Destination tourism	Social-developmental climate

THE DEVELOPMENT PROCESS

The Development Team

In the development of a large-scale tourism project it is likely that both the private and the public sectors will be involved. The involvement of the public sector is important for two reasons. First, because of the gap between the amount of investment required and the revenue expected, it is unlikely that major projects can be funded initially solely by the private sector. Second, because of the income-producing potential of tourism development, investment by the public sector can act as a boost to the involvement of the private sector.

Typically, the public sector is involved in preparing the master plan, acquiring land, marketing the development of the project to potentially interested parties, developing and maintaining infrastructure, and monitoring development by the private sector. The private sector conducts feasibility analyses of specific projects and plans, and constructs and operates those deemed financially feasible. The respective roles of the private and public sectors and the time gap between investment requirements and revenue expectations are illustrated in Figure 8–1.

Steps in the Development Process

The development process begins with an analysis of four areas—the market potential, planning and engineering, socioeconomic, and legal and business. From this basic data, areas that are ripe for development are selected. Objectives, principles, and standards are developed and area-wide master plans prepared. For each area under development consideration, the environmental impact is assessed together with an estimate of the overall costs of development. From this a preliminary assessment of economic feasibility can be made. If it is decided to proceed with the project, a multiyear development plan is prepared in conjunction with more detailed financial and economic analyses. Marketing and administrative

190

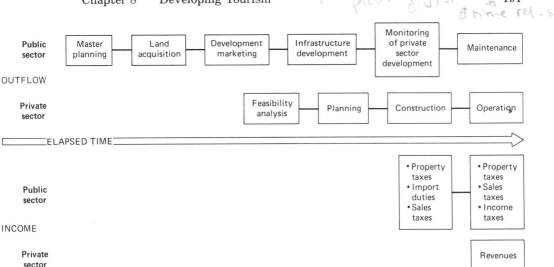

Figure 8–1. Time-related relationships between investment requirements and revenue expectations in tourism development. *(Source:* Charles Kaiser, Jr., and Larry E. Helber, *Tourism Planning & Development,* [Boston: CBI Publishing Company, 1978], p. 53.)

plans are prepared to support the chosen projects. The overall financial feasibility and economic impact can then be determined. This process is illustrated in Figure 8–2.

MARKET ANALYSIS

The purpose of the market analysis is to provide an estimate of long-term tourist flows to the destination. This is done by examining the tourist resources of the area compared to those of the competition in light of present and potential tourist demand.

Inventory of Tourist Attractions

Core and Supporting Attractions.   The purpose of the inventory is to summarize the current stage of tourism development in the area. The key question to be answered in this section is, "What do we have that would cause a tourist to come here?" Figure 8–3 contains a listing of various attractions. Often what is regarded as "ordinary" by local people will be of interest to outsiders. One way to approach this subject is to distinguish between *core* and *supporting* attractions. A core attraction forms the theme for the area. It is the principal reason tourists will visit the destination. It may be a natural attraction such as Niagara Falls or a way

Figure 8-2 Steps in the development process.

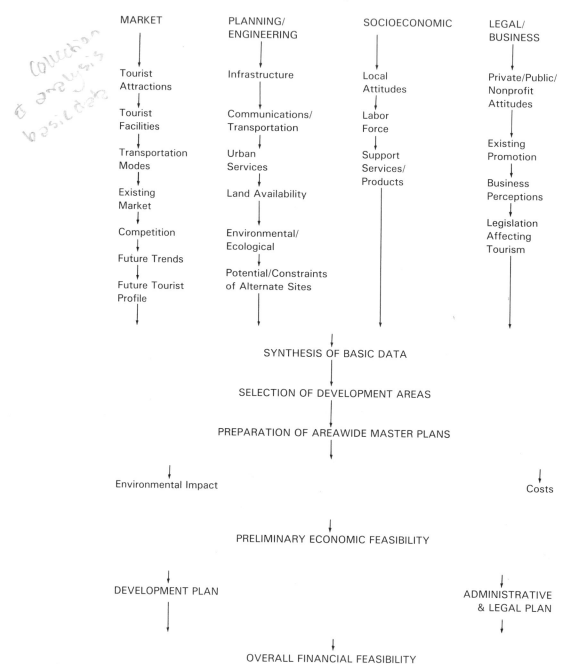

Source: Adapted from *A Proposal to Prepare a Feasibility Study of Tourism Development in Nicaragua,* Laventhol & Horwath, Leo A. Daly Company, and Osorio y Teran, 1975.

Figure 8-3   Attractions Checklist

Natural, Scenic or Environmental	Attraction currently exists	Area has potential to develop this attraction
Beaches		
Botanical gardens		
Canyons and gorges		
Caves		
Cliffs		
Climate (low humidity, low rainfall, sunny, warm, etc.)		
Deserts		
Fall foliage		
Farms, ranches, dude ranches		
Fishing streams and lakes		
Forests		
Geysers		
Golf courses		
Islands		
Lakes		
Marinas		
Mountains		
Nature trails		
Oceans		
Orchards and vineyards		
Panoramic picturesque views		
Parks, national, state and local		
Picnic areas		
Playgrounds with equipment		
Rivers		
Sand dunes		
Ski slopes		
Springs		
Swamps		
Unique geologic formations		
Valleys		
Volcanoes		
Waterfalls		
Wildlife sanctuaries		
Man-Made Attractions		
Airports		
Amusement parks		
Antique shops		
Arenas		
Art galleries		
Ball parks		
Beauty spas		
Big-name entertainers		
Bridges		

Figure 8–3   Continued

Natural, Scenic or Environmental	Attraction currently exists	Area has potential to develop this attraction
Campgrounds and trailer parks		
Candles		
Childrens' parks		
Churches		
Covered bridges		
Craft shops		
Dams and power stations		
Fish hatcheries		
Ferry boats		
Gambling casinos		
Government buildings		
Handcraft and homecraft industries		
Harbors		
Health resorts		
Large city attractions		
Libraries		
Local industrial plants		
Lumber camps		
Military installations		
Night clubs		
Nuclear reactors		
Observation towers		
Planetariums		
Rest stations		
Roadside parks		
Ships		
Shopping centers		
Showboats		
Souvenir and curio shops		
Stage shows		
Swimming pools		
Telescopes		
Theaters		
Universities and colleges		
Unusual buildings		
Unusual restaurants		
Wharfs		
Windmills		
Zoos		
Historical Attractions		
Battlefields		
Birthplaces of famous people		
Burial grounds		
Famous historical buildings		

Figure 8–3   Continued

Natural, Scenic or Environmental	Attraction currently exists	Area has potential to develop this attraction
Ghost towns		
Historic tours		
Landmarks		
Markers		
Memorials		
Missions		
Monuments		
Museums		
Newsworthy places		
Old forts		
Pioneer churches		
Pioneer homes		
Reconstructed historical towns		
Re-enactment of historical events		
Ruins		
Cultural and Ethnic Attractions		
Antiquities		
Archaeological sites		
Art galleries		
Ceremonial dances		
Conservatories		
Costumed events		
Early settlements		
Ethnic celebrations		
Exhibits		
Ghost towns		
Indian culture		
Indian reservations		
Mansions		
Museums		
Native folklore		
Prehistoric items		
Re-creations and restorations		
Special "nationality" days		
Trading centers		
Unique lifestyles		
Recreational Activities		
Archery		
Beach combing		
Bird watching		
Boat rides		
Body surfing		

Figure 8–3   Continued

Natural, Scenic or Environmental	Attraction currently exists	Area has potential to develop this attraction
Bowling		
Camping		
Canoeing		
Fishing		
Fossil hunting		
Golf		
Hang gliding		
Hiking		
Horseback riding		
Hunting		
Ice skating		
Mountain climbing		
Nature trails		
Racing and regattas		
Rock hunting		
Sailing		
Scuba diving		
Skeet shooting		
Skiing		
Spelunking		
Swimming		
Tennis		
Trap shooting		
Water skiing		
Special Events (too numerous to list all possibilities)		
Air shows		
Antique auto shows		
Arts and crafts classes		
Barbeques		
Barn dances		
Boy Scout Jamborees		
Country and folk music festivals		
Excursions		
Fairs		
Fishing		
Hayrides		
High-school band days		
Hobby weekends		
Hog calling contests		
Home tours		
Jazz festivals		
July 4th celebrations		
Pageants		

Figure 8-3 Continued

Natural, Scenic or Environmental	Attraction currently exists	Area has potential to develop this attraction
Parades		
Photo contests		
Pie-eating contests		
Plowing tractor contest		
Queen coronations		
Races, auto, motorcycle, horse		
Rodeos		
Shows, dog, cat, horse		
Sightseeing tours		
Tournaments, sports		
Turkey calling contests		
Turkey shoots		

Source: University of Missouri, *Tourism U.S.A., Volume II, Development: Assessing Your Product and the Market* (Washington, D.C.: U.S. Government Printing Office, 1978), pp. 33–37.

of life such as the Amish in Pennsylvania. Supporting attractions are those built around the core theme. In Niagara Falls, for example, the *Maid of the Mist* boat trip, which takes people to within yards of the bottom of the falls, and the museum of daredevils who attempted to go over the falls are examples of supporting attractions.

Sources of Information.   Information can be collected from several sources. These include:

1. Telephone directory
2. Chambers of Commerce
3. Local historical societies
4. Area historian
5. State tourist and travel offices
6. People in the various tourist industries
7. Local elected officials and regional planning and development staff[1]

Collecting such information requires leadership from the appropriate national, state, or provincial leadership and a coordinated effort throughout the region. At the local level this might be coordinated by representatives of the local chamber of commerce, people in businesses associated with tourism, or elected officials.

Figure 8–4   Tabor, Czechoslovakia. An inventory of
attractions is part of the
market analysis. (Courtesy
Cedok.)

Tabulating the Data.   Once data are collected, the information should be
stored in some usable form. Data can serve as the basis for preparing a
marketing plan, for determining the strength of the area attractions, and
for identifying areas of weakness that must be attended to. One format
for such a display is shown in Figure 8–5. Dividing the attractions into
their various types can help determine what the core attraction of the
destination is. The capacity together with the actual number of visitors
will determine the need to expand. The price charged will give an indication of the market segment being served while a judgment of the quality
will show where resources have to be improved.

Inventory of Tourist Facilities

An inventory similar to the one above would be prepared for tourist
facilities and would include information on lodging, food and beverage
outlets, and retail stores aimed at tourists. Information would be collected on the location, number of rooms or seats, amenities and services
provided, and the markets served.

Figure 8–5 Tabular Inventory Form for Sample Survey Questionnaire

Name and Address of Attractions	Scenic	Historic	Recreational	Man-Made	Capacity Per Day	Admission Rate				Services	Should/Should Not be Expanded	General Condition			
						Adult	Child	Group	Other			good	fair	poor	needs improv.

Source: University of Missouri, *Tourism U.S.A., Volume II, Development: Assessing Your Product and the Market* (Washington, D.C.: U.S. Government Printing Office, 1978), p. 41.

Transportation Modes

Transportation to, from, and within the destination is covered in this section. For commercial carriers, the cost and frequency of service, cities served by direct connections, and future plans for service will be covered.

Existing Market

The end product of this inventory is to answer the following questions:

1. Whom do we attract?
2. When do they visit and how far in advance do they decide?
3. Where do they come from and how do they get here?
4. Why do they visit?

Marketing is more art than science. Yet one rule of thumb in marketing is to "attract people similar to those who already visit." A certain type of person already visits the area. By identifying the characteristics of existing visitors it is possible to identify similar target markets. By answering the question "Whom do we attract here?" in light of tourist trends it is possible to determine the most appropriate markets to approach.

Market Segmentation.   Because the travel market is made up of people who have diverse needs it is necessary to think in terms of different segments of the market. *Market segmentation* is the process of dividing a market into distinct groups who have relatively similar needs and developing separate marketing strategies for each one.

Demographic Segmentation.   Markets may be segmented demographically, geographically, psychographically, or on the basis of behavior. Demographic variables might be such factors as age, marital status, number and age of children, stage in the family life cycle, education, income, or occupation. Such a profile might determine that the visitors to a destination area are primarily between the ages of 25 and 35, married with children between the ages of two and six. The parents have attended some college and are professionals with a family income of $20,000 to $30,000. Demographic variables have long been the basis for segmenting markets. However, in recent years, tourist markets have become more complex and demographics alone cannot explain tourist behavior. Many students, for example, journey to Europe. They may buy a Eurail pass and sleep on the train to avoid hotel costs as they take in the history and culture of foreign lands. On the basis of age and income their travel to Europe could not be predicted.

Geographic Segmentation.   We have seen earlier that both travel distance and time impact on the decision to travel. Thus, it would appear that segmenting a market geographically would make sense. Target markets can be identified by means of a four-step process.[2] In the first step, the attracting powers of the area's attractions are estimated. Attracting power is a measure of the amount of effort people will spend in getting to the area. Attracting power depends on the amount of time a visitor would have to spend seeing the attractions in the area and the degree of interest the individual has in these attractions. One way to do this is to classify the attractions of the area into those with local, state, regional, national, or international appeal. Disney World, for example, has international appeal, whereas a weekly farmer's market might draw folks from 20-mile radius. A second method involves estimating the amount of time it takes the average person to visit the attractions of the area. The minimum measure of the area's attracting power is the time taken to see and enjoy the highlights of the destination. The total amount of time to see all or most of the attractions is the maximum measure of the destination's attracting power. It may be that these measures would vary by season. From these figures an estimate can be made as to whether or not visitors would take more, the same, or less time to travel to the area than to appreciate its attractions.

The second step in targeting a market geographically is to take the above estimates of attracting power and estimate the distance, travel time, and travel expense for someone to drive or otherwise reach the destination. From this a radius of potential markets can be drawn with the area at the center.

The third step in this four-step process involves using a map. The maximum distance that people would be willing to travel is estimated and towns and cities within these boundaries are identified. It is important to consider also the tourists who might stop en route to another destination. An examination of tourist flows can uncover this data.

In the final step the potential competition for each geographic segment is identified. If it is determined, for example, that tourists from a particular city will drive up to 200 miles to vacation, then be sure to examine all other competing destinations up to 200 miles from the area. The destination area under development consideration can be compared to the others in terms of number and type of attractions. This may allow us to eliminate certain market segments because of the strength of the competition.

Time and money permitting, it is also possible to survey existing tourists as to where they come from in order to establish the attracting power of the area.

Figure 8-6 It is important to know your market. (Courtesy Hong Kong Tourist Association.)

Psychographic Segmentation. While demographic segmentation divides the market into segments based on socioeconomic characteristics, psychographic segmentation divides tourists on the basis of personality. Segments are identified in terms of:

1. Why does the tourist travel?
2. What does the tourist like to do on vacation?

A demographic segment of the market can be thought of as a skeleton that provides the framework and shape of the visitors. Describing the segment in psychographic terms is like adding the flesh to the skeleton— it completes the features and makes the tourists recognizable.

Behavioral Segmentation. Segmenting a market on the basis of the behavior of the visitors would cover such things as how they traveled to the area, how many were in the party, when the trip was taken, when the decision to travel was made, and how long the trip was.

Competition

It is vital that a realistic assessment be made of competing destinations in order to determine the future numbers of expected tourists. A competing destination is one that seeks to attract the same tourists as the destination under development. Ideally, each competing destination would be subjected to the same level of analysis as that being developed.

Future Trends. A variety of secondary sources of information exist that identify changes in the marketplace. Many of these are listed in Appendix 1. From documents that cover changes in the segments of the market being attracted, it can be seen which segments are growing, changing, or declining. Appropriate changes can then be made in the forecast of future tourist numbers.

The end result of this will be a profile of the numbers and types of tourists expected in the future.

PLANNING AND ENGINEERING ANALYSIS

The objective of this analysis is to study existing conditions in a number of potential sites and to collect, for these sites, information on factors and regulations that impact the development of these sites for tourism purposes. Areas covered include quality of infrastructure; prevailing government practices and regulations; and environmental and ecological conditions for each potential area.

Infrastructure

Information on the infrastructure covers such items as when it was originally installed, the reserve capacity of the system, programmed improvements for increasing the capacity of the system, or the programmed extension of the system to serve additional areas.

Communications and Transportation. Visitors must be able to get to and from the destination. Even the enormously successful Disney World required an investment of $5 million by the state of Florida for access highways. As the nation's interstate highway system developed, many smaller communities that attracted tourists en route elsewhere lost that business. Some communities did not recover while others were able to develop attractions to lure people off the interstate. Asbury Park, New Jersey, was bypassed in the 1950s by the Garden State Parkway. The parkway allowed visitors quick access to better beaches farther south. The town of Asbury Park developed a new attraction—Grand Prix racing—as a way of getting people to visit. The same situation was faced by towns in Georgia that, for years, had captured visitors on their way to Florida. Interstate 95 bypassed them. Local people worked with state and federal authorities to develop codes for limited advertising along I-95. Today, directional signs identifying travel service facilities, areas of scenic beauty, and public attractions are permitted. As a result, many travelers continue to stop there en route to Florida.

The principal areas for which information would be evaluated would include:

1. *Roads:* existing roads providing access to a given area or service within an area; number and width of lanes; paved or unpaved; planned extensions, widening or other improvements; extent and quality of parking; adequacy of signs.
2. *Airports:* location and quality of existing airstrips and airfields; type of runway, lighted or not; accessibility of terminal to tourist areas.
3. *Ports and marinas:* location, size, number of slips or berths; depth of channel; extent of marina facilities; accessibility to tourist areas.
4. *Telephone, telegraph, and postal service:* availability and adequacy of telephone, telegraph, and postal service; planned improvements or extension of service.

The interdependence of these facilities should be considered. For example, if an expansion is considered at the airport, there will also be increased ground traffic. How will this be handled? Will ground transportation and/or road capacity be increased? What will this do to street traffic?

When looking at transportation in and out of the region it is necessary to examine the time-zone preferences of the visitors. People generally prefer departure times convenient to their everyday schedules. In flying from the United States to Europe it is common to leave in the evening and arrive early in the morning. On the other hand, it is not unusual for British visitors to many European resorts to have to check out of their hotel by midday and find something to do until their plane leaves early the next morning to return to Britain.

A major problem often is that, by improving the access to a destination, demand increases and the area loses its attractiveness to visitors. Destinations may be forced to limit or ban traffic from certain areas, even set speed limits or institute one-way scenic loops to keep traffic flowing.

Parking is another major problem related to congestion. Increased road traffic tends to force the elimination of parking places. On-street parking can be increased through such things as instituting one-way traffic or changing from parallel to angle parking. Parking can be handled in several ways.[3] It may be provided privately by the attraction, as in the

Figure 8–7 Transportation can take many forms. (Courtesy Texas State Department of Highways and Public Transportation.)

case of major attractions where the cost is often included in the price of admission. For new businesses locating in low-density areas the community may require that attractions and facilities—through zoning and provision of business licenses—provide off-street parking on some ratio of spaces per room, per seat, or per square foot. Private lots may be set up by entrepreneurs. Visitors pay but local businesses often will stamp the customer's ticket if a purchase is made. The cost to the business is passed on to customers in higher prices. However, a problem occurs when the owner of the parking lot wants to turn the land into a more profitable use. This type of conversion can be deferred by placing low property assessments on land used for parking. Another way to handle parking is to provide public lots. The expense may be picked up by the community, or motorists may pay through parking fees or meters.

Urban Services.   An inventory must be taken to ensure the adequacy of such support services as water, electricity, sewage collection and disposal, and the provision of police and fire protection.

Land Availability

Development of tourist attractions and facilities obviously requires the availability of land. However, the question goes beyond the physical availability and into such areas as:

- who owns the land?
- are the owners willing to sell or allow development?
- can foreigners own and develop land?
- how much does the land costs?

The situation can be illustrated by the ski industry in the United States. Approximately half of all privately operated ski areas are on federal land. To expand these areas further or to develop new areas requires the permission of the federal government.

Environmental and Ecological Aspects

Any major development will require some form of environmental impact statement. Oftentimes the success of a particular tourist area depends upon the quality of the physical environment. This may include such factors as sunshine, temperature, isolation, surf, snow, beaches, water, natural drainage, or vegetation. The impact of development on the natural features of the environment must be considered as they relate to the planned use for each site.

Safari development in Africa has increased the close shadowing of lions by tourists. As a result, many kills are missed by the lions and lion cubs starve to death.

At this early stage of analysis it is appropriate to evaluate, in a preliminary fashion, the alternate sites. The dominant characteristics of each would be arranged, evaluated, and graded on a matrix in order to allow an evaluation of their relative merits and limitations using the criteria noted above.

SOCIOECONOMIC ANALYSIS

A socioeconomic analysis covers two areas—the local people and the support services and products.

Local People

An analysis of the residents of the area is important for three reasons. First, tourism will impact the lives of the area residents. There will be more visitors to the area; prices of certain items may increase; services may improve. The point is to determine the prevailing attitudes of people in the community toward the development of tourism. If there is an overwhelmingly negative attitude about the development of tourism it may be unrealistic to plan for its increase. If partially negative attitudes emerge, it may suggest the need for an educational program on the benefits of tourism to the community.

A second reason considers the identification of numbers and types of people most likely to be interested in working in the tourism industries. In some instances it has been necessary for countries to institute training sessions in order to upgrade the level of skills in the community as part of a tourism development program.

A third part of the analysis is concerned with the role of residents as part of the tourism "product." Often the hospitality of the local residents is a major attraction in itself. Local hospitality is well known, for example, in such places as Scotland, Ireland, and Hawaii. How hospitable to visitors is the local population? Moreover, are local people aware of the potential attractions available in their community? The author recently asked a waitress in a restaurant in Aberdeen, Scotland, "What is there to do here for the afternoon?" The answer: "Go to Inverness" (a town some 60 miles away!). At the other extreme is Niagara Falls, Ontario. In the two months on either side of the summer tourist season the Chamber of Commerce organizes visits by local groups to tourist attractions, Admission to the attractions is free to groups who make reservations through the chamber. As a result, local residents see why tourists visit their community. They develop civic pride. And when anyone comes into town and asks "What can I do here?" there is a ready answer.

Support Services and Products

Tourism requires many support systems—food items, bedding, furniture, fixtures, etc. To maximize tourism's economic impact, backward linkages to other sectors of the economy should be encouraged. At this point it is important to determine the following:

1. Are these support services and products available locally?
2. If not, can they be developed locally?
3. If not, can they be easily imported?

BUSINESS AND LEGAL ANALYSIS

The purpose of this section is to determine the need for changes in the legal and business environment for tourism development to be successful. This involves a study of the business and legal environments as they relate to tourism.

Business Environment

The environment for tourism business is made up of private businesses, both tourism related and nontourism related, the public sector, and the service and civic organizations in the community.

Figure 8–8 Tourists require many support services. (Courtesy Hong Kong Tourist Association.)

Information Needs.   Three types of information are needed:

1. What are the attitudes of the private, public, and civic sectors toward increased tourism?
2. What is presently being done to promote tourism?
3. What are the perceptions of the community regarding the existing economic impact and relative importance of tourism to the community?[4]

This information is vital to the development process. If organizations underestimate the present role of tourism it will affect their attitudes about the amount of effort they will put into future development. Equally, if increased development is perceived as a negative, the process of development will be slowed or stopped altogether. If the specific perceived problems of increased tourism are identified an action plan can be formulated to educate community residents if their perceptions are wrong or to ensure that problems in developing tourism are controlled. A survey of what is presently being done is necessary to determine what remains to be done. This information can be collected by means of a mail survey or through personal interviews.

Financial Institutions.   Of particular importance is the attitude of financial institutions toward tourism. The growth of tourism requires the availability of capital. And if extensive development is envisioned, funding from outside the community may be necessary. This is a two-edged sword. On the one hand, financing is available. However, the price paid (apart from interest payments) is that control of the project is moved outside the community. Decisions are then made by those outside the community that affect those within the community. Thus, it is important to determine the extent to which the local banking community supports the growth of tourism, the extent to which it will lend financial and moral support to efforts to increase tourism, and the kinds of incentives it would give to expand tourism within the local area.

Financial incentives for tourism development include loans, loan guarantees, fiscal incentives, and subsidies. Private banking institutions could be involved in giving loans. Many governments have also underwritten matching loans. The other incentives, if offered, would come from the public sector. A loan guarantee occurs when the host government co-signs or guarantees the loan. Fiscal incentives can take the form of reduced taxes on investments or income. This may also include such things as the relaxation or suspension of import or real estate taxes. In other cases, cash contributions, namely a subsidy, have been made to private businesses to encourage their development.

Such incentives should be made carefully and selectively. Too often communities have given financial incentives to businesses on the promise of future economic benefits to the community. But many times these benefits—jobs, taxes, and revenue—did not materialize. Communities have to weigh carefully the up-front costs of incentives against the likely future benefits.

Legal Environment

Government regulations have increasingly affected all businesses, and tourism businesses are no exception. The objective here is to determine the extent to which government affects tourism development and to identify legislation that would hurt the development process. This analysis will serve to guide developers through the legal maze to the right agency, office, or person to approach regarding regulations that affect the development under review. It will also point out to entrepreneurs the cost and risks involved in a developmental effort.

A framework for investigating the impact of the legal environment is suggested in Table 8-1. This table identifies the basic categories of the legal environment that impact tourism development.

TABLE 8-1. Legal Environment

Factor	Implication	Source of Information	Location	Method	Personnel
1. Existence of agencies a. Planning Commission b. Parks and Recreation c. Transit Authority d. Health Department e. Airport Board f. Building Commission g. Sanitation h. Other	Presence requires analysis of rules and regulations	Records of County Commissioners County official and residents	Courthouse City Hall	Examination of records Personal inquiry of individuals	Administrative Assistant County Commission City Manager, Clerk of County and City, President of County Commission
2. Environmental Protection a. bird sanctuaries b. littering	Preservation of the "environment"	State Code Environmental Protection Agency (EPA)	N/A	Examine written laws and rules and regulations of EPA	N/A
3. Zoning laws and land use plans a. building codes b. BZA	Site selection	Planning Commission (Reports), USDA Soil Conservation (Maps), Chamber of Commerce (Proposals)	USDA Office Chamber of Commerce Courthouse	Personal Interviews Chamber of Commerce USDA, County Comm. Planning Comm.	Administrative Assistant Clerks of county and Director of Chamber of Commerce

Item	Purpose	Source	Location	Method	Officials
4. Sanitation a. Dumping facilities b. Sewage systems	Protection of health	State Code Department of Health Local Health Office Sanitation Department	State Capitol Local Health Office	Examine law Rules and regulations of State Health Department Interview personnel of local agencies	Directors of health and sanitation locally
5. Guests and Innkeepers	Safeguarding comfort and enjoyment	State statute Case law	N/A	Examine written law	None
6. Transportation and Public a. countywide or districts b. private, public, quasi c. fire protection	Availability of services	Public Service Commission Local utilities	State or Regional Utility Co. office	Written inquiry to Public Service Commission for rules and regulations. Interview of local utilities	Officers/Directors of local utilities
7. Licenses and Permits a. Fishing b. Hunting/game preserves c. Gambling d. Alcoholic beverages e. Food	Availability of certain activities to visitors	State Code County Officials Alcoholic Beverage Board Health Department Rules and Regulations	State Courthouse	Examine statutes Interview clerks Rules and regulations	Clerk of County Commission

TABLE 8-1. Continued

Factor	Implication	Source of Information	Location	Method	Personnel

8. Regulation of Attractions and Activities
a. art
b. music
c. waterways
  (1) boating
  (2) swimming
	Public protection; availability fosters tourism	State Code
		Arts & Humanities Councils
		State and Local Historical Society
		Department of Recreation
			N/A	Research
				Written inquiry to State
				Personal interview, local
					Directors, Arts Councils, Historical Society, Recration Department Personnel

9. Sunday closing laws	Tourism's weekend activity	Minutes of County Commission, Sheriff, Prosecuting Attorney	Courthouse	Examine record of certification of last local option vote: (Statistics)	Clerk Prosecuting Attorney Sheriff
10. Advertising a. Billboards b. Signs, roads c. Signs, streets	Public education plus aesthetic values	State Code City ordinance County ordinance Department of Highways	State Courthouse City Clerk's office	Examine written material	None
11. Taxation-local a. sales b. B&O or privilege c. property	Encouraging or prohibitive	Local ordinances State Code	Courthouse City Hall Assessor's office	Examine ordinances Interview of clerks and assessor	Clerks of City and County Assessor Assessor
12. Wages and Compensation	Impact on development	State Department of Labor State Code	State Capitol	Written inquiry Examination of statutes and rules and regulations	N/A

Source: West Virginia University, *Creating Economic Growth and Jobs Through Travel and Tourism: A Manual for Community and Business Developers* (Washington, D.C., U.S. Government Printing Office, 1981), pp. 122–124.

Environment and Land Use.   In recent years controls by the federal government on the quality of air and water have increased significantly. Appropriate permits are necessary if the quality of the environment may be put at risk. An example concerns campgrounds or recreation facilities located near lakes or streams. Under the federal Water Pollution Control Act anyone who discharges pollutants into navigable waters must obtain approval by means of a permit from the Environmental Protection Agency or the Army Corps of Engineers. Such a permit might be necessary during the building and/or operation of a facility centering around a body of water.

Land use in many countries is controlled through a system of zoning. Zoning laws can require that certain areas be solely residential, can regulate the size and type of buildings or industry in an area, and can even specify the maximum size of buildings and the minimum space surrounding the building. Planning commissions, county commissions, or

Figure 8–9   (Courtesy California Chamber of Commerce.)

city councils generally govern the system of zoning in a community. Local government can be petitioned to alter zoning requirements.

Both the National Park Service and the Heritage Conservation and Recreation Service of the U.S. Department of the Interior can furnish information on the procedures necessary to designate specific buildings or sites as historic landmarks. Sites or buildings so designated will be protected against future development.

Public Safety and Health. Businesses that deal with the public have greater responsibilities than those that do not. Customers and visitors to the business are either licensees or invitees. Examples of licensees would be salespeople, people coming in out of the rain, or those taking a short cut through the property. The legal obligation to licensees is to warn people of any risks on the property. Additionally, the property owner cannot attempt to cause injury to the licensee.

Obligations toward invitees are greater. Invitees are those using the premises as a result of an apparent invitation. Customers fall into this category. The owner's duty to invitees is not only to warn the invitee of potential dangers but also to inspect the premises for potentially dangerous conditions and to take reasonable care to prevent harm to the invitee.

Enforcement is usually done at the state level. Restaurants, for example, must undergo health inspections that cover cleanliness, sanitation, lighting, plumbing, and ventilation. Emergency exits and fire extinguishers are checked against the state fire code. Food-handler permits may be required from the state health department.

Transportation. Transportation companies are regulated by various federal agencies. Each state, in addition, has regulations regarding height, width, and weight limits. State public service commissions are involved in regulating taxi and limousine companies.

Recreational Activities. The law impacts on recreational activities in such things as liquor laws, gambling, and racing regulations as well as restrictions on various recreational pursuits such as hunting, fishing, and boating.

State regulations typically control the legal age of an individual to be served alcohol, when alcohol can be served, and the presence or absence of gambling machines on the premises. Similarly, states regulate the type of betting or racing allowed in the community. It is difficult to change community laws enacted to "safeguard" the morals of the people. The type of tourism developed must be in accordance with local mores and customs.

Licenses for hunting and fishing are usually controlled at the state level. Temporary licenses are usually available for out-of-state visitors.

Taxation. The common forms of taxes are income tax, privilege tax, consumer sales tax, excise tax, and licensing fees. Income tax is paid at the federal, state, and often the local level. Companies are, in addition, often taxed for the "privilege" of conducting business. Often called a business and occupation tax, this can be enacted at the state and local level. Most states have consumer sales taxes on various goods and services. There are usually exceptions to this tax—such as for food. Excise taxes are placed on items not considered essential to life, such as cigarettes and beer. Most businesses will have to have an annual license to conduct business. The business license must usually be displayed in a prominent place at each unit of business.

Business Organization. Businesses may operate as a sole proprietorship, as a partnership, or as a corporation.

A sole proprietor exists when one person operates a business without incorporating it. Business taxes are paid as part of the owner's taxes. Business income is regarded as the individual's income and losses are treated the same way. The owner is liable for any debts of the business to the amount of his or her personal assets.

A partnership is similar except that it involves more than one person.

To incorporate, a business must obtain a charter and meet the requirements of the state in which it is incorporated. Business income, losses, and taxes are treated separately from that of the owners, who have limited liability for business debts.

Employment. When employees are hired, the business must adhere to regulations designed to protect the employee. Employees must be paid at least the minimum wage. If the employee works more than 40 hours a week, overtime must be paid at the rate of time and a half. (There are some limited exceptions to this rule including the requirement of 44 hours for employees of hotels, motels, and restaurants.) Additional regulations aim to prevent employers from discriminating against employees on the basis of age, sex, race, color, religion, national origin, or handicap.

Employers are expected to withhold taxes from employees' pay checks. They must also pay half the Social Security (FICA) tax of each employee. Workers' compensation mechanisms have been established as a no-fault method of compensating employees who are injured on the job. All employers pay into this fund based on the amount of hazard associated with each employee's job and the safety record of the employer.

Child labor laws must be adhered to. These place limits on the minimum age of and hours to be worked by young people. Generally, youngsters under the age of 16 cannot be employed without a special certificate,

Figure 8-10 Many tourist operations are small businesses. (Courtesy Hong Kong Tourist Association.)

and restrictions are placed on the number of hours anyone under 18 can work.

Employers have a responsibility to protect the safety and health of their employees in the workplace. The Occupational Safety and Health Administration (OSHA) regulates and inspects business premises to ensure that employees are not made to work in an unsafe environment.

SYNTHESIS OF BASIC DATA

In bringing together the information collected to date, two questions must be answered: Where are we? and Where do we want to be?

Where Are We?

Position statements should be developed in the areas of development, marketing, industry organization, tourism awareness, and support services and activities. These statements should not be long and involved. An evaluation of "Where are we?" might indicate, for example,

TABLE 8–2.   Synthesis of Basic Data

Where	– – – – –	Relative Importance of Objectives	– – – – –	Where Do
Are	– – – – –		– – – – –	We Want
We?	– – – – –	Relative Stage of Tourism	– – – – –	to Be?

that: "Our destination area has traditionally relied upon the summer market; facilities and support infrastructure to attract and service tourists at other times of the year have not been developed; the market has evolved to where more people have the time and money to take off-season vacations; a number of potential sites are available that could attract such tourists; yet there is a lack of appreciation among community leaders for the role that tourism can play in the economic and social development of the community; this lack of appreciation manifests itself in legislation that often discourages tourism development."

Where Do We Want to Be?

A similar position statement would then be developed on "Where do we want to be?" Such a statement would cover the areas mentioned above and would be related to working to solve the problems of the community while being realistic about the existing role of tourism. A region with chronic unemployment might stress the type of tourism that would produce large amounts of jobs while another with unbalanced regional growth would seek to develop tourism in those areas where the economy is weak. The point is that the answer to the question "Where do we want to be?" should be related to solving the problems unique to that region.

Those in the region will have to determine to what extent they want tourism to:

● maximize the opportunity for tourism development to raise the level of the national and regional economy;

● maximize the opportunities for harmonious integration of tourism development with the local life style, culture, and environment;

● maximize the opportunities for the creation of more jobs;

● maximize the opportunities for essential tourism infrastructure to improve the level of services for local people.[5]

The position statement should also realistically reflect where the region presently is in terms of tourism. It is pointless to develop a goal that has no chance of being met.

SELECTION OF DEVELOPMENT AREAS

Based on the information collected, a tentative selection can be made of the most suitable areas for tourism development. The suitability of a tourist area is the likelihood that its development will contribute to meeting the needs of the region. Development areas selected will bridge the gap between where a destination area is and where it wants to be. At the same time the development process will be guided by the objectives deemed most important to the destination area itself.

PREPARATION OF AREAWIDE MASTER PLANS

For each area in which tourism will be developed a master plan should be prepared. The plan will aim to meet the objectives deemed most appropriate for the region. Typically, such a plan will have a five-year horizon. It should be emphasized, however, that the plan, once drawn, is not carved in granite. It should be updated as circumstances dictate. In fact, the major benefit is not in the preparation of a final document, but rather in the process itself. When people get into the habit of looking several years ahead and in considering how development in one area affects the needs of the community then the benefits of planning are felt by all.

Elements

A master plan will have four elements to it. First, the *land use* element of the master plan will suggest appropriate uses for land within the region—agriculture, tourism development, marinas, industry, etc. One important use may, in fact, be not to use the land. That is, for certain areas, a decision may be made to leave open space in the region. Second, the *transportation* element includes suggestions on roads, railroads, airports, and harbor facilities. Finally, the *supporting facilities* and *infrastructure* elements of the plan identify the additional development required to service the expected influx of visitors and workers to the region.

Land Use.   Land is probably the most important resource to be managed in a tourism development plan. Five elements are particularly important. First, the *location* is important in terms of accessibility of the site itself and proximity of accommodations to the attraction.

Second, the attractiveness of the *view* can either enhance the attraction or be the primary attraction for the visitor.

Third, the planned use of the area must be *suitable to its environment.* Many elements of the environment—sunshine, hills, isolation, etc.—are part and parcel of the tourism experience. Developing activities appropriate to the characteristics of the land will enhance the tourism experience for the visitor. This includes taking the terrain into account. Terrain affects such things as drainage in addition to the cost of excavation and construction.

Fourth, land must be *available* to be used. Consideration must be given to the cost, time, procedures, politics, and public relations associated with the acquisition of land deemed important for development purposes.

Finally, the *usable area* of the land must be addressed. Planning should take into account not only the present-day development needs but also the availability of land for future development if expansion is necessary.

Transportation.   The importance of transportation in tourism has been stressed several times in this text. It is important to think of traveling from the tourist's point of view—the trip from home, travel at and around the destination, and the return trip home. Of particular importance are the positioning of gateways for arrival and departure and the routing of ground transportation networks.

If tourists arrive at a destination after a long plane journey it is unlikely that they will want to, or be able to, travel great distances on the ground. Accommodation facilities must be developed close by. Ground transportation should, wherever possible, avoid doubling back on areas covered and should be routed away from destinations where tourism is not wanted.

For travel by automobile, the importance considerations include:

- comfortable, safe and attractive roads that avoid overcrowding;
- directional signs that are clear, large enough to be visible to the traveler, placed to give the driver time to react, and, where the visitors are foreign, use of universal picture-type signs to communicate;
- promotional signs that balance the need to attract and inform while avoiding unattractive signs that are a blight to the environment.

Taxis should be modern and the drivers able to speak at least a few words of the tourist's language. Strict control should be exerted over regulations regarding fares.

Buses should be appropriate not only to the segments of the market being attracted but also to the type of travel. If an area seeks to attract tourists to international-class hotels, buses used to transport the visitors should also be of this caliber. At the same time, different kinds of buses are needed depending on the use. Buses for city sightseeing trips should be designed for frequent stops, ease of entry and exit, and maximum pas-

Figure 8–11   Safe, comfortable roads are an important part of the tourist destination. (Courtesy New Zealand Tourist & Publicity Office.)

senger capacity. Luggage space is not important. Touring coaches, on the other hand, need to provide for passenger comfort, baggage facilities, and passenger amenities such as lavatories. Many European coaches offer videos and hostesses who serve drinks.

Rail transportation is ideal for many destinations and offers a relaxing way to reach an area. Of special importance are such things as transportation between the terminal and local hotels, the provision of sufficient baggage handling, customs and banking facilities if the terminal is a port of entry, and the provision of bus or taxi facilities sufficient to handle heavy arrival and departure loads.

Cruise ships have similar concerns. There must be ease of access from metropolitan areas at the departure points and proximity to attractions at the destination. Only a few parts of the destination will be affected by cruises—shopping, attractions, and local transportation.

A recurring transportation problem is that of transfer—from one mode to another or from transportation to hotel. There can be startling contrast when visitors arrive in a modern jet and stay in a modern hotel but must travel between the two, complete with baggage, by less than adequate means.

Supporting Facilities: Accommodation.   There must be enough accommodation facilities of the right kind to appeal to the visitors being attracted. Ideally, facilities will be designed in accordance with the traditions and customs of the area. The more the local products can be incorporated into the design, the more money will stay in the area.

Accommodations also have to be tailored to the type of tourist. Facilities at a destination, as distinct from a pass-through, area will require larger rooms as guests will be staying longer. The quality of accommodation provided by the competition has also to be taken into account.

Accommodations are of many types. Hotels offer a number of facilities and generally have food and beverage service and may even offer such amenities as room service, laundry and valet service, and various shops or facilities such as auto rental and tour reservations.

Motor hotels are hotels with integrated parking facilities where guests park free of charge. They tend to range from 50 to 300 rooms.

Motels offer room accommodations only. As a result, their room rates are less expensive. Motels are found primarily at roadside or heavy traffic areas in places that have a high volume of visitors who stay a short period of time.

Resort hotels are located to take advantage of natural or developed recreational attractions. Rooms are large and of high quality. Many amenities are offered as guests tend to stay longer; many resorts are in remote locations. Often a guest service director is appointed to organize an activities program.

Condominiums and apartment hotels have been developed to provide full apartment-type living facilities. Such properties appeal to families and small groups.

Other facilities might be recreational vehicle parks, campgrounds, pensions, or bed-and-breakfast homes, hostels, and even houseboats. The type of accommodation developed, as noted above, will depend upon the type of tourist being attracted.

Other Support Industries.   Support industries are all the services, goods, or activities required by tourists. They tend to be highly fragmented. Examples of these businesses are:

LOCAL OR DAY TOURS	RETAIL SHOPS
ART GALLERIES	RESTAURANTS
NIGHT CLUBS	MUSEUMS
RECREATIONAL FACILITIES	MOVIE THEATERS
HANDICRAFT STUDIOS	SPECTATOR SPORTS
FESTIVALS	LAUNDRIES
PHARMACIES	GAS STATIONS

Note that many of these examples are businesses that are used by both residents and tourists alike. In fact, the development of tourism may encourage the development of facilities that would not otherwise be available to residents.

Opportunities for support services fall into two areas—impulse or entertainment purchases, or staple items or requirements. The former is pleasure-related and includes such things as tours, festivals, and museums. The latter is subsistence-related and includes such things as gas stations, pharmacies, and restaurants. It is important that a certain amount of integration occur between both types. People attending a festival will require some place to eat, for example.

The number and type of facilities must be appropriate to the number and type of expected visitors. High-income tourists will wish to shop in high-quality stores. The type of retail store in Aspen is much different from that at Coney Island. Typically, facilities are clustered. Restaurants with different themes or retail stores selling different merchandise, when placed in close proximity, attract a mass of visitors because of the number of different facilities available.

The number, quality, and type of support facilities can be controlled through two techniques—zoning and operating regulations enforced by law, and ownership control through the leasing of facilities to entrepre-

Figure 8–12 Tourists love to shop. (Courtesy Hong Kong Tourist Association.)

neurs. Many areas have had great success through controlling a large facility and leasing portions of it to individual entrepreneurs. In this way a particular theme can be established for the area. Control might be extended to such things as:

- height restrictions for buildings
- density of buildings
- green-belt requirements
- restrictions on the design of signs
- parking requirements
- architectural styles

To keep tourists in the area there must be something for the visitors to do. Through careful coordination by a number of individual small businesses, a major attraction may result that could increase the length of time visitors remain in the region.

A difficulty that many tourist areas have had to face is the tendency by many small entreprenueurs to take a short-term view of the business of tourism. For these business people the motivation is to maximize short-term profitability at the expense of long-term consequences. In a mind-set like this, tourists may be overcharged and costs cut to give less than adequate service. Someone has to look out for the interests of the tourist area. Depending upon the philosophy of the residents regarding individual rights, this can take the form of education, regulation, and/or enforcement—educating owners to take a longer view of their business and its impact on the region as a whole; regulating what they can and cannot do individually for the good of the whole; and enforcing the regulations in an evenhanded way.

Infrastructure.   In developing the infrastructure for a tourist area the needs of the residents must be considered. Because of this, in addition to the high cost of infrastructure, the cost tends to be borne by the public sector.

A common problem in the development of tourist regions is that infrastructure is not properly provided. If done properly, infrastructure will not be noticed by the tourist. It is the lack of sufficient services that will be noticed.

At this stage in the project it will be necessary to bring in the expertise of engineers—largely civil engineers. A problem may be one of educating engineers to see things from the tourist's perspective. A highway engineer, for example, is primarily concerned with the most efficient means of moving people from point A to point B without regard to views from the road. Utility lines can be put underground—greater cost, more aesthetically pleasing—or strung on poles. The point is that a coordinated effort is necessary to develop services and utilities that enhance the area for tourists as well as being within the budget of the public sector.

Some of the most common infrastructure concerns are outlined below.

Water.   A typical resort requires 350 to 400 gallons of water per room per day. Large quantities of pure water must be available in a convenient and consistent manner.

Power and Communications.   Electric power and communications must be adequate and continuously in service. Peak-load requirements can be identified through forecasting, and systems designed to meet these needs.

Sewage and Drainage.   Drainage requirements within a typical tourism destination are approximately 1,800 gallons per day per acre of developed land.

Streets and Highways.   A basic question to be answered in the development of streets and highways is the extent to which tourist attractions and accommodations should be isolated from normal traffic-flow patterns.

Parks and Recreation.   In providing recreational space the key is to find the right balance between use of the facility and preservation of the resource. Parks can provide excellent opportunities for residents and visitors to meet one another. In urban areas an important concern is the mix between buildings and open space. It is vital that parks be designed to accommodate the uses to which they will be put.

Health-Care Facilities.   Appropriate health-care facilities will depend upon the numbers, age groups, and expected activities of anticipated visitors in light of the geographic factors unique to the area. A greater than normal incidence of broken bones can be expected at ski areas, for example.

Education.   Educational facilities will be required, not for the tourist, but for employees and local people. Workers may require training in skills necessary to serve the visitor, whereas educating the local people on the benefits of tourism to the area may be necessary to get local support for the development of tourism.

Employee Housing.   Where the tourist area is in a remote area it will be necessary to provide employee housing. It is preferable that such housing be located away from guest accommodations. Employees want to get away from their work when off-duty, while guests will not be pleased to have off-duty employees use the same facilities for which they have paid so much.

Security.   Visitors must feel safe when on vacation. Local police officers should be aware that tourism often tends to bring an increase in certain types of crime—theft and prostitution, for example—and to plan accordingly.

Environmental Impact

In any plan that considers development of a tourist region, the impact on the environment is particularly important. Because the environment itself is often the attracting force, care must be taken to ensure that development does not detract from that which attracted visitors in the first place. The environmental impact would include consideration of such factors as:

- alternative land uses precluded by tourism development;
- effect upon the area's resources such as water, prime agricultural land, beaches, etc.;
- effect of an influx of service personnel on such things as housing, water supply, sanitation, schools, recreation, etc.;
- effect of tourism development on local culture and life styles;
- effect on general public safety, health, and welfare.[6]

Costs

At this point a preliminary determination of likely costs can be made. This would include costs to both the private and the public sectors.

ECONOMIC FEASIBILITY

Based on projected costs and environmental impact an initial assessment of economic feasibility can be made. Analysis is predicated upon the anticipated investment and maintenance costs for both private and public sectors compared to estimates of revenues gained and jobs created.

If an initial assessment indicates that development should occur, two processes will result—a detailed development plan and a supporting administrative and legal plan to ensure the success of the development. Both will be discussed in the sections that follow.

Figure 8–13   Recreational areas balance use and preservation. (Courtesy New Zealand Tourist & Publicity Office.)

Development Plan

Clare Gunn has identified several principles of tourism planning to guide the development of any tourism project.[7]

Clustering.   As mentioned above, the clustering of facilities and attractions makes it more convenient for the traveler by avoiding the need to make many brief stops along the way. Clustering has also been shown to be more efficient in the provision of infrastructure. The per-unit cost of such things as water, waste, and power is less with clustered facilities.

Attraction-Services Linkage.   While minimal facilities—snack bars and rest rooms, for example—need to be provided at attraction sites, major clusters of services are better located at the nearest community. The exception would be at major attractions such as Disney World where full services are expected.

Natural and Cultural Resource Dependency.   The basis for much of the success of a tourist attraction lies in the natural and cultural resources of the area. Each area is unique and, to maximize the development opportunity, the attraction should build upon, without destroying, the uniqueness of the resource.

Access.   Access to and from attractions must be planned for as an integral part of the development. This is particularly important for linkage from the highway and air network to destination areas.

Population.   For most tourist areas a relationship exists between visitation and distance. Tourist development is most successful when the attraction is within reasonable distance of major population areas. While there are exceptions—activities highly oriented to place (for example, winter skiing)—this rule tends to hold true.

Capacity.   Attempts have been made to develop carrying capacity theories. The rationale is that a physical resource can handle a certain maximum number of people before the resource quality is diminished. Concerns over capacity are threefold—physical (not enough room), biological (overuse of fragile sites), and managerial (lack of staff or budget to cope with the number of tourists). It appears that the principle of capacity is elastic. That is, a site can handle an increase in visitors without a corresponding loss of quality experience if proper design and management practices are put into effect.

Cities.   Cities are important to the development of tourism for several reasons. Cities are the prime location for services and facilities; they provide the destination for transportation modes; they are attractions themselves; and they contain "friends and relatives," a major motivation for tourist visits.

Social-Developmental Climate.   As pointed out earlier, the attitude of the local population toward the development of tourism can mean the difference between success and failure.

Flexibility.   The dynamics of tourism are constantly changing. New destinations become the "in place"; a shortage of fuel limits travel plans; changes in the value of the dollar make it less attractive to vacation abroad. This does not violate the idea of planning, which attempts to predict and develop alternatives for the future. It does mean that planning must be a continuous activity, constantly being updated to meet new conditions.

Figure 8–14   Madrid, Spain. Cities are important to the development of tourism. (Courtesy National Tourist Office of Spain.)

Types of Tourism.   For developmental purposes, tourism can be defined in terms of *touring* and *destination tourism.* Touring involves visiting several locations during the vacation period. There is a heavy reliance on the linkage between attractions, transportation, services, and facilities, and the traveler's need for information and directions. Attractions are closely associated with the highway and are usually visited only once by the tourist. Activities tend to be more passive, and time constraints are of major concern. The vacation is a curcuit rather than a point.

Destination tourism is more tightly self-contained geographically. Activities are often repeated and tend to be more physically demanding.

People.   Destination areas must be designed and developed with the tourist in mind. As noted above, there must be a blend between "protection" of the area and the provision of creature comforts suitable to the type of tourist being attracted.

Heterogeneity.   Tourism is place-oriented and all places are different. Destination areas cannot be treated the same. What may work for one will not necessarily work for another. Each region must be looked at individually in light of its opportunities and problems.

Facility Operating and Revenue Projections

Within the overall development plan, feasibility studies will be performed for individual properties.

A typical objective is to provide enough rooms to accommodate 130 percent of visitors while generating 70 percent occupancy rate on an annual basis. The occupancy rate for a hotel is the number of rooms sold divided by the number of rooms available. For a 160-room property, an occupancy of 70 percent means that 112 rooms (160 × 70 percent) are occupied. Ideally, hotel room rates should be structured so that the property will break-even at 50 percent occupancy. At the break-even point the property is not making a profit or a loss—it is holding its own. The break-even point is the point at which revenue generated is exactly equal to costs incurred. With fewer guests the property makes a loss; with more guests it makes a profit.

Typically, an accommodation facility has a relatively high percentage of fixed costs. Fixed costs do not vary as volume of business varies. The rent or mortgage must be paid irrespective of the number of guests who stay in the hotel; so must the manager's salary. These are examples of fixed costs. Certain costs, on the other hand, are variable—they vary as the volume of business varies. There are, for example, certain variable costs associated with the rooms department. Variable costs are those incurred in getting a room ready for occupancy by another guest. These would include:

- the cost of cleaning the room;
- the cost of supplies (soap, shampoo, etc.);
- the cost of laundering sheets and towels.

The relationship among fixed costs, variable costs, and sales volume can be seen in Figure 8–16. A business with a high proportion of fixed costs tends to have a relatively high break-even point. However, once the break-even point is reached the only costs incurred are variable costs. The difference between revenue and costs is great. Hotels and other accommodation facilities place a great emphasis on getting in as much business as possible beyond the break-even point. If a property can achieve the break-even point it may be willing to discount rooms in the off-season because the revenue generated will still contribute to profit as long as the variable costs are being met.

Another way to think of the break-even point is as follows: Suppose a 160-room hotel incurs $1 million in fixed costs for the year; a room typically sells for $40 and the variable cost of that room is $5 (for cleaning, soap, laundry, etc.). What happens when the first room is sold? The guest pays $40. Five dollars goes toward getting the room ready for the next

Figure 8–15   Hotels must know their break-even point. (Courtesy New Zealand Tourist & Publicity Office.)

guest. The remaining $35 is call the *contribution margin*. It goes toward (or contributes to) paying off the fixed costs for the year. After the first room is sold the fixed costs remaining are $1 million minus $35 or $999,965. Every time a room is sold for $40, $5 gets the room ready for the next guest and $35 goes toward paying off the fixed costs. The fixed costs remaining after succeeding rooms have been sold are $999,930; $999,895; $999,860, etc. Eventually, if the property gets enough guests the fixed costs will have been paid for the year. This would occur after 28,572 rooms have been sold ($1 million ÷ $35). At this point the hotel is breaking even. When the next guest comes in he or she pays $40. From that, $5 goes to get the room ready for the next guest. The remaining $35 is profit! Each additional sale adds $35 in profit to the operation. However, as long as the variable costs are being covered, we are adding profit, In fact, we could sell the room for $5.01 and still make a profit, albeit only 1 cent.

This, however, is the rationale for selling rooms in the off-season or to groups at less than the regular rate. As long as the break-even point has been reached, rooms can be discounted and additions to profit will still occur. This should be done only if it is impossible to get the regular rate for the room.

What, then, is the break-even percentage for this hotel? The break-even percentage is the number of rooms needed to reach the break-even

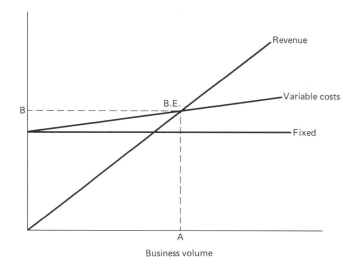

Business volume

Figure 8–16   Break-even chart.

point divided by the number of rooms available. The number of rooms to break even is 28,572. The number of rooms available is 160 rooms times 365 days, or 58,400. The break-even point is 28,572 divided by 58,400 or 49 percent.

Administrative and Legal Plan

Certain administrative functions are necessary to ensure that the development plan is carried out to its fullest potential. Such items would include:

1. Determining whether or not the proposed facilities are adequate to meet projected demand.
2. Establishing quality-control standards and means of determining whether or not they are being met.
3. Maintaining liaison and cooperation between the private and the public sectors.
4. Ensuring the protection and preservation of the quality of the environment.
5. Directing appropriate marketing efforts toward potential tourists. This would include a determination of the type of promotional campaign and selection of the channels of distribution that would most effectively market the destination to tourists, intermediaries in the channels of distribution, and investors. (The channel of distribution refers to the link between destination and the market. Intermediaries in the channel would be those busi-

nesses that act as conduits between destination and tourist, such as tour wholesalers, retail travel agents, etc.).

6. Coordinating ongoing research and analysis to support market research in both the private and public sectors.

7. Coordinating the various public-sector agencies that have some degree of involvement in, and responsibility for, tourism.

8. Determination of employee training needs. Tourism is a "people" business. The development of tourism requires those who can deliver service at a level expected by the tourist. In some cases this may mean the establishment of training centers at the destination to bring local skills up to the standard expected.

These and other points will be expanded upon in the following chapters.

OVERALL FINANCIAL FEASIBILITY

A project is economically feasible if it provides a rate of return that is acceptable to the investors in the project. Most people favor time-value measures. The net-present-value and internal-rate-of-return techniques assume that money has a time value. A dollar received today is worth more than a dollar received a year from now, since the dollar received today can be reinvested to produce a higher overall return.

Cash flow projections provide a basis for determining the amount of money available in the future. Future flows of money are then discounted at assumed rates of return to give an overall estimate of the return on an investment.

Lenders want to know if the project will produce sufficient operating profits and cash flow to cover interest and principal payments when they become due.

Public officials are principally concerned with a project's impact on:

1. Employment
2. Personal income
3. Living standards
4. The balance of payments
5. The physical environment
6. The sociocultural environment
7. Tax revenue
8. Secondary demand for agricultural products and locally produced goods

If a project looks positive to investors, lenders, and those in the public sector, it will go forward. Organization at the local or community level will ensure its success. Managing tourism at the community level is, then, the subject of the next chapter.

ENDNOTES

1. *Creating Economic Growth and Jobs Through Travel and Tourism* (Washington D.C.: U.S. Government Printing Office, 1981), P. 34.

2. *Tourism U.S.A.,* Volume II, Development: Assessing Your Product and the Market (Washington D.C.: U.S. Government Printing Office, 1978), pp. 42–43, 46.

3. Ibid, p. 77

4. *Creating Economic Growth and Jobs Through Travel and Tourism,* p. 88.

5. Adapted from *A Proposal to Prepare a Feasibility Study of Tourism Development in Nicaragua,* Laventhol & Horwath, Leo A Daly Company and Osorio y Teran, 1975, p. III-19.

6. Ibid, pp. III-23–III-24.

7. Clare A. Gunn, *Tourism Planning* (New York: Crane, Russak & Company, Inc., 1979), pp. 307–317.

S T U D Y   QUESTIONS

1. Why is the involvement of the public sector important in the development of a large-scale tourism development project and what is its role?

2. What are the steps in the tourism development process?

3. What are the key questions that should be answered as a result of a market analysis?

4. How can target markets be identified using geographic segmentation?

5. List the ways that the development of parking can be accomplished.

6. Why is an analysis of the residents of the proposed development area important?

7. What information is necessary during the analysis of the business environment for tourism?

8. What factor determines the suitability of an area for development?

9. What are the four elements of a master plan?

10. What factors are important regarding the parts of a master plan?

D I S C U S S I O N   QUESTIONS

1. What roles should the private and public sectors play in the development of a tourism destination?
2. What information must be collected to provide an estimate of the long-term flow of tourists to a destination?
3. What role does a planning and engineering, socioeconomic, and legal and business analysis play in the development of a tourism development plan? What kinds of information must be collected as part of the process?
4. Give examples of how collected data is synthesized into statements of where a destination is and where it wants to be.
5. Identify the importance to tourism of the factors that are part of an areawide master plan.
6. Identify and give examples of the principles of tourism planning that can be used to guide the development of any tourism project.

9

THE MANAGEMENT OF TOURISM

At the end of this chapter the reader will be able to:

- Describe the importance of community leadership to the management of tourism and show how leadership emerges and can be developed within a community.
- Describe the roles of leadership within a community.
- Develop a program to coordinate the community components of tourism.
- Understand the importance of visitor services and discuss how that function should be organized.
- Organize an effective program strengthening the public's awareness of tourism.
- Be able to define and correctly use the following terms:

Autocratic leader	Democratic leader
Laissez-faire leader	Self-selection
Promotional mix	Advertising
Publicity	Public relations
Sales promotion	Personal selling
Visitor services	Hosting
Tourist information center	

How to Develop Leadership

The Value of Leadership to Tourism Development

Competent, motivated leadership is vital in the planning and development of tourism as an economic force within the community. Sufficient facilities, finances, and all the other aspects necessary to produce a comprehensive, coordinated tourism program stand still unless adequate leadership can direct the human, physical, and financial resources into a comprehensive, coordinated tourism program.

However, leadership is often the least-considered aspect in tourism development. The concept itself has a variety of meanings. Some people think of leadership as an innate personal attribute. Persons may become "symbolic" leaders because they are presidents of banks or the managers of motels, but they may be completely wrong for the job of leader of a tourism council. The "symbolic" leader has the power associated with a particular role and its expectations. The "symbolic" leader is powerful because people expect him to be.

Effective leadership is a learned behavioral skill which includes the ability to help others achieve their potential as team members. Strong leadership is vital and every effort should be made to recruit leaders who have already gained the respect of the citizens and are capable of efficiently using all of the available resources.

In general there are two types of individuals who obtain leadership positions: (1) those who have something to gain from the development, and (2) those

In 1978, the then United States Travel Service published a series of booklets titled *Tourism U.S.A.* The project was cordinated by Glenn D. Weaver, Department of Recreation and Parks Administration, University of Missouri-Columbia. The series was updated in 1987.

This chapter consists of a reprint of sections of Volume II, *Development: Planning for Tourism,* and Volume III, *Implementation: Visitor Services.*

who want to see the community grow and develop. Of course, one person may fit into both groups.

Leadership Emergence and the Organizational Process

A common pattern of leadership emergence can be found in many communities. Suppose you are involved directly with the tourism and travel business, as manager of a resort. You see that tourism would increase through more publicity, better streets, or a better reservation system. You share your ideas with friends from the Chamber of Commerce or the local service club who have similar interests in increasing visitors to the community. Your friends agree to then organize a group to seek a larger support base and additional help. Visits with governmental or community committees, such as a planning and zoning committee, or the city council, might result in financial, physical, or human resources needed to accomplish your goals. *This is the first phase of leadership emergence.*

The initial thrust to develop tourism will likely come from one individual organization or special interest group, e.g., resort owners, hotel or motel managers, Chamber of Commerce members or an historical society. Regardless of who stimulates the development, strive for early commitment from leaders already in place within the community. The tourism industry will affect either directly or indirectly most community interests.

When your group sets out to achieve your objectives you see other things that could be accomplished to im-

prove tourism. A group larger than the original three is needed. You might organize a subcommittee of the Chamber of Commerce on travel and tourism, a committee of the Rotary Club, or an ad hoc committee on tourism, either as a part of the industrial development group in the community or as a part of the city council. *This is the second phase in the organizational process.*

The third phase comes when the committee realizes that some jobs can be done only by someone who shares your priorities. So you form an association and invite all people of similar interests to join. In many communities this is done through the Chamber of Commerce, particularly in those communities that have tourism as a major economic resource. Certainly many if not most of the enterprises benefiting from visitors would be members. This is the most common type of organization; other types may be directly under the city council as a part of the local government, or independent, such as the Jonesville Resort Association.

This process may be completed in any time from a few months to a number of years. The originators may now be encouraging others to take over positions of leadership, or, in the situation of phase three, official and formal elections may be held, officers elected, and committees established.

At some point the workload begins to be exceedingly heavy in distributing publicity, answering incoming mail, soliciting memberships—too heavy for a volunteer operation. Time does not permit some of the members with other job responsibilities to continue to meet all the demands of the association. Therefore, a regular office is established and a secretary is employed.

Many communities stop here. Others desire full-time tourism leadership and go on to hire a full-time executive secretary or executive director. *This is the fourth phase of organizational development.* It is then that the community begins to see its greatest growth, not necessarily because of the employment of a professional, but because the ground work has been completed and the relationships involved in organization and cooperation have gradually been smoothed out. With a knowledgeable and experienced person working full-time, the planning process can be implemented at increased speed.

Not all communities will even want to consider a full-time director of tour-ism; they may want to include these duties with those of the present Chamber of Commerce. It might do well at this point to suggest, however, the advantages of a strong tourism association with a full-time director.

While an individual operator can advertise and promote his facility through a number of means, there are some aspects of tourism development that are either too costly for an individual or that lend themselves to attracting people to an area, rather than to an individual facility. An organized approach can accomplish a number of things that could not be done individually.

Leadership, whether volunteer or hired, should be responsible at all times to a policy-making board or group. The leader should not make all the ultimate

Figure 9–1   Chambers of Commerce help promote tourism. (Courtesy Jamaica Tourist Board.)

decisions. Rather he should share suggestions, perspectives, and recommendations and implement policy, planning, and direction. Never should he be in the position of being the principal advisor to the group to which he reports. This will cause inevitable problems in the long run.

The roles that local governments and Chambers of Commerce have played in providing leadership for local tourism are almost as diverse and numerous as the cities having tourism programs. In Springfield, Illinois, the local city council appointed an historic sites committee which ultimately led to an extensive tourism program. While in other communities such as Decatur, Alabama, Boise, Idaho, and Asheville, North Carolina, the Chamber of Commerce has provided the leadership for tourism. In Asbury Park, New Jersey, a corps of newly elected city officials took the lead in promoting tourism, while in Boise and Decatur newly appointed directors of the Chambers of Commerce took the leadership role. Even in those communities in which the Chamber of Commerce is not providing the major leadership for tourism, the Chamber of Commerce usually cooperates with the tourism leadership. In most communities there is a strong working relationship between local government and the Chamber of Commerce.

In summary, no one type of organization or leadership is better than another. It depends upon the tradition, the resources available, the organizational structure in the community, the strength of the Chamber of Commerce, or the confidence in the local elected officials. Many ways are used and all ways have found success in some areas.

Whichever type of organization is chosen, there are a number of leadership roles which can be identified with particular organizational structures. Leadership roles are the activities and responsibilities to be assumed by the organization providing the leadership. Some of these, by category of leadership organization, are listed here.

Leadership Roles

Leadership Roles—Where There Is Either a Separate Tourism Organization or One Functioning as a Part of the Chamber of Commerce

- **Gaining Public Support or Awareness.**

  Create community awareness and acceptance of tourism through public information activites including: news articles, editorials, and public speeches to demonstrate the positive effects of tourism to local residents.

  Keep all those involved in tourism aware of current and future plans and maintain high levels of identity and motivation through the use of news letters, newspapers, radio, and television coverage to publicize the activities and achievements of those involved in tourism.

  Work to promote and support local, state, and federal legislation beneficial to tourism. Maintain a harmonious relationship with local political officials and both state and national legislators.

  Gain support from auxiliary facility and service providers, such as hotels, motels, restaurants and service stations.

- **Coordination**

  Develop a tourism staff having technical knowledge of tourism, the ability to relate to others effectively, and commitment to the tourism program.

  Establish short and long range goals and map out plans to achieve them.

  Coordinate independently managed attractions and events in tourism development and promotion.

  Develop programs to measure tourist satisfaction with attractions, events and support facilities, and services such as hotels and motels, restaurants, service stations and other businesses serving tourists.

  Work to achieve a feeling of unity through the development of goals which appeal to broad community membership, particularly where local, regional or state tourism programs may be adversely affected by sectionalism, provincialism, and jealousy. Organizational activities must include representatives from all groups.

- **Operational**

  Seek funds from local, state, and federal governments and private resources.

  Provide and direct visitor information centers.

  Attract conventions, sporting events, cultural and other activities, by working with those in charge of local, state, and national organizations.

  Research the impact of tourism on the local community.

- **Promotion**

  Prepare and coordinate all advertising and promotional pamphlets, brochures.

  Prepare or direct the preparation of feature stories about local tourism for newspapers, journals, or travel magazines.

  Develop close working relationships with radio, television and newspaper media to assure thorough coverage of tourism projects, events, and attractions.

  Promote local tourism through activities with professional travel associations, attendance at travel shows, working with professional travel brokers, and advertising in national travel magazines.

Leadership Roles—Chamber of Commerce, When There Is a Separate Tourism Association

- **Gaining Public Support or Awareness**

  Encourage Chamber members to actively participate in the development, promotion, and operation of the community's tourism program.

  Develop community publicity materials which relate community economic development to the tourism industry and the success of a tourism program to overall community development including economic, social, and cultural.

- **Coordination**

  Create a committee or council to advise the tourism association and to present Chamber interests.

  Develop membership which includes

representatives from the economic, political, social, historic, cultural, educational, and religious interests in the community.

- **Operational**

  Develop, if not otherwise provided for, a visitors information center.

  Provide, or work with local government to provide, adequate rest areas and related facilities for visitors and tourists.

- **Promotion**

  Participate in regional and state programs to promote tourism.

Leadership Roles—Local Government, Where the Tourism Association Is a Part of Chamber or Separate

- **Operational**

  Provide zoning ordinances and building codes which facilitate the development of tourist attractions, protect historic structures or sites, and provide maximum assurance against alienating citizens with regard to tourism.

  Implement ordinances which tend to maximize the effectiveness of advertising signs without detracting from the scenery, tradition, decor, or heritage of the community.

  Establish regulations which protect important resources for local residents, for example, scarce water supplies.

  Provide ordinances for effective crowd control to minimize disturbances which would be distasteful to both local residents and tourists.

Develop effective parking and traffic controls to minimize congestion.

Landscape public areas to enhance the beauty and attractiveness of the community for both tourists and local residents.

Provide adequate refuse control.

Give adequate financial support to the community's tourism program, for example, pass a lodging tax for funding the local tourism association.

Provide or work with other community organizations to provide adequate rest areas and related facilities.

Imposed Organization

A word about imposed organization. Because tourism is many times regional or statewide in nature, and because states are sometimes willing to share some of their financial resources in the form of matching funds, some specific types of organizations may be dictated in order to qualify. For example, to qualify for state matching funds Huntington County, Pennsylvania, had to develop a formal organizational structure which met the requirements of the state. A travel promotion agency had to be organized with its directors appointed by county commissioners. The directors, in turn, appointed all staff members including a full-time executive director. Thus the operations of the tourism effort are subject to some political control.

To facilitate the restoration of New Harmony, Indiana, a county trust commission was formed with an operating unit, the tourist council, to activate

Figure 9-2   Local areas can landscape tourist areas. (Courtesy New Zealand Tourist & Publicity Office.)

state support. Historic New Harmony, Inc. was founded as the operating arm of a new state memorial commission. While there had been state influence involving the leadership of the restoration project, significant state financial support was also provided.

Regional leadership in developing tourism may be imposed at the state level as in Utah or may be voluntary as in the sixteen county Alabama Mountain and Lakes area. There is no single approach to developing regional tourism. For example, in Chattanooga, Tennessee, the tourism program was taken from the Chamber of Commerce and placed under a newly organized Chattanooga Area and Convention Bureau. In the coastal area of Georgia, a number of Chambers of Commerce organized the Coastal Area Planning and Development Commission to take a regional approach in developing tourism. Regional requirements then may dictate the type of local organization for tourism.

Developing Leadership Within the Community

Now that we have a picture of how leadership emerges and the types of organizational structure that provide the vehicle for that leadership, let's look at leadership itself. **Leadership begins with people creating a mental picture of what they want to do for themselves or the community,** who then sell this to others to gain their support. Leadership begins to be a part of planning: resources must be obtained, goals and objectives set, work assigned, accepted, and evaluated. The type of leadership can affect success. The traditional categories of leadership, autocratic, democratic and laissez-faire, may be appropriately discussed here.

There probably is little place in the tourism development process for an autocratic leader. Shared leadership improves the quality of decisions. **Those who will be affected by the ultimate decisions should be involved in the decision-making process.** The question should not be who makes the decisions, but how they can be made more sensibly. This suggests more of an "operational leadership" method rather than leadership as a "status" or "symbol." Leadership, as a function within commu-

nity processes, can be shared and does not have to be concentrated. People can be leaders in some situations and followers in others. Development of tourism in a community results in diverse objectives, plans, and methods of implementation. These occur at different times and places and require a variety of leadership styles, skills, and structuring. The leadership patterns, therefore, have to vary with the nature of the function.

It is not a question of who should lead the process, professionals, politicians or interested citizens, but how to group the abilities needed for the leadership function. It can be a partnership in which professional, political, and citizen roles can all be delineated.

The interaction among these various elements, each with its own perspective, provides the motive for getting things done. There should be no question as to what is most important. All participants must work together. Cooperation is not everyone doing the same thing, but doing different things together.

This positive interaction among professionals, officials, and citizens does not imply total agreement or lack of controversy. In fact disagreements can increase understanding of situations. What is necessary is that the parties accept the legitimacy of each other's activity in attempting to influence and exercise leadership. Many things in tourism are private matters. They depend on individual or firm business decisions on investments, operation, and management and are not subject to group decisions. At the same time many things in tourism development involve public decisions and public investments.

Remember . . . in the public sector

keep the democratic process open—public policy is involved. This doesn't mean that everyone must be involved in every decision. Further, there are many operations that do not require committees or extensive involvement. Some jobs can be done best by an individual or select team. People don't want to participate in everything.

In fact, when things are going well, participation decreases. But when there are difficulties, questions, and anxieties, people make an effort to get involved. The key is to keep the process open so that people can see how things are going. Be responsive to concerns, suggestions and information from citizens. The democratic process, then, whether with the public or with the tourism group, is not marked by unremitting participation. Involvement tends to be distributed at different intensities at different points in the system. It usually is intermittent. Most people simply don't want to be involved in the actual day-to-day working operations of the association, or in those matters of widespread interest. The responsibility will usually fall on a relative few. These few should make every effort to keep the lines of communication open with their constituencies.

Reconnaissance

It is important that any leader take reconnaissance of other organizations, individuals, or people in like businesses to see what they are doing before taking initial steps. A leader may automatically assume that he must create an organization to meet his goals. He should be aware, however, that communities are already organized, and no matter what ideas he has, someone else probably has had similar ideas and might be pursuing similar objectives.

Resistance

Every leader has faced resistance, whether a leader of a small informal group, or a community-wide leader with an interest in tourism development. The consideration of planning or of strategies for enlisting participation or legitimization will bring resistance—someone is sure to dispute the idea or the timing.

It is necessary to understand the source of the resistance if it is to be overcome to any degree. Strong resistance may mean discontinuing the project.

Apathy is the greatest problem to be overcome by those involved in leadership situations. Nevertheless, effective leadership must not develop a tendency to give up when a lack of interest is encountered.

To reduce resistance and enhance participation, the leader must meet others halfway; avoid taking total control of the circumstances and work out ways to get others to participate.

Citizen Involvement

A successful tourism development has the support of the citizens in that community. Many people, however, feel that citizen participation complicates the planning and implementing process. This is a short-sighted philosophy. While it may be a problem, in the end it will pay off in support and other types of dividends, such as development of new supporting facilities and attractions.

Citizen participation does not substitute for having experienced, trained, specialized professionals involved. But the leadership must enlist the support and blessing of those who seem untouched by the tourism development process.

Representation

Another basic tool of the good leader is to achieve adequate representation. There is usually considerable pressure to establish a representative arrangement rather quickly when plans begin to move. This is one reason why those who are to be represented in the system may not be consulted about how this is to be done. Adequate representation and shared leadership will improve the quality of decisions.

Division of Labor

This is the cornerstone on which good leadership is based. For any substantial task within communities there are many things to be done, ranging from minor housekeeping to sensitive and demanding negotiations. Tourism development work takes time and the duties required to adequately support it continue, adjusting to meet new situations and stages. In any sizeable effort, the work-load has to be shared. No one person or group has the time, energy, or the range of skills to do it all. **A system for dividing the labor is essential.**

The key to division of labor is in cooperation. *Cooperation is doing different things together.* The leader, then, must find practical and equitable ways to divide up the work among those willing to take part. It may seem impossible to do fairly and efficiently. Certainly it is a thankless responsibility to carry the task of assigning specific work to particular people and organizations and then following up to see if it is done when promised.

In tourism development, seldom is there any clear or formal basis on which to direct authority over others. Most of those involved are working on their own volition, voluntarily, and are not subject to commands. This even applies when a director of tourism is in place. Most of the work has to be done by persuasion and influence. If someone is assigned a job he does not like, has not the time, or feels ill-equipped to perform, he probably will not do it.

Rather than attempting to put the burden on one person or organization to separate and assign the specific jobs, it should be a group responsibility. A small group of active and concerned people should decide what needs to be done. When a job list is developed and a sequence established, the total active group can be informed. Assignments then can be made on the basis of *self-selection.*

When people know the range of jobs and are given some choice, they will likely pick things they can and will do. This does not assure every job will be selected or that there will not be clusters of the most- and least-popular jobs. Experience, however, does indicate that in a reasonably sized group there will be a diversity of interests and preferences enough to cover a great many jobs.

Some people prefer to be assigned to jobs. In the process of self-selection they are likely to let this preference be known. The existence of these persons will help in assigning every job. It is important that you exhibit confidence in the willingness and ability of people to pick jobs for themselves.

In the process of self-selection and/or delegation, it is implied that unless otherwise stated, the individual is free to do the job the way he wants and to his expectations. Many leaders have fallen from grace because they expected the individuals to do a job as a leader would have done it. Particularly in volunteer organizations, the leader must be willing to accept the effort of the individual if it is satisfactory at all. This is not a business where employees must please the boss to receive a salary. It is very difficult for the leader not to react or respond negatively when things do not meet his expectations, but it's also the quickest way to eliminate the volunteer leader or to ruin the self-selection process.

Supervision and Follow-up

Once the projects have been assigned, and procedure is agreed upon,

the leader must check periodically to see whether or not the work has been completed. This is a vital aspect of leadership. All of us are aware of the many projects which people agree to do and then just don't seem to find the time. Establish a deadline at the time work is selected or assigned. If it is not completed by that time, the leader must then go to the individual and ask about progress and whether the individual intends to do it. If he does, additional time may be allowed, or the work should be reassigned. The follow-up function is one of those vital parts of the leadership process which many times is forgotten or ignored, causing a breakdown in the planning process.

Coordination of Tourism

A community's tourism industry requires a diversified organizational structure capable of handling many responsibilities. Promotion, budget and finance, training and education, research and data collection, and communications are also responsibilities of the tourism organization. Coordination of this organization is not a process which just happens, it has to be planned; each element in the organization should contribute to the success of the master plan. Whoever leads the program must be responsible for coordination—the tourism council, a tourism committee in the COC, a tourism committee in the city council, or a hired director of tourism.

One aspect of coordination is flexibility—the ability to change objectives

as needed. Close coordination between organization elements helps avoid duplication of efforts. Clearly defined objectives and assignment of responsibilities will also be beneficial to the coordination process.

The problem faced in overall coordination is to see that each goal established fits into the master plan and that committees work toward goals at the proper pace. Usually, the overall plan will call for certain priorities. To avoid bottlenecks certain actions have to happen before other things can happen. The coordinator must be aware of this process and organize the plan of action so it is done in the proper sequence.

In its simplest form coordination is a communications issue concerned with the two-way sharing of information at each level of development (initiating, developing, implementing, evaluating) and by each component of the tourism industry. These components will be discussed in the section that follows.

Communications

Coordination requires efficient ways of communicating. Channels should be as direct and simple as possible; they must be well-defined and understood by everyone involved in the organization. Each person in the program should know how word about each activity is to be spread to those who need to know.

Channels need to be established; within the community; between the community and the tourist; between the community and external segments of tourism such as other organizations, travel agencies, and tourism organizations; and among the various interests that make up the tourism industry.

Some of the most common methods for constructing an effective communications function follow.

- **The tourist center** is most effective for welcoming tourists, providing information about all attractions in the area, local customs, and laws. Community attractions literature and fliers for special events can be distributed here.

  The visitor center can provide a communications vehicle between tourist and community. Compliments and complaints should be handled with equal ease. Complaints should be given special attention, however, because poor handling indicates a disregard for the tourist.

- **Well-trained service people.** In many communities service personnel will interact with more tourists than the visitors' center. It is most important that they know the community and current events.

- **Good signing on the streets and highways.** This is a basic type of communication. It says to the tourist, "We are concerned that you do not waste your time finding our attractions."

- **Meeting, forums, discussion groups, board and committee meetings open to the public,** and special planning or problem solving meetings. These are especially important in communicating with people in the community.

- **Organized dissemination of information** through newsletters, special reports, local newspaper editorials, radio and television news reports. Publicity (non-paid advertising), though generally administered through the promotion committee or department, may also emanate from local government and political sources, private business, and other organization sources. When they are issued by other organizations, it is important that the tourism organization be informed beforehand so that potential conflicts do not occur.

Obviously, *communications and coordination must go hand in hand if the organization's efforts are to succeed.* Good communications require good coordination and good coordination demands good communications. Therefore, in planning the communications and coordination functions, one must be careful to select those persons who can cre-

Figure 9-3   Tourists like a warm welcome. (Courtesy Hong Kong Tourist Association.)

ate the environment in which these functions may effectively occur.

Research and Data Collection

The process of determining what is happening and what is most likely to happen is a continuous one and basic to good organization and management. Managers also need to know what their best alternatives are for each decision. Supplying these types of information is the responsibility of the research arm of the organization.

Size and degree of sophistication of this arm depends upon the amount of resources the organization feels it can, or wants, to devote to it. Small communities can use fairly simple ways of collecting information, but should keep in mind that the results are likely to have some errors. The study of the section on data collection will reveal a number of basic rules which can be employed to cut error in the results.

Likewise, the amount of analysis to be expected from the research arm depends upon the quality of personnel working there. For many uses, the analysis can be quite simple. For others this may not be true. Information is basic to good decision making and every possible effort should be made to get the best information available and have it delivered in the most usable form.

The following are illustrations of problems where good information is important to the solution:

- **Promotion:** the kinds of promotion, geographic areas in which it is done, and timing depend upon a knowledge of the potential market for a community's attractions. It wouldn't do much good to advertise in a magazine having only national circulation, if your only chance to draw customers was from within 500 miles of your community. You don't usually advertise a ski area in the spring. Certain kinds of attractions appeal to older people, so promotion of these in media they read gives you the best return on advertising dollars.

- **Visitor Satisfaction:** You always want to know if you are sending away satisfied customers. The only way you can really find out is to devise some way of asking them or of keeping track of repeats and referrals.

- **Changes in numbers of tourists:** Season to season comparisons enable managers to determine how much change to expect in the present year and when to increase promotion efforts. Expenditures by tourists for various goods and services combined with some knowledge of size of the local multiplier would enable administrators to communicate the importance of tourism to the local economy. This will help to gain community support.

- **Knowing types of people visiting your community** could be of help in planning for future operations, understanding some of the problems you are facing, and improving your communications. Knowing changes in the supply of tourism attractions and facilities in your region, state, and nation could help you gauge plans for expansion in your community. This may not now be a problem in your area, but it would be well to know when it might be.

Each community has to decide how much importance to attach to research. The general inclination seems to be to do too little of it. Making decisions based on inadequate or erroneous information leads to waste. Many communities never know whether their operations are getting results or not since their research is inadequate to tell them.

Education and Training

Since tourism is a hosting industry, methods of training those who come into contact with tourists are very important. The development plan should examine ways of doing this most efficiently and lay out a blueprint for its accomplishment.

A major problem in training employees of service stations, cafes, motels and retail stores is reluctance of employers to give them time (with pay) for such training. Even though most of these firms are regarded as part of the industry, they sometimes fail to identify their welfare with that of tourism. The tourism organization needs good communication on this point with employers.

In addition there should be methods developed to have a well-informed

Figure 9-4 Know the types of people who visit your community. (Courtesy Hong Kong Tourist Association.)

public. Both of these functions should be allowed for in the organizational structure.

Data collected on the number of tourists visiting the area, what they do, how much money they spend in the community, and where the money goes, should be explained to the general public. This assures that the public will be aware of the importance of tourism to the local economy and that their contacts with tourists could also affect its success.

For the tourism organization to be effective, it must not only communicate the information the community wants, but also communicate with the community itself. Here, residents as well as special interest groups must have a mechanism available for communicating complaints, ideas, and opportunities, and for reporting on changes that should be made in some aspect of the tourism program. A good mechanism would be periodic public meetings of the Tourism Council. Having the tourism director or an associate available for discussion at regular times could also help.

Promotion

Although promotion is really a part of the overall communications concept, its importance in most tourism programs indicates that it should be viewed in the organizational structure as a separate and specialized function requiring professional expertise. It includes:

- Advertising
- Publicity and Public Relations
- Sales Promotion
- Personal Selling

The manner in which these are integrated is called the promotional mix.

Advertising involves developing a campaign theme, selecting those media that best reach target market audiences, and preparing or ordering the necessary art work, copy, printing and other production materials to meet media schedules.

The publicity function manages all matter relating to the issuance of news releases to local and national media; staging publicity events; and performing supportive services for the other functions comprising the promotional mix.

When a community commemorates a special day, occasion, or historical event, it uses the vehicle of publicity to promote interest in it. The main purpose of publicity is to focus immediate attention on the subject. If the event is well staged, the news releases are well written and placed with appropriate editors, and are of real news value, they will be published or presented by the media. If it is a gimmick of little news value, and is an obvious attempt to focus attention on a minor event, it will be ignored.

Many communities hire publicity agents to create and publicize various events such as beauty pageants, contests, auto shows, and Easter parades. A good publicity agent can get a great deal of "mileage" out of a well-presented event. He can also get a lot of bad publicity for the community if the event is a flop or if something unfortunate happens as a result of the event. Some events have been so well publicized that they attracted too many people to the area, and this resulted in fighting, drunkenness, and considerable police action which turned a good event into a bad one. Several "rock music shows" and some state fairs have had such negative experiences.

While publicity and public relations are usually considered simultaneously, they tend to have different perspectives and responsibilities in contributing to a successful promotional mix. Whereas publicity is generally designed to focus attention on special events and communication of specific information, public relations is designed to be an ongoing function that performs a supportive service for the entire tourism organization as well as the community.

In public relations (PR), the concern is with the various "publics" whom the organization has identified as being important to the accomplishment of its mission. Those "publics" that usually require special relationships and programs are:

- General public
- Media
- Governmental agencies
- Employees of the tourism organization and support facilities

- Special interest groups (historical societies, attractions and amusement operators; hotel, motel, restaurant groups, and others)

The PR function may also be a trouble-shooting function in problem-solving situations, or it may be a function that helps spread community good will, and provides the "grease" in implementing the decision process.

Sales promotion is the sub-function responsible for strengthening the advertising and personal selling function. This function is also described as the "enhancer" or the "extender" of the advertising and selling of the community's satisfactions at special shows, such as recreational vehicle shows, boat shows, hotel, motel and restaurant association shows. It also develops exhibits, displays, and other materials that encourage tour directors and travel agencies to include the community in their patrons' travel plans. It provides for concessionaires and the distribution of promotional items such as T-shirts, maps, directories, souvenirs, and other special promotional devices that add to the overall program.

The personal selling part of the promotional mix addresses its efforts to the personal contact work that must be done with tour directors, travel agents, and private organizations that may want to vacation in a community. The selling function is also utilized along with public relations' efforts and trade shows and other activities where it is advisable to have personal community representation available to provide added sales pressure in selling the community to others.

Budget and Finance

The organization structure must have a sound system of fiscal management. This system will include provisions for generating or receiving funds as well as sound policies and practices for expenditures and accounting.

All organization structures require operating funds. The funds for salary and wage, office space and equipment, supplies, postage and funds necessary for accomplishing special responsibilities such as promotion and advertising, education and training, research and data collection, are a part of the normal operating expenses of the organization. The amount of funds needed will depend upon the size and scope of the organization and its responsibilities. Inadequate funding can kill a good program.

A good accounting system will identify where money is spent, how much, and for what purposes. The system needs to include features and procedures which demand honesty and periodic accurate reporting.

Initial planning for the organization's responsibilities and objectives must consider the method of financing the program. You waste time planning something for which adequate funds are not available. Careful consideration should be given to the conditions and procedures through which funds are collected and allocated to the tourism organization.

An example of how this issue could be a concern may be found in the collection of the lodging tax by a city with allocations made to the tourism organization by the city council. From year to year the attitude about tourism may fluctuate and funds may be directed to streets, sewers, and other municipal concerns. Although these projects may be deserving, the problem is that the tourism budget remains uncertain and dependent upon the whims of individuals with other interests.

Method of funding fall into two major groups: funding of operations and promotion and funding for capital improvements or development. These probably represent 75% to 80% of the ways in which communities support tourism development and promotion. The list is by no means exhaustive and continued investigation turns up many unique and creative methods of funding Chamber of Commerce and tourism associations.

Several of the methods to be discussed will require state, regional, or local legislation or ordinances. Some of these methods may not be legal in some areas because of lack of state "enabling authority." Investigation will be required in each specific locality to determine whether or not some of the alternatives suggested are available. This is not to say, however, that groups local, regional or statewide could not together promote such efforts in the future.

Funding of Tourism Operations and Promotion

Communities vary widely in how they organize to provide ongoing and sustaining emphasis for tourism both internally and externally. In many communities the Chamber of Commerce provides the vehicle, in others it is a committee of that group, a separate visitors and convention bureau, a department of the city for tourism development, or in other cases a privately organized group representing tourism-related business. Some of the options listed below will not be available or appropriate for each group, others may apply more directly to some groups than others. For example, allocations from the general fund would be more likely to fund a city organized department than a private group.

The Transient Guest Tax is gaining popularity as the desired method of financing operation and promotion. It goes by many names including bedroom tax, lodger's tax, hospitality tax or resort tax, but basically it levies a tax, generally from 2% to 5% on hotel rooms, in some areas on apartments rented less than a year, or on restaurants or bars. This can raise considerable sums of money. In many smaller areas from $50,000 to $300,000 per year can be raised. In almost all cases this requires passage of an ordinance by the city which may require a local public vote, and in many cases, requires state legislation authorizing such a tax. Communities are advised to check the state authorization before preparing campaigns on the local level.

In some cases these funds are earmarked. This method of financing is usually resisted by local motel and restaurant groups as unfair taxation and imposing an extra burden on their business, while the larger chains usually see the benefit of it. The local residents usually will support such a tax since it is paid by visitors.

Mill Levy on Real Estate Property. This is not a commonly found method of financing local tourism operation and promotion. This method of financing, like the previous method, gives

Figure 9–5 Taxes on meals can help fund tourist projects. (Courtesy New Zealand Tourist & Publicity Office.)

a consistent, permanent source of revenue. This method tends not to reflect inflation as would general fund allocations or a percent of the room cost, but stays at the same relative level except when new real estate property or new hotels, etc. are constructed.

General Revenue Funds from City, County, or Region. This source of funding is probably used more widely than might be expected. A number of local tourism promotion agencies, whether they be Chamber of Commerce or other, receive allocations from the general funds of the city or the county, or in some cases, the state. Cities have excel-

lent opportunity to expand the general revenue funds through statutes. The advantage of a general allocation is that the allocation can increase in size as the amount of funds coming into the city increases.

Some forms of the specifically earmarked general revenue funds include:

- Earmarking of funds, such as, in Rapid City, South Dakota, where the state gasoline rebate funds go directly to the tourism promotion agency, and
- Nashville, Indiana, which has merchant's license tax of $50 which goes directly for tourism purposes.

Limitations of this type of financing would be that the city is normally reluctant to allocate general revenue funds to agencies outside the city government framework over which they have little or no control. In some areas this may not be legal.

Matching Funds. A number of states have programs where local funds can be matched by state or regional departments of tourism primarily for outside marketing and promotional efforts. Several states allocate funds to regions, which in turn match funds with local tourism promotion agencies.

In those states where matching funds are not now available, it is sometimes extremely difficult to get the legislature to pass legislation authorizing this arrangement, or to get them to fund the state department of tourism at sufficient levels to allow funds to be available for this purpose. However, this provides an excellent incentive and seems to provide a good deal of cooperation in the marketing area in those states which have it.

Membership Dues and Assessments. The most common method of financing the local tourism promotion agency or visitors' bureau is through membership dues, the method the Chambers of Commerce have used for years. In many locations the visitors' bureau is a function of the Chamber of Commerce and a portion of the membership dues is allocated for that prupose. In other locations the visitors' bureau is a separate agency, and is made up primarily of resort owners and/or other businesses that receive a major portion of their income from the tourist dollar. Their membership dues operate the cen-

ter. In addition, there may be assessments for specific programs, activities, or projects.

Many times the membership dues are on a sliding scale depending upon the size of the business, the number of employees, and the benefits derived from tourism. The amount of funds received, of course, depends upon the size of the community and, to some degree, the success of the director of the bureau or center in convincing the secondary businesses that they are receiving benefits from the tourist dollar. Many communities have less than 50% of their businesses as members of the Chamber of Commerce which presents a problem of limitation on the membership dues' method of financing.

The number of tourism businesses, resorts, or enterprises that are members of the local tourism organization will depend upon how high a priority the tourism industry has within the group in which it is organized. If the primary purpose of the Chamber is tourism promotion, more tourism-related industries will be members. If it is a secondary function, the number will be consistently less. The number of members also depends a great deal upon the ability of the executive director or secretary to educate the businessmen as to the value of the organization, its purposes, and the extent to which the businesses and enterprises benefit from the tourist dollar.

Special Events and Other "Direct Income Producers." A number of communities use special events to provide or supplement their budgets for tourism operation and promotion. Asbury Park, New Jersey, has an annual Grant Prix Race by the local Chamber of Commerce primarily for fund-raising purposes. Hermann, Missouri, has an annual Maifest as well as periodic antique auctions sponsored by the local tourism and visitors' bureau to help fund the operations and provide funds for promotion. Numerous examples could be used to illustrate how events of a festival or special event nature can be used for these purposes. Cheyenne, Wyoming, has a tourism program financed by the receipts from "Frontier Days."

Festivals U.S.A., a bulletin from the United States Travel Service, lists numbers of these by state which are organized by the local bureaus for the purpose of raising funds for tourism.

The disadvantage of this method of financing is that it requires an exceptional amount of work to organize and promote, as well as requiring the cooperation and support of a majority of businesses and organizations in the city. The amount of funds raised may fluctuate depending upon the weather, the interest of people in the activities, and such things as the availability of energy.

Advantages, however, include the fact that it does provide a focal point for community cooperation.

Other direct income producers would include such things as the following:

• Many communities have visitors' bureaus with souvenirs and other items for sale.

• Frankenmuth, Michigan, has guided tours for a fee.

• Several communities contact local commercial tour businesses to arrange for tours to stop in the community and have handled all of the lodging, food, and sightseeing arrangements for a standard fee.

These few ideas are samples of the potential in this area. Local creativity could add many more.

Funding of Capital Improvements or Development

Sources of funds for capital development differ somewhat from those available for operation and promotion.

Local Resort Tax. A number of communities earmark a certain percentage of the local resort tax to be spent for capital development projects related to tourism. This insures a balance between internal expenses to upgrade the product to be sold as well as external expenses for marketing to bring the public to the facilities.

City Capital Improvement Budgets. Another related form of capital funding is the inclusion of some building projects on the capital improvements development list of the city. While some facilities, such as historic redevelopment of homes, and for the most part of direct benefit to tourists, other capital developments such as golf courses, tennis courts, and restroom facilities, while primarily for the local public, can be of equal value to the tourist. The local park and recreation department may have a number of capital project needs which could be related to tourism development and their cooperation should be sought. Tourism concerns should be included in all planning of community facilities, particularly park and recreation areas, but also construction of other schools, buildings, and com-

Figure 9-6 Some resorts earmark a percentage of the local resort tax for capital projects. (Courtesy New Zealand Tourist & Publicity Office.)

munity facilities which might indirectly lend themselves to tourism appeal.

Voluntary Contributions. Traditionally, voluntary contributions are more available and easier to generate for capital projects than for operation and promotion expenditures. In some communities asking for contributions is not considered at all, while in other communities, such as New Harmony, Indiana, over $21 million has been generated through various kinds of grants, contributions, and solicitations. Contributions are usually more substantial and consistent when a local historic foundation is involved, which can be the recipient of these contributions for tax deduction purposes.

Disadvantages of this method of financing capital improvements are the inconsistency of funds over a long period of time and the effort required to generate them.

Foundations. A very significant source of funds for capital projects and tourism development is the historic or museum foundation. Several communities visited had foundations that had as their primary purpose the acquiring and restoration of historic places, or the development and operation of a museum or both. Historical Savannah (Georgia) Foundation, Historic New Harmony (Indiana) Foundation, Historic Williamsburg (Virginia) Foundation, Greater Memphis (Tennessee) Foundation, Historic Lexington (Kentucky) Foundation, and Historic Fredericksburg (Virginia) Foundation are examples of foundations working in close association with local tourism councils to develop tourist attractions. One of the advantages of such a foundation is that it usually has a program of fund solicitation which is independent from the tourism council or the city. It is attractive to those who want to leave part of their estate to the foundation, or as a tax advantage for contributions. The independence of the foundation gives the donors additional assurances that their donated funds will be used to the best advantage of the community, and will be cared for in years to come.

Other types of foundations may also be of help. The Blandin Foundation in Grand Rapids, Minnesota, has $4 million of annual income which has to be spent on projects to enhance the local community. Much of this goes for projects which have tourism potential.

New Harmony, Indiana, received a grant from the Lilly Foundation of $25,000 for planning Historic New Harmony. Several years later, as they were progressing in their plan, this foundation contributed an additional $3.5 million.

Miscellaneous Sources of Funding for Capital Development. Sources un-der this heading may be for both operation and/or capital projects and are from a variety of sources. For example:

- USTS provided a grant of $10,000 to Fall River, Massachusetts, to promote Bristol County to foreign tourists.
- Bishop Hill, Illinois, received a National Endowment for the Humanities Grant to develop an orientation film.
- Bishop Hill also received a federal community redevelopment grant from the Historic Preservation Act of 1956, National Park Service.
- Several agencies have received CETA funds for personnel salaries, consumer research programs, and evaluation of agency activities.
- One community received a HUD 701 Grant to establish a new master plan for tourism.
- Another community received 50% matching funds for a water system from the Farmers Home Administration.

Once tourism has been established, funded, and coordinated and public facilities have been provided, you have something to sell the tourist.

Visitor Services

What Are Visitor Services

Visitor services are probably the single most important group of activities that a community offers its visitors because these activities are what make the visitor feel welcome and well served. They include all the normal city services that pertain to police and fire protection, health and sanitation, public utilities and facilities, as well as the range of services provided by local businesses, civic organizations, and others involved in making your community a pleasant place to visit. Of paramount importance among all the services provided are those included under the heading of *hosting*.

What Is Hosting

Hosting is one of the functions of communication. It provides information for visitors on where to go, how to get there, what to see, and what to do to enjoy their visit. It includes being *hospitable, knowledgeable,* and caring on the part of all members of a community whether or not they are actually involved in tourism activities. It is an *attitude* that pervades the community, making the tourist-visitor feel comfortable as a guest of the community. Being a good host wil bring visitors back to the community because they will talk to their friends and neighbors about their experience, urging them to visit the community to receive these same satisfactions.

It is the purpose of this publication to address the *need* for having a visitor services plan as a part of the tourism master plan; the necessary service training that must be given to all persons involved in tourism in the community; and *evaluation* of the adequacy and nature of the services provided.

Identitfying Visitor Service Needs

Tourists sometimes present special problems and not all tourism activities run smoothly. Tourists do get sick, some will have heart attacks and heat strokes, others create accidental fires, cause civil disturbances, and have boating and auto accidents. Some of them will even die. Therefore, a community and its attractions must be prepared to deal with these problems efficiently and effectively.

Consider, for example, that a special event, a sailboat regatta, is being being planned in your community for the 4th of July. Inquiries, reservations, and tickets sold indicate that this one event could attract in excess of 70,000 persons.

It will be a long weekend and those attending will have probably driven 100–300 miles on a 90° day. By the time they arrive, they will be hot, tired, thirsty, adventurous, fun seeking, careless, anxious, and impatient!

How does one prepare for all of the possibilities of things happening that may not only affect the success of this event, but which might also destroy much of the goodwill and community image building your community has worked so hard to develop? How do you prepare for this onrush of humanity so that each visitor will feel that he is being treated hospitably? How do you look out for, comfort and protect, manage and control, all of these forces, and make it appear orderly, convenient, organized and efficient? You . . .

Develop a Visitor Services Plan

You plan for

- The number of police and firemen needed and their positioning.
- A special crowd control force.
- Parking and crowd movement.
- Concessionaries to feed your visi-

Figure 9-7 Visitors require many services. (Courtesy Hong Kong Tourist Association.)

tors, adequate lodging facilities to house them.

- The sanitation department to pick up litter and provide facilities for personal needs.

- Paramedics, doctors, nurses, and a treatment station to handle emergencies.

- Trained tourist information personnel to answer innumerable questions.

- Programs and souvenirs to be distributed and people to do it.

The plans list seems endless.

While the above examples might seem exaggerated, the point is that things do happen during the tourist season which can tarnish a community's image; which can result in inept handling of crowds, traffic, parking, and sickness; which can turn a happy event into a disaster.

. . . And that is what visitor services programs are about . . . **the preparation and implementation of a specific plan to insure that visitors are well served by trained personnel when they visit your community.** This plan should not only be developed for special events, but also should cover the spectrum of services needed for *continuing* tourism development.

The manner in which these services are performed affects visitor satisfactions, the image that the community projects, and the very valuable word-of-mouth advertising that brings new tourists.

The Visitor Services Program

The development of visitor services programs generally progresses through four stages:

Stage I—Anticipating and planning service needs.
Stage II—Determining how these needs will be coordinated.
Stage III—Training Visitor Services personnel.
Stage IV—Evaluation of training and services performed.

These stages will be discussed in the sections that follow.

Anticipating and Planning Service Needs

Every community has tourists—a motorist who stops for gas, people visiting their relatives, or the vacationer who spends his holidays at your lake resort. Some visitor services are already provided in your community. While visitor service base plans and programs may differ slightly from one community to another, almost all tourism development is structured on a service base that includes most of the following considerations:

Public and Private Support Services
Business
Food-lodging-entertainment-recreation-auto-amusement concessionaires
Information
Visitor information centers-local and state organizations and associations.

Security
Police and fire protection
Lifeguards
Beach patrol

Crowd control
Traffic control and accident prevention

Health and Sanitation
First aid stations
Emergency and rescue
Hospital and clinic
Garbage and litter disposal
Personal facilities

Pubic Utilities and Facilities
Water-Electricity-Telephone (Primarily for campers)
Campgrounds
Parks and Recreation Areas

Before you can plan more or improved visitor services you must first evaluate quantity and quality of present hospitality in your area.

Your preliminary assessment of existing visitor services should include the following questions:

● Does your community have a tourist information center (or does the state or region have one in your area)? Where are these located (major transportation terminals, office buildings, the university, convention center)?

● What travel agents, auto clubs, travel clubs offer services to tourists and what do these services include?

● What hosting services are provided by hotels, motels, hostels, campgrounds?

● How do the attractions themselves help tourists? the ticket offices? cultural institutions? historic sites? recreational facilities?

● Are the food services (restaurants, street vendors, fast food chains) showing hospitality to their tourist customers?

● What services are provided by postmen? policemen?

● What services are provided by the many other people and businesses who interact with tourists—gas station attendant, librarian, newsstand clerk, 7-11 shopkeeper? everyone in your community?

As you can see, there are many people in your community who can and do help host your visitors. When you have inventoried and evaluated what your community offers and reviewed problems and solutions from previous years, you can plan to meet present and future tourism demands.

Effective visitor service programs must be carefully planned, and while most parts of the service base are already in place, they probably will not be adequate for the tourist season. Additional personnel may have to be hired and trained and a *coordinative* system of organization will have to be created to insure that services are available when needed. And an evaluation methodology must be designed to continually measure and improve the effectiveness of the services rendered.

Coordination of Visitor Services

Coordinating visitor services requires not only a knowledge of how these services are performed, and by whom, within the framework of each service area, but also understanding the problems that these various service organizations face.

Coordination is the control function that establishes what the channels of communication are going to be among the various service agencies and organizations, the community at large, and the tourism organization. To achieve good coordination and control, *everyone* involved in tourism must understand what are the tourists' needs and services required and be prepared to respond to these needs . . . effectively.

Close cooperative effort among all agencies and organizations is vital, and the coordination of this effort is best managed by an individual who is a "perfectionist" on details, has insight into, as well as a firm grasp of, all facets of tourist service problems; be able to analyze how these services may be better performed; recognize the needs for new services; and evaluate past performance to assess future needs.

Furthermore, he should concen-

Figure 9-8   Recreational services are part of visitor services. (Courtesy New Zealand Tourist & Publicity Office.)

trate on making contacts in the community, making sure that the program meets the needs of the people involved, and that all phases of management are running smoothly. He must be able to plan, to organize, to conduct seminars, to manage, and to coordinate all visitor service activities.

Who Pays For and Provides Visitor Services?

Obviously, the community itself will be paying for most of these services, but many of the dollars will be coming from the tourists themselves through parking fees, admissions, local sales and use taxes, and from the hotels, motels, restaurants, theatres, and other tourist businesses. Community development grants and some state and federal programs also assist in providing funds for visitor services' programs, as well as lo-

cal businesses and civic organizations and those involved in the tourism program.

Special Service Needs

As international travel expands, American communities are being discovered by more foreign tourists. There may be communications problems unless specific services are planned and provided. Persons within the community who speak foreign languages should be identified and be ready to service foreign visitors when needed.

There are standard signs and symbols, recognized by people all over the world. Small communities may consider themselves too isolated to invest in such signs. But such signs are very important in offering specific directions and instructions to *all* tourists regardless of what language they speak. What's more, the symbols are more explicit than words and require less space than most phrases which they replace. Symbols adopted by the National Park Service

are in the public domain and can be used for local application without any charge or prior permission.

Training for Visitor Services

Visitor services training programs must extend into almost every area of tourist interface, from the unskilled but important jobs of busboys, bellmen, porters and ticket takers to those who have the more sophisticated jobs of arranging tours and giving out tourist information, as well as to the citizens of the community. Furthermore, the program must be continuous because people change jobs, or get careless or forgetful, and need refresher course training.

The primary focus of the visitor services training program is always on *hosting:* How to be a good host when entertaining or serving strangers. Sound easy? It's not. Hosting is much more than putting on one's best smile, being cordial and courteous, or just being "nice." To be a good host, one must understand the tourism philosophy of the community as well as the individual tourist on his level of intellectual and emotional being.

Tourists are complex beings. Away from their own familiar environment, they are trying to relate to a community's environment as quickly as possible so that they may absorb, ingest, and partake of everything that a community has to offer them to satisfy their needs. They are guests in the community, and they expect to be treated as guests.

Who Needs to Be Trained?

Everyone! In differing degrees, everyone in a community should receive some training, even though the training

may only be informational. Generally, the segments in the community which must receive training are:

- *Those who render personal services,* are highly visible and have frequent opportunities to speak with tourists such as hotel, motel, restaurant and service station employees; city employees; and those involved in the attractions, amusements, and tourist businesses who give out tourist information.

- *Those who must perform specialized services* for the community as well as for tourists. These persons include police, firefighters, sanitation employees, security guards, health services personnel, and the bankers, and shopkeepers and their employees.

- *The general community* itself must be informed about tourism development, so a spirit of friendliness prevails, and so tourists feel they are welcome. The better they feel about a community, the longer they will want to stay and the sooner they will wish to return.

- *Persons staffing the Tourist Information Centers.* (TIC).

The general training focus should be on hosting and hospitality, but there should be some specific tourism training for each of the above groups. Specifics of training personal and specialized ser-

Figure 9-9 Training is necessary for personnel who have tourist contact. (Courtesy New Zealand Tourist & Publicity Office.)

vices personnel are discussed in Hospitality Training. Specifics for training members of the community are in The Public Awareness Program, for TIC staff in Establishing Tourist Information Centers.

Training for Personal Services Personnel

Because personal services personnel have frequent opportunities to interface with tourists, their training program should include the following:

- *The impact of tourism on their jobs and on the community* should be discussed. The more they realize how

important tourism is in terms of dollars, jobs, and community betterment, the more they will develop a respect for the need to be hospitable and to give good service.

- *They should receive hospitality training.* Learn to answer questions, how to be polite, how to be friendly toward strangers, and how to make strangers into friends.

- Some will need training in *personality development* so they will automatically show the best side of their personality. Visitors get a poor impression of a place if they are ignored, or if they are confronted with rudeness or sullenness.

- They should learn how to do their own jobs with greater efficiency and effectiveness. They should develop *an attitude of "professionalism"* about what they do, say, or how they act.
- They should be aware of their *general appearance and impressions that are created* by being clean, well groomed, dressing appropriately, and speaking clearly.
- They should *become informed about the community* and area in which they work. They should know the highway system and know about the natural resources, history, attractions, special events and places of interest so they can answer tourists' questions.
- Specifically, they should be given a one-day tour through the community which highlights the area's attractions and services. (Employers should be willing to grant this one day with pay to improve their employee's ability to interact with tourist customers.)
- They should know *what to do in an emergency* whether it be a fire, robbery, fainting spell, heart attack, or someone choking on food (applying the Heimlich Hug); whom to call *first;* how to, and how not to, react in an emergency situation.

Training for Specialized Services' Personnel

In addition to knowing their own specialized jobs, service personnel should receive additional training as it relates to tourism and to the individual tourist.

Here again, the training should emphasize the impact that tourism has on their job or business. They should welcome tourists as they would any other guest. Their hospitality training should emphasize "doing the extras" that tourists like, but may not expect:

- Extra help in giving directions.
- Extra time to explain the nice things about your community and specific things that tourists should do while visiting the community.
- Extra explanations that help tourists find whatever they are seeking.

Training the Members of the Community

Community training programs may be accomplished in two ways.

- Normal communication channels, for example, press releases, public meetings, or progress reports may be used.
- Special presentations to community interest groups by tourism personnel or by the community's leaders may be made.

What instruction should the members of the community receive? The most important training should tell citizens about the economic and social impact of tourism. They should know how tourism affects their taxes and where these dollars go in schools, hospitals, street repair, and community beautification.

The community members also must be taught the importance of civic pride, clean-up campaigns, and maintaining a good community image. Citizens must learn to understand tourists.

Who Should Do the Training?

Ideally, the training should be done by experts in tourism training, or by the tourism organization personnel. Frequently, however, tourism training is handled by employers, or by osmosis, and, of course, is only minimally effective.

The tourism organization, if it does not provide the necessary training, should prepare a list of the training needs, based on the community's tourism objective, and establish a mechanism for training that it can coordinate or supervise and evaluate.

Some communities offer tourism courses in local high schools and colleges. The tourism organization should encourage all tourist-oriented businesses and their employees to take these courses. In other communities, the Chamber of Commerce or other civic organization or association may offer instruction-orientation in tourism.

The Public Awareness Program

Successful implementation of a tourism program involves two distinct promotional efforts. Naturally, you must promote your community to the traveling public, a task discussed in Marketing Tourism. Less obvious, but of equal importance is promoting tourism to your own community. This is accomplished through the **community awareness program.**

The purposes of advertising have been described as *to inform, to persuade,* and *to remind.* It is helpful to think of the community awareness program along the same lines. The community should be informed of the benefits of tourism and the nature of the tourism organization's activities. They may need to be persuaded these benefits are worth the cost. Finally, they must be reminded of the program from time to time and brought up to date on its progress, just to keep them "in the fold."

Some might question the allocation of resources to this task. A possible challenge is "Spend the dollars or time devoted to the public awareness program on advertising to tourists; the benefits will speak for themselves." This seems ill-advised for several reasons.

Community leaders are likely to have mixed feelings toward tourists and tourism. An early effort to bring people on board may be necessary before a concerted effort at promoting the community is possible.

The benefits people receive from tourism differ in degree and kind. For those actually collecting tourist dollars, the advantages are obvious. Second order, or multiplier effects are more subtle and difficult to identify; even experts do not agree as to their magnitude. These may not be recognized without careful and thorough explanation. It may appear community resources are being spent to benefit the owners of a few attractions, restaurants and hotels.

The public awareness program is extremely important and should be planned and initiated before beginning to promote the area to vacationers. A manufacturer wouldn't advertise a product until he had a product to advertise. **In tourism, an important part of the "product" is the community's recep-**

tiveness. Developing, or reinforcing the friendly, helpful attitudes that are so essential is a task of the community relations program.

Value of Tourism

A central purpose of the public awareness program will be to educate the community as to the value of tourism to the community.

Relevance

The term "community" has been used as if its population were completely homogeneous. In fact, a community is a collection of individuals, families and groups with diverse attitudes, goals and aspirations. This diversity must be recognized in planning and conducting the public awareness program. It is important to identify the audience for a particular communication and tailor the message to its needs. A critical factor to be considered in explaining the benefits of tourism is relevance. One must analyze the interests, aspirations, backgrounds and life styles of the audience one is addressing. Only benefits which are relevant to a particular group should be selected for emphasis.

Taking an example, an increase level of banking activity might be a benefit of tourism of interest to the financial community. It would be a ridiculous theme for a campaign directed toward disadvantaged youths; it is not a concept that is relevant to their world. Even a reduction in the unemployment level might be too remote a notion, since this audience may often have been left unemployed in periods of rapid economic expansion. A discussion of the number and kinds of new jobs this group can fill

would be focused on a benefit to which they can relate.

Tourism offers many values to the community and nearly everyone gains from some of them, either directly or indirectly. While the public awareness program should help citizens recognize these benefits, not all can be explained to all audiences. It is necessary to select and stress those a particular audience experiences and to explain it at a level they can understand.

Importance

Time, resources, and the audience's capacity to absorb, will limit the amount of information that can be presented in any one message or in a total campaign. In selecting benefits to be promoted, it is necessary to consider not only their relevance, but, their importance. Given limited resources, it is necessary to concentrate on educating the public about those which it will feel to be most desired.

Some benefits, such as economic growth, would be counted as important by most communities. The ranking of others, such as diversifying the economic base, would be more situational. People in most communities might acknowledge this to be desirable. Among those recognizing its desirability, persons in areas whose economies were subject to wide cyclical swings would probably rate it as highly important. Were the local economy "recession proof" diversification would probably be of minor interest.

The importance attached to particular values may vary widely among groups within a single town or city. Again, it is necessary to tailor the message to the audience. All may agree ex-

Figure 9–10 Many retail outlets benefit from tourism. (Courtesy Hong Kong Tourist Association.)

panding the property tax base would be a good thing. Homeowners and businessmen are likely to feel this is a highly important benefit while apartment dwellers would probably place it far down on their list of priorities.

Every benefit is of interest to someone. In communicating with an audience, it is necessary to concentrate on those they are likely to consider important.

A sort of filtering process has been described. First, all benefits of tourism are considered. In developing a message for a particular group those values that are relevant to their lives and goals are identified. This reduced list is then ordered as to probable importance and the

important values are emphasized in the public awareness program.

Understanding the Tourist

In addition to building acceptance of tourism, the public awareness program must help the community to understand the tourist. This involves two separate topics: understanding who the tourists are, and their problems, and understanding their motives for journeying to the area.

Tourists and Their Problems

It is important for residents to know what kinds of people are coming into your area. This will involve various methods of informing the community of the demographic and economic characteristics of visitors and of their geographic origins. In many instances these profiles will show travelers do not differ markedly from the area's own population. Similarities can be emphasized to facilitate acceptance of visitors.

Where differences affecting tourists relations with the community do occur, they should be explained so as to be understood and accepted. These may be ilustrated with two differences that are certain to be encountered: the tourist is from somewhere else and he is on vacation. Geographic differences exist and affect individual tastes and preferences as well as speech and behavior. Northerners' brisk manner and more rapid speech may seem rude, and even insulting to natives of a southern locale. The most sophisticated of southerners may be branded as a "hick" in the north because of his drawl. To the uninitiated, a New Yorker's praise may sound less friendly than a Georgian's insults. Residents must be educated to expect and respond appropriately to these differences.

"The tourist is you" has been mentioned several times as a possible theme for a public awareness program. We frequently observe those on vacation acting differently than they would at home. Those visiting your community are probably no worse, and no better than your own residents vacationing elsewhere. Realistically, the theme should be qualified to *The tourist is you, on vacation.*

Three factors seem helpful in understanding these modes of behavior: normlessness, strangeness and pressure. We will illustrate these with a simple case of undesirable behavior: dumping trash in a park.

Normlessness. Solid citizens, who live amidst meticulously trimmed suburban lawns and complain about school children dropping an occasional gum wrapper, can be observed indiscriminately strewing trash when on vacation. Normlessness is frequently offered as an explanation. The idea is that once the individual is away from the restraining influence of friends, neighbors and associates, his true (animal) nature emerges.

This explanation obviously rests upon a pessimistic view of human nature. If it is appropriate, there is little the community can do to prevent the behavior. Yet it is important for the community to understand some visitors, like some residents, will respond in this manner. As in raising children, it helps to know about the various phases you should expect, even if you can do little to influence them.

Strangeness. The traveler is in a new and strange environment. Odd, and normally unacceptable acts may merely be a response to unfamiliar circumstances. Taking the trash example, the visitor might willingly have deposited his litter in a garbage receptacle if he had known where to find one. He may even have carried it around for a while looking for a place to put it. Admittedly, this example seems a little far-fetched. The important thing is to realize people respond differently and, perhaps unpredictably, to unfamiliar circumstances.

Pressure. Americans supposedly go on vacation to relax and get away from the restraints and pressures of everyday life. They then set a grueling pace for themselves. The resulting pressures may be as great as those they face during their normal routine and of a sort they are not accustomed to handling. An executive who competently manages tens or hundreds of subordinates may be completely frustrated by the pressures of controlling his own children on a full-time basis. The trash dumper may have been a person who is normally neat and orderly responding to unfamiliar pressures. Similarly, kind and considerate individuals may behave rudely as a result of cumulative frustrations.

While the example, trash, seems trivial, there is an important principle involved. The more the community understands and attempts to alleviate the problems of tourists, the fewer the problems the community will have. Normlessness can be reduced if the tourist feels those he meets are interested in him. If he has been befriended by someone in the area he is less likely to act objectionably. Emphasize the necessity of responding readily to questions, even if they seem absurd; they are very real to the person making the inquiry. It may not be apparent to everyone passing through that the cute op-art frogs with gaping mouths are trash cans. By easing the frustrations and pressures of traveling, your community can reduce the number of unpleasant incidents with tourists. Maybe the litter in the park didn't get there by careless dumping. Maybe, to borrow a term from the late sixties, it was a case of (subconscious) trashing!

Understanding Tourists' Motives

We are all familiar with the golden rule. George Bernard Shaw's comment is less well-known, "Don't do unto others as you would have them do unto you; they may not share your taste." Both are relevant to understanding and responding to the tourist. It is important

for the community to understand tourists are families much like their own, rather than a mob or rude, intrusive litterbugs. Visitors appreciate and will respond to friendly, courteous treatment.

On the other hand people differ. The area's primary appeal might not be one that would attract its own residents, were they vacationing in the region. People in the community must be helped to understand, and accept as legitimate, the various reasons visitors do come.

Suppose the major attraction is a geological feature that is only of real interest to those with formal training in geology. Residents would not be likely to share visitors' enthusiasm. They might even feel anyone willing to spend good money to come and "look at the silly rock" is a little weird. A task of the public awareness program is to help the community understand and be supportive of travelers' interests even though they do not share them.

Further, even though an area may have a central appeal, say flat water recreation, different aspects will appeal to different travelers. The community must be made aware of the multifaceted nature of its offering. Imagine the plight of the tourist who hates fishing and is only seeking a little solitude, when he is cornered for a 30-minute discourse on the best fishing techniques.

This facet of the public awareness program is largely a matter of promoting the area to its own citizens. Residents must understand the reasons visitors come to their community: what it has to offer. Strategies for the public awareness program are discussed below. Those encouraging the local populace to sample the area's offerings seem most appropriate for this step. These could range from distribution of brochures

Figure 9-11 It is important to understand what tourists are looking for. (Courtesy Hong Kong Tourist Association.)

within the local community to programs encouraging citizens to visit its attractions. The latter might include tours, off-season rates, resident passes and other devices encouraging local tourism.

Methods for Communicating With the Public

In the preceding paragraphs we discussed the message to be conveyed to the public and the necessity of tailoring these to specific audiences. Attention will now turn to methods or channels for delivering these. Channels will be categorized as passive spokesmen, personal communications, mass media and direct experience. Before turning to specific strategies, one other, more general item should be considered.

One-Sided versus Two-Sided Arguments

How many times have you heard "There are two sides to every story"? This is as true of tourism as of any other complex issue. The problem for a communicator is whether to present only one side—"Tourism helps the economy"—or both sides: "Admittedly, tourists create congestion but they help the economy." The evidence is mixed as to which strategy works best. On the one hand, a two-sided argument seems to make the communicator seem more credible. On the other, the speaker risks delivering his opponent's view to people who had not heard them.

The decision as to which strategy to adopt shoud be based on the prevalence of opposing views and the strengths of your counterarguments. If opposing views are not widely held or your arguments may sound weak by comparison, a one-sided approach is safer. This situation could be encountered when your case depends on complex arguments and your opponent's rests on simple, but erroneous assumptions. If negative views are commonly accepted but you can muster strong reasons for your position, there is little to lose and much to gain by a two-sided approach.

The Refutational Approach. If a two-sided campaign is selected, the following sequence, termed the refutational approach, has proven superior.

- State the Negative. Briefly, but honestly, identify the issue you are addressing. Focus the audience's attention, but don't argue the opposing case. "It has been stated that tourists will create congestion and put a drain on public services."
- Give the Counterarguments. Forcefully present your case. Be explicit. "Tourists contributed X million dollars to the area's economy" is better than "The economic benefits of tourism are immense."
- Draw the Conclusion. Clearly state the conclusion you wish your audience to draw. "The benefits of tourism are more than worth the costs."

Two-sided campaigns have often failed by stopping after step two. Communicators apparently felt their case was so strong any thinking person would come to the desired conclusion without assistance. Many didn't!

Passive Spokesmen

Some strategies involve using objects, rather than words to communicate. An anecdote will explain. The commander of a major military installation was dismayed at the hostility citizens of the neighboring community displayed towards the post and his troops. Having tried various public relations' activities that failed, he hit upon one final idea. He secretly arranged to have the entire command paid entirely in two dollar bills. The program was conducted without comment. This mass of currency silently flowing through the community demonstrated the installation's importance more powerfully than words could ever have. Best of all, the program involved almost no direct cost. It was free.

Several communities have employed variations on this theme.

- One actually encouraged tourist establishments to make change in two dollar bills.
- Tourist establishments in another stamped one-dollar bills, "tourist dollar."
- For a time establishments in a third had "tourist dollars" printed on their checks.

Other silent salesmen, such as souvenir buttons and bumper stickers distributed free or at cost, can effectively highlight the number and importance of tourists to the economy.

Face-to-Face Communications

Communicating on a face-to-face basis is the most effective method of delivering a message. Most communities rely heavily on this mode in their public awareness program. This may either take place in an informal one-on-one setting or in the more structured atmosphere of a group. In the latter instance there is usually an implicit notion of a two-step process: tourism representatives meet with, or address, groups hoping the members will, in turn, convey the message to their friends and associates.

Meetings. Meetings offer an opportunity for one, or a few tourism representatives to discuss their plans, programs and problems with the citizenry. In areas where formal tourist promotion organizations exist, officials usually consider attending or addressing meetings to constitute a major portion of their responsibilities.

Examples of how this approach may be used are listed below. These fall into one of two general categories: (a) meetings held specifically to discuss tourism with interested parties, or the general population and (b) providing speakers and programs for groups formed for other purposes.

- Hold town meetings to discuss and obtain reactions to the general topic of tourism.
- Hold public meetings focused on particular problems with tourists or tourism.
- Organize booster breakfasts or lunches to bring supporters up to date on tourism's progress and problems.
- Tourism leaders meet with the community's business and financial leaders.
- Tourism representatives get together with elected officials and other political leaders.
- Organize a formal speakers' bureau where a file of representatives willing and able to address groups is maintained.
- Arrange programs specifically tailored to the desires and needs of particular groups.

Personal Communication. Except for meetings with key influentials, the purpose of the strategies outlined above is seldom only to deliver the message to the few people who attend. As we noted, there is usually some notion they will pass it along in that most effective of all communications situations: direct, one-to-one personal communication.

More structured efforts also exploit the advantages of face-to-face communication. Tourism leaders often have programs of meeting privately with key influentials on a regular basis. In other instances personal contact has been effective in membership drives or fund raising efforts where supporters agree to quotas of new members or contributions. This is often a particularly effective method for reaching those who have recently allowed their membership or support to lapse.

Mass Communication

Face-to-face communication is the most effective mode since listeners have an immediate opportunity to respond, question and clarify. Unfortunately, the time available for this task is never as great as the need and part of the task must be accomplished through the use of mass communication.

Opting to use mass communications involves trading off effectiveness for efficiency. Admittedly, the message is not delivered as *effectively* and completely by mass means. Yet, it is *efficient* in that larger numbers can be reached for a given allocation of time or money.

In discussing mass communication, it is conventional to distinguish between advertising and publicity.

Advertising. Advertising differs from publicity in that advertising is paid for while publicity is free. The most obvious use of advertising is the purchase of space in newspapers or time on radio or television. An alternative is the publication of newsletters or brochures.

Media advertising seems to be used less frequently than other modes in public awareness programs. The amount of information that can be conveyed is limited, the relative cost is high and the amount an organization can afford is frequently viewed as being so small as to have a negligible impact.

In the communications program, paid advertising seems best adapted to one-shot efforts such as countering specific criticisms. Since the use of public resources to influence the public is politically sensitive, a tourism organization may not wish to pay the cost from its own funds. Often it will be advisable for the organization's officials to coordinate a campaign that is underwritten by one or several members.

Brochures and newsletters are more frequently used since their relative cost is low and larger amounts of information can be included. Examples include

- Information sheets and newsletters for distribution to the general public
- Newsletters for members or members of sponsoring organizations such as a chamber of commerce.
- Brochures describing the benefits of membership to prospects.

Public service spots made available by radio and television stations resemble both advertising and publicity. They are like publicity in that the time is free. Like advertising, there are costs involved; the advertiser usually must pre-

pare, or pay for the content. These can be valuable if they are offered at times when desirable audiences are available. Otherwise, the organization may find itself in the situation experienced by one federal agency.

The department was prohibited by Congress from using paid television advertising, and relied entirely upon public service time. They still had to pay the considerable cost of preparing and distributing commercials. A study revealed that, since few were watching, the total cost per viewer worked out to be greater than if the organization had purchased prime time.

Publicity. Publicity is free and is carried among the regular articles, stories or programming of the medium. Sometimes it is unsolicited. Dodge City residents' consciousness of their heritage was raised immeasurably by "Gunsmoke." The Poconos area was pleasantly surprised to be the subject of a five minute interchange about second honeymoons on "All in the Family." These cases are exceptions. A successful publicity program usually requires at least as great an effort as advertising.

In considering publicity, remember media representatives are anxious to find newsworthy items of interest to their readers. This sentence contains two key ideas: "newsworthy" and "their readers." Those who have experienced difficulty getting an item published have frequently ignored one or both.

An item must be news. The day to day activities of the organization or its officers usually do not qualify. The appointment of a new director may be an exciting event for those in tourism, but most of the community will not share their enthusiasm.

Media have different audiences with different interests and items must be tailored accordingly. An agency's news releases may often be ignored because they are intended for mass distribution in the hope someone will see fit (or be desperate enough) to notice them. Higher success rates will be experienced if items are tailored for specific audiences.

Some examples of successful publicity efforts follow.

- Arrange for and assist media representatives in the coverage of tourist events as *news* items.
- Arrange for documentary type coverage of the area's attractions and events.
- Participate in the development of a documentary or series of articles on the impact of tourism.
- Prepare news releases with individual outlets in mind.

- Try to stimulate editorial coverage of tourism and its impact. If the editor is friendly, great! If not,
- Write and submit thought-provoking letters to the editor.

Direct Experience

No method of building the community's appreciation of its attraction and of tourists' motives for visiting is as effective as direct experience. Many methods might be pursued to develop the public's understanding of the area's offering. Those listed below have proven effective in successful public awareness programs.

- Special resident rates.
- Off-reason rates and privileges that are particularly attractive to natives.
- Passes and tours for school children.
- Open houses.
- Behind the scenes tours of hotels, restaurants and attractions.

Figure 9–12 Some resorts offer special prices for residents. (Courtesy New Zealand Tourist & Publicity Association.)

- Making brochures prepared for the traveling public easily available to residents.

- Displaying a booth designed for a tourism show in a mall, shopping center or at a local fair.

- Giving residents, particularly students, priority in filling jobs.

Summary

The public awareness program is largely a matter of educating the members of your community in the value of tourism. In this process it is important to tailor the message to the audience and emphasize benefits that are relevant and important to the listener. The necessity of developing an understanding of who the tourists are, their problems, and motives was noted.

The public awareness program is a communication task. One may use any or all conventional methods: personal contacts, advertising, and publicity. Facilitating resident visits to the area's attractions was viewed as particularly appropriate to building an understanding of the area's appeal and tourists' motives.

One opportunity for the community to show the tourist that he is a welcome guest in the community is to establish a Tourist Information Center.

Establishing Tourist Information Centers

Tourist Information Centers (TIC) are the most important visitor service facility in a community. They are important because they frequently provide the initial contact with most tourists who visit a community, and because they have the opportunity and the responsibility for creating the first impressions a tourist will perceive. Therefore, it should be one of the first duties of the tourism organization to establish TICs in and near the community, provide them with complete information on the area, and staff them with well-trained personnel.

The Community TIC offers specific information about the local area, its attractions, events, facilities and services. It also assists in gathering data about tourists, such as where they come from, how long they will stay, what brought them to the area, and other significant data that a community needs to assist in the development of its tourism plan.

As pointed out in a guide published by the Texas Tourist Development Agency, most visitors or "passers-by" are strangers to the community and unaware of the variety of attractions offered. Therefore, the TIC must be able to provide *complete* information about the community. Types of information which should be available to tourists should be classified for easy reference, and could include most of the following major categories:

Accommodations (Hotels, Motels, Campgrounds, Hostels)
Auto repair garages
Attractions-amusements
Children's services
Churches
Cultural attractions—museums, galleries, lectures, musicales.
Complaint referrals
Community events
Directional information
Directories of

Emergency information
Employment information
Entertainment
Foreign visitors and interpreters
Health services and hospitals
Historical sites, places, buildings
Local industry
Local government services
Local newspaper, radio and television
    services
Maps
Parking
Parks and recreational places (tennis
    courts, swimming pools, golf courses,
    horseback riding stables, and other
    sports information)
Restaurants (showing type, price
    range, reservations needed etc.)
Shopping information
Sightseeing services
Special tour services
24-hour services
Transportation services

Of course, the TIC may expand this list of categories, or use only those which represent a large portion of the questions that are most often asked by tourists.

The initial compilation of the information represents a major commitment of staff time for researching, organizing, and determining the form in which the information is to be presented to the tourist. Therefore it is important that the information be inclusive, accurate, up to date, easy to understand, and attractively presented.

The TIC makes it easy for travelers to get reliable answers to their questions and provides an excellent opportunity to sell them on the area's attractions as well as gather information about them. By placing a facility of this type in a cen-

tral, easily reached location, one stands a good chance of stopping many travelers who might otherwise just drive through the community.

The information center should be placed strategically along the major route through your community—or at the intersection of major routes. It should be conveniently located at ground level with plenty of free parking space available. In congested areas reserved parking areas adjacent to the center should be arranged. By all means, keep the building and grounds attractive. If possible, provide for well-landscaped grounds.

The center could be located in a store, hotel/motel, or the Chamber of Commerce office. However, it is preferable to have it in a building of its own. It is not necessary to have much space as long as the center is attractive, easily recognized, and large enough to provide display racks for brochures on local and area attractions.

One approach is to have a center with an unusual type building—a tepee, covered wagon, log cabin, grist mill, replica of historic building (The Alamo or Judge Roy Bean's saloon perhaps). The center should be unusual and attractive on the inside as well as the outside. It must draw attention to itself. A large sign should identify it. Posters, photographs, and historic artifacts are appropriately displayed inside. Welcoming signs on the major routes to town should give the location and hours of operation. It is important that your staff, volunteers or paid employees, be well-informed and enthusiastic individuals who understand their purpose and have a knowledge of and pride in their community.

Figure 9-13 Tourist centers must carry information on area activities. Panning for gold near Queenstown, New Zealand. (Courtesy New Zealand Tourist & Publicity Office.)

Visitor centers can double as a reservation bureau for your hotels and motels. Often the hotels and motels help finance such projects and their operation. Alternatively, a leading hotel or motel can be sought out to donate the necessary space to the community or at least provide rent at a minimum rate.

In sum, hospitality and tourist information facilities are important in promoting the attractions of the community. Additionally they serve the important purpose of providing a method for surveying the tourist population. These are the places where valuable information can be gathered through registrations, questionnaires, and interviews with little contamination of data from the nontourist or the risk of alienating the visitors (in this latter case they have voluntarily stopped which is far different from being stopped or interrupted as would be required in some information gathering situations).

The number and quality of the information centers in your community should be assessed. Do you have an information center and is it adequately attracting people to stop? Is the exterior and interior attractive and is it strategically placed and indentified so visitors can be enticed to stop without feeling they have to go out of their way? Comparing registrations at lodges, various attractions, or restaurants with the registrations at tourist information facilities will give a good index of how many take advantage of such facilities. Various questionnaires may be used to assess tourism and can include questions about visitor center usage and usefulness.

An additional role and service that the visitor center can play is providing the visitor something to do and see. The economic rewards of delaying the visitor one extra day is well known. The Texas Tourism Development Agency suggests that the community should encourage visitors to use the community as a base

of operations for seeing all of the attractions within easy driving distance.

Evaluating the Visitor Services Program

In evaluating the visitor services program, there are two perspectives to consider:

- Monitoring on a continuous basis
- Analysis of specific complaints and preferences (formal and informal).

The first perspective is an ongoing activity, a process, a measuring system. To make the system operate smoothly, it must have rather subjective standards in terms of "good," "bad," or "needs improvement." Here, the person making the evaluation simply prepares a complete checklist on which he rates the various qualities that are important to having an effective system. The more subjectivity, however, the more disagreement there will be about accuracy.

Another similar method is to establish a rating scale ranging from "very good" through "very bad," on which persons doing the evaluation can each offer their own subjective ratings, and then discuss or average them to arrive at a specific rating.

Ultimately, however, in any monitoring system, the one(s) doing the monitoring is searching for details, and with this type of system, there is continuous and detailed input that inevitably leads to an improved output. If it is a good system and if it has the continuous attention of key service program personnel, it will yield a smoothly functioning and polished visitor services program.

Analyzing and evaluating visitor satisfaction in terms of visitor complaints and preferences is a more objec-

tive measurement approach and allows the tourism organization to focus on major and specific problem areas; to identify new attractions and promotional opportunities; to recognize trends in community tourism; and to study tourism's impact on the community.

Generally, evaluation procedures rely on surveys or observations. Whatever procedure is used, the data or information on the situation, program or service must be as objective as possible, must be verifiable, must be usable in the decision process and have some degree of predictability as to decision outcome and/or results expected.

For example, using observational procedures, a person or team of evaluators may observe tourists enjoying themselves on the ski slopes of Aspen. They observe what tourists do when they are not skiing. They observe how tourists relate to each other. They observe what tourists are purchasing. They observe the lift operation to see how well it is functioning. They observe access routes, traffic patterns, accidents . . . everything literally that may affect tourist satisfaction.

The scene is played and repeated daily, and after numerous observations, they are able to arrive at general measurable conclusions on skier behavior patterns, adequacy of service facilities, and additional opportunities for improvement of skier services.

In evaluating visitor satisfaction, one would classify and analyze the types of complaints received, or one could ask tourists a list of questions that develop

Figure 9-14   Evaluation: Are tourists satisfied? (Courtesy New Zealand Tourist & Publicity Office.)

answers from which conclusions can be drawn.

The steps involved in designing a survey of visitor satisfaction follow.

- Determine objectives of survey
- Determine survey procedure
- Design Questionnaire
- Test Questionnaire
- Design and select sample of persons to be interviewed
- Conduct the interviews
- Code and tabulate the questionnaires
- Analyze the results
- Prepare report of recommendations

Probably the most important point to be made is that evaluations should be performed repeatedly to offer continuity of information. Providing reliable data over a period of time allows comparisons with previous evaluations and makes the evaluation process a continuous one.

Remember too, that as you are evaluating visitors services, the visitors themselves are doing their own evaluating based on how they perceive your community and its attractions, your approach to tourism development, the manner in which you manage and provide service for visitors, and the satisfactions they have received during their visit.

Watch them, listen to them, and respond to what they want and like. They will talk to others about your community, and what they tell others will depend upon how well the visitor services program operates. Make it a good one!

S T U D Y   QUESTIONS

1. What are the four phases of leadership development in the organizational process?
2. What are the leadership roles where there is
   a. a separate tourism organization or one that functions as part of the chamber of commerce?
   b. a chamber of commerce and a separate tourism association?
3. What are the three common leadership styles?
4. What is the greatest problem to be overcome in leadership situations?
5. What is the biggest problem in coordinating the tourism effort?
6. What are the most common methods for constructing an effective communications program?
7. Identify the various methods used to fund tourism operations and promotion and capital improvement or development projects.
8. What items should be included as part of a visitor services plan?
9. In what ways can the benefits of tourism be communicated to local residents?

D I S C U S S I O N   QUESTIONS

1. How does leadership emerge within a community? What are the components of successful leadership?
2. How should the following components of community tourism be coordinated?
   - communications
   - research and data collection
   - education and training
   - budget and finance.
3. Compare and contrast the advantages of the various methods of funding the development and operation of tourism at the community level.
4. What is a visitors services program? What questions need to be answered when planning and coordinating such a program?
5. Develop a visitor services training program for (a) those who work in a tourism business and (b) the general public. What topics should be covered? How should the information be presented?

10

TOURISM PROMOTION

LEARNING
OBJECTIVES

At the end of this chapter the reader will be able to:

- Identify the unique challenges of marketing tourism.
- Discuss the importance of the steps involved in the development of a marketing plan.
- Be able to define and correctly use the following terms:

Marketing	Selling orientation
Product orientation	Intermediaries
Marketing orientation	Channel of distribution
Profit margin	Cognitive dissonance
Brand loyalty	Promotional theme
Marketing strategy grid	Noise level
Unique selling proposition/point	Pass-along rate
Life span	Market selectivity
Geographic selectivity	Timing flexibility
Cost-per-contact	
Cooperative advertising	

INTRODUCTION

Marketing is the sum total of the activities involved in getting products and services from producer to customer. This means ensuring that the right *product* is developed at the right *price* and *promoted* through the right *places* to produce a satisfied customer at a profit for the producer. In the case of tourism, a producer might be a destination, an airline, or a hotel, for example.

Marketing Challenges

The marketing of tourism is different from marketing in the manufacturing industries because of the special characteristics of tourism.

1. Tourist supply cannot be easily changed to meet changing tastes. This puts increased pressure on planners to make the right development and marketing decisions.
2. Tourist demand is highly elastic. This means that changes in tourist income will produce a proportionately larger change in the demand for tourism.
3. Tourist services are consumed on the spot. There is no opportunity to maintain an inventory of goods to compensate for soft periods of demand. There is constant pressure to sell every room, every seat, and every ticket every day because the sale that is lost today is lost forever.
4. The tourist product is an amalgam of services—a plane seat, a hotel room, restaurant meals, sightseeing tours, etc. Lack of service in any one of these areas can ruin the entire vacation experience for the tourist. Any one producer lacks control over tourist satisfaction for the entire vacation.

Orientation.   In addition to being a series of activities, marketing is also a way of looking at a business—namely through the eyes of the tourist. Historically, tourism marketing has been product oriented. The focus of the marketing effort was to provide the best beaches, the best rooms, etc., and to assume that, because these were the "best," tourists would automatically visit. This "product orientation" focuses on providing a "better" (as defined by the producer) product. Where there is more demand than supply, such an orientation might work.

However, when supply (of destinations, airline, hotels) is greater than demand, the focus tends to switch to a selling orientation—where the emphasis is on convincing tourists to visit a particular destination. The trouble here is that the focus is on the needs of the producer to sell rather than on the needs of the tourist to buy.

A marketing orientation focuses on the tourist. "What does the tourist want? Can I provide it?" This orientation—or way of looking at the business—sees the vacation through the eyes of the tourist. Decisions

Figure 10-1   Product orientation—because the mountains are here, people will come. (Courtesy New Zealand Tourist & Publicity Office.)

regarding what to provide (product), what to charge (price), how to advertise our message (promotion), and how to communicate with the tourist (place) are taken with the tourist firmly in mind.

In tourism we are dealing with a "living product"—a destination. While the focus of our efforts must be on satisfying the tourist, the physical, social, and cultural environment of the destination must be protected. Destinations that satisfy tourist needs to the exclusion of their own soon end up having lost the very thing that made them attractive in the first place. The task for the marketer is to satisfy the needs of the tourist while protecting the integrity of the destination.

Previous chapters have covered product and pricing issues within the context of the development of tourism. This chapter will focus on promoting tourist destinations and services, and the two chapters that follow will zero in on the fourth "p"—place, or, as it is referred to in tourism, the channels of distribution.

DEVELOPING THE PROMOTIONAL PLAN

Promotion consists of the activities undertaken to increase sales.

There are various steps in the development of a promotional plan. These are:

1. Select target audience.
2. Determine objectives.
3. Develop an appropriate message.
4. Select the promotional mix.
5. Set a budget.
6. Evaluate the campaign.

These steps remain the same whether a destination, a company, or a specific tour is being promoted.

While the last step is that of evaluation it should be noted that the campaign should be evaluated at each stage of the process. The reason a promotion might fail can be because the wrong segment of the market was chosen, the objectives were inappropriate, insufficient budget was given to do the job, the wrong message was sent through the wrong media, or the right message was sent but through the wrong media. The only way to keep the promotion on-track is to evaluate it at each stage.

Select Target Audience

Tourism marketing involves the extensive use of intermediaries—people or companies who operate in the channels of distribution between the producer and the tourist. While this will be covered in more detail in later chapters, the subject is raised here because a promotional campaign often needs to be aimed at both the tourist and one or more intermediaries.

For example, an airline sells its seats through retail travel agents as well as directly to the public. Any campaign to sell seats to a specific destination would be aimed at the potential tourist as well as the travel agent. A destination might advertise directly to the general public. It would also put together packages to sell the destination. These packages would be assembled with the help of tour wholesalers and sold through retail travel agents. The promotional campaign by the destination is at least three campaigns: encourage the wholesaler to package the destination; encourage the retailer to sell it; and encourage the tourist to buy the package.

The development of a marketing orientation involves targeting a message to meet the needs and wants of the audience. Yet, within tourism, the producer, the intermediaries, and ultimately the tourist have different needs and wants. The producer wants tourists, repeat business, a high return on investment, low selling costs, and maximum attention given by those in the channel of distribution to the products and services being promoted. The wholesaler is concerned with high volume of business, high profit margins (the difference betwen sales price and cost), reliable producers, packages offering low risk and little novelty, and products that will motivate retailers to sell them. (There is, of course, a market for unusual packages that appeal to a smaller, more sophisticated audience. However, wholesalers make their profit by selling volume. The way to do this is to produce products that have a better chance of appealing to the mass market.)

The retailer also seeks high sales volume and margins, wants to see a regular stream of innovative products to offer clients, and is concerned with the reliability of both wholesaler and producer. British vacationers relate horror stories about booking a package through a travel agent and arriving at the destination only to find their hotel has not yet been completed. Upon their return home, it was the travel agent who faced angry customers.

Tourists are looking for vacations to excite or to soothe. They want a lot of information about what they are buying; a variety of experiences, constantly updated, to choose from; help in deciding where to go; how to get there; where to stay; what to do; etc. They want to be treated as individuals by hospitable people who are knowledgeable about the various choices and can book their vacation choice with a minimum of time and effort.

It can be seen that, for the same product (say a vacation package to Tahiti), a completely different promotional campaign would be necessary for the tourist and the retailer.

Determine Objectives

The objectives of promotion are to inform, to persuade, and/or to remind. They come into play at different stages of the tourist's buying process. To get the tourist to buy and to buy again, successful promotional campaigns must

- get the tourist's attention;
- develop an understanding about the benefits being offered;
- create positive attitudes about what is being promoted;
- develop tourist preferences for what is being sold;
- get the tourist to buy;
- convince the tourist to return.

It is extremely unlikely that one campaign can achieve all of these things. The important point, however, is that a tourist moves through (or must be moved through) these stages prior to making a purchase decision. Tourists can be at different stages in this buying process. For example, London is a fairly well-known tourist attraction. While a potential visitor might not have visited London, enough may be known about it from watching travel programs, reading articles, and talking to friends and relatives that the tourist has a positive attitude about vacationing there. The objective, then, is to create a preference for London as a destination and get the potential visitor to buy a vacation there. Further messages can work on getting the tourist to return.

Less is known about India as a travel destination. Promotional efforts have to interest the tourist in India, create understanding about the benefits of visiting India, and put forth positive attitudes about India before moving onto the other stages of the buying process. For a new destination the efforts to get the tourist to buy will be longer and more time-consuming.

Attention/Comprehension.   At these stages the objective is to inform. This means, during the *attention* stage, exposing the message to as many of the right kinds of people as possible. Specific objectives can be set in terms of numbers of people to be reached within a specified period of time. The goal might be to have our message seen by 5,000 golf enthusiasts within the next month. Most media have excellent records of the reach (number of readers/viewers in particular categories) of their newspaper, magazine, television, or radio station and can give these figures.

It is one thing to have our message in a place where it can be seen. It is quite another to have it noticed and remembered. Thus, at the *comprehension* stage the objective can be stated in terms of message retention. We need to know what percentage of the target audience remem-

Figure 10–2   Aberdeen Harbor, Hong Kong. Informing people about the destination. (Courtesy Hong Kong Tourist Association.)

bered the important parts of the message. This can be measured through recall instruments.

Attitude/Preference/Action.   The next stage of the buying process involves persuasion. The promoter is seeking to create or strengthen existing positive attitudes or to change negative attitudes about a destination, airline, etc. This can be measured by means of before-and-after surveys of the audience. Before the campaign, for example, attitudes toward an airline can be measured on a "positive-negative" scale. The campaign is run and a similar survey taken to determine whether or not the campaign was effective. The same is true at the preference stage. The objective here is to convince the target group that what is being promoted has attractions or services superior to those of others. A before-and-after survey can, again, demonstrate how effective the campaign was.

At the action stage the objective is to encourage purchases. This can be measured through increased bookings or sales.

Adoption.   At the adoption stage, tourists have developed what is known as "brand loyalty." For example, the next time they fly, they will use Continental; whenever they are out of town they will stay at the Holiday Inn.

Promotion does not end with the sale. Even after the tourist has made a purchase, advertising is necessary for two reasons—to combat "cognitive dissonance" and to encourage repeat business. Cognitive dissonance refers to the feelings of anxiety felt after a decision is made to buy. It is a feeling that, perhaps, the choice made was not the right one. It is similar to that felt in a restaurant after having ordered prime rib and seeing a juicy chicken at the next table. The more expensive and important the purchase the more the anxiety. Consequently, it is necessary to further convince customers that they made the right decision. This might take the form of a note congratulating the customer on the purchase or advertisements with enough information in them so that vacationers can convince themselves that the right decision was made.

It is less time-consuming and less expensive to convince customers to buy again (if they were satisfied the first time) than to convince new customers to make the purchase. "Reminder" advertising seeks to encourage repeat sales. The incidence of repeat purchasers is an indication of how successful we are in satisfying the customers and convincing them to return.

Which Stage?   It is vital that appropriate objectives be set. To people who know little about New Zealand as a travel destination, a campaign aimed at "the hard sell" will be fruitless. Once target markets have been identified, their "place" in the buying process can be determined by means of some simple research.

- Have they heard of New Zealand?
- What are New Zealand's major tourist attractions?
- What are their attitudes toward New Zealand as a tourist destination?
- Given a list of possible destinations, where would they rank New Zealand?
- How likely are they to visit New Zealand next year?

Such a survey will indicate the appropriate objectives to stress in a promotional campaign.

Marketing Grid.   Another method for determining appropriate objectives is suggested by Ronald A. Nykiel in his book *Marketing in the Hospitality Industry*.[1] Nykiel uses a marketing strategy grid to identify appropriate campaign objectives. The grid is depicted in Table 10–1. The grid shows the relative strengths of the market and the competitive posi-

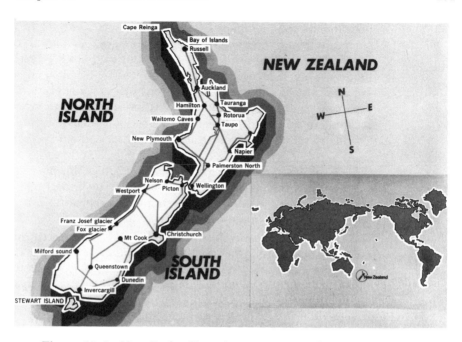

Figure 10–3   New Zealand's major attractions. (Courtesy New Zealand Tourist & Publicity Office.)

tion of a destination or firm. The position on the horizontal axis is an indication of how strong or viable a particular segment of the market is. The vertical axis is a measure of how we compare with our competition in vying for that segment of the market. To what extent do we have a strong competitive advantage in attracting that segment of the market?

Given an honest, albeit subjective, appraisal, an X can be placed in one of the nine squares. For example, if "conventiongoers" is seen as a strong market segment, but we are perceived as in a weak competitive

Table 10-1   Marketing Strategy Grid

Market Potential				
Strong	Moderate	Weak		
1	2	3	Strong	Competitive Position
4	5	6	Moderate	
7	8	9	Weak	

position for the segment of the market, an X would be placed in box seven. In general, numbers 1, 2, and 4 are seen as favorable positions and occur when one or both factors are strong and neither factor is below the moderate level; 3, 5, and 7 are seen as less favorable, and occur when one factor is weak, and one is strong, or both are moderate; and 6, 8, and 9 are seen as unfavorable positions to be in and occur when one or both factors are weak and neither is above the moderate level.

Different objectives are suggested for each of the squares:

1. *Strong market–strong product.* Protect this position through special progams designed to recognize the importance of this market segment; increase prices to maximize profits; add or upgrade services to remain competitively ahead.

2. *Moderate market–strong product.* Attempt to increase market share through competitive pricing.

3. *Weak market–strong product.* Promote to more segments of the market with multiple pricing strategies and a variety of service offerings; strong emphasis on cost control.

4. *Strong market–moderate product.* Price slightly below the competition; stress "value for money"; advertise as acceptable replacement for competition.

5. *Moderate market–moderate product.* Utilize specialized promotions to increase the market segments attracted; attract market share through competitive pricing.

6. *Weak market–moderate product.* Expand the number of market segments attracted.

7. *Strong market–weak product.* Upgrade the product and then increase prices.

8. *Moderate market–weak product.* Build market share through special rates.

9. *Weak market–weak product.* Sell or turn to alternate business.

Both the market and the competitive situations are constantly changing. As such, the marketing grid can also be used to determine which way the market and the competitive situations are moving in order that objectives can be formulated based on likely future situations.

Develop Appropriate Message

The promotional theme comes from a comparison of the analyses of the product, the market, and the competition. An analysis of the market will tell, among other things, what the market wants—what is important to the people in that market. For British vacationers it may be sunshine and beaches; for West Germans it may be friendly, local people. By taking the factors important to the potential tourists and comparing ourselves to the competition, a campaign theme can be developed. *The theme should consist of factors that are important to the market segment being sought and where we do a better job than the competition.* In marketing this is referred to as the *unique selling proposition* or, more simply, the *unique selling point.*

Perception vs. Reality.   A complicating factor arises when we consider how we are perceived by the market on the factors the market considers important. People act on their perceptions of a situation rather than on the reality of the situation itself. Suppose, for example, that historical sites are important to the market. The United States has a number of interesting historical sites. Mesa Verde National Park in Colorado has more than 200 dwelling rooms and 23 sacred kivas (ceremonial structures) in Indian cliff dwellings dating back to the first century B.C. However, if the market *perceives* that the United States lacks historical sites, people will not visit.

A comparison of image versus the actual situation is displayed in Table 10–2. Box 1 represents a situation where, on a factor that is important to the tourists being attracted, their image of the company or destination is positive and, in actuality, we *are* positive. (For example, friendly people are important to the tourists; they think we have friendly people compared to the competition and we do.) This, then, becomes our message—our campaign theme. In effect, we say: "Friendly people are important to you; we do a better job than does our competition in this regard."

Box 2 illustrates a situation where the image is negative but the actual is positive. Friendly people are important; we do have friendly people but tourists do not perceive our locals as being friendly. The message is essentially the same, but we will have to work harder and longer to change this image. Perhaps advertisements can be developed that show letters written by the local people inviting tourists to visit.

Boxes 3 and 4 indicate problems for the destination. In box 3, tourists believe the locals are friendly toward tourists but in actuality they

Table 10–2   Developing the Campaign Theme

Tourist Image			
Positive	Negative		
1	2	Positive	Actual Situation
3	4	Negative	

Figure 10-4   Are the locals friendly? (Courtesy Australian Tourist Commission.)

are not. Tourists could be attracted but, as soon as they arrive, they will realize that their perceptions were wrong. They will not return and will spread negative word-of-mouth advertising to others. In box 4, tourists do not believe that the locals are friendly and, in fact, they are correct! In both cases the "product" must be changed before the situation can be improved. Perhaps some educational seminars can be put into place to show the local people how important tourism is; surveys can be initiated and meetings held to discover why locals do not like tourists and to use this to address their concerns.

Select the Promotional Mix

Many methods can be used to get our message across. The most widely used method in travel and tourism is advertising—both to the consumer and the trade; personal selling; publicity or public relations; and promotional literature and merchandising, such as posters and window displays.

Each has advantages and disadvantages in terms of cost, selectivity, and ability to convey the message.

Newspapers. Newspapers are relatively inexpensive, both on a total cost and cost-per-contact—the cost of reaching one person—basis. Newspapers offer geographic selectivity and high frequency (most are dailies). Coverage is good in that approximately 80 percent of the U.S. adult population reads at least one newspaper a day. The lead time required to schedule an ad—flexibility—is low, and most papers have specific travel sections on Sunday.

Market selectivity, however, is low. In addition, newspapers have a high "noise level"—the amount of stimuli competing for the reader's attention—while the life span and pass-along rate are both low. Although there have been recent improvements in the quality of color photographs in newspapers, the quality is still rather poor.

Magazines. Magazines have a much higher total cost and cost-per-contact than do newspapers. They also have fairly long lead times for advertising. However, because of their specialized nature, magazines are highly market selective while regional editions offer some geographic selectivity. Life span and pass-along rates are both above average; print and graphic quality are excellent; and, through coupons or inserts, magazines have direct-response capabilities.

Direct Mail. While the total cost of a direct-mail campaign tends to be rather high, the cost-per-contact varies considerably depending upon the quality of the mailing list and the quality and quantity of the materials used. For example, geographic mailing lists containing the names of readers of *Golf* magazine or those of affluent travelers can be purchased.

Both market and geographic selectivity are the highest of all media. Both the life span and the noise level are low, as is timing flexibility owing to the need for production lead times.

Television. Television is an excellent medium for promoting tourism because it can utilize sight, sound, and movement. It is very expensive although the cost-per-contact may be low. The noise level is very high because people usually watch television with other people. To a certain extent it is possible to be geographically selective. However, the level of credibility or trust is low and timing flexibility is below average.

Radio. Radio offers the advantages of low cost and high timing flexibility. It is highly selective geographically and offers above-average market selectivity. Its credibility and noise level are similar to that of television. In addition, unlike newspaper or magazine advertisements, radio (and television) ads cannot be referred to afterwards. Because of this, and the fact that listeners are usually doing something else while listening to the radio, ads must be heard over and over again if they are to have an impact on potential tourists.

Outdoor Signs. There are two types of outdoor signs—billboards and transit signs. Billboards are placed along highways and at places where there is a high concentration of people. Transit signs are to be found on the sides of vehicles, such as buses.

Outdoor signs offer good geographic selectivity and low cost. However, they are limited in the amount of information that can be taken in by passing motorists. Additionally, there are increased restrictions on their use owing to laws regulating their placement.

To be most effective the message should be short, have high visual impact, and should be repeated.

Community Attractions Literature. Community attractions literature, often called *collateral material,* consists of brochures, pamphlets, maps, and directories. They can be promotional, informational, and directional.

Brochures should contain the following information:[2]

- Identification of the facility, including the logo.
- Descriptive facts on the facility.
- Directions on how to get there.
- A map with commutation times.
- Address and phone number.
- Person to contact for more information.
- Amenities within the facility.
- Nearby attractions and items of interest to the visitor.
- Transportation information.

The cover is the most important part of the brochure. Most people read only the headline in an advertisement or the cover of a brochure. To get the reader into your message, the cover must attract attention. The cover should contain:

1. The name and location.
2. The selling message.
3. A consumer benefit.
4. An identification of the target audience.

Next to the cover photo, captions are the best-read part of the brochure. Make sure that captions sell the personality and the unique features of the facility or destination.

People like to see other people. In the photographs include pictures of guests enjoying themselves. The exception to this rule is food. Readers prefer seeing close-up pictures of the finished dish.

Directory Advertising. There are over 5,000 different reference directories ranging from the Yellow Pages to specialized listings. Operators or destinations often undertake directory advertising because "everyone else does it." The decision to be listed or not should be based on an analysis of the business brought in from the listing compared to the cost involved.

Travel Videos.   The recent increase in the number of households with VCRs has offered a new opportunity for promoting tourism—the travel video. Some destinations will, for a small refundable deposit, send a video to interested customers. The video, viewed in the comfort of one's home, can be an effective sales tool. Promotional pieces can be repeated, and the noise level is low because the potential tourist has requested the video. While the initial cost is high, the combination of color, sound, and movement makes for an effective sales technique.

Public Relations.   Public relations (PR) is usually thought of as free advertising in that the company or destination does not pay for it. Yet there is a cost. To be effective, a PR campaign must be well planned and executed. Public relations should have objectives, ways to reach these objectives, target markets, timetables, and evaluative techniques to measure the results. And that costs money.

Public relations consists of the efforts involved in creating a positive image for the company or destination in its dealings with its publics—visitors, the local community and businesses, the media, and suppliers.

Figure 10–5   Providing photographs like these is an example of public relations. (Courtesy Hong Kong Tourist Association.)

Included in PR activities are such things as press releases, press conferences, appearances on radio and television shows, and familiarization trips for travel agents or travel writers. In the case of the latter, travel writers are given subsidized or free travel to a facility or destination in the hope that positive travel articles will result. In the case of travel agents, the hope is that the agent will be better able to sell the destination because of increased familiarity with it.

Films.   The cost of travel films is very high. As a result, their use is limited to large companies, cities, states, and countries.

Trade Shows.   There are two types of trade shows—those open to members of the trade and those open to the general public. In domestic and international travel trade shows, destinations and companies buy booth space and meet with wholesalers or retail travel agents in an attempt to sign business deals. This can be an excellent way to meet many travel trade people in one place over a few days.

Shows open to the public tend to be geographically regional. They offer the opportunity to see many potential tourists in the same short period of time. Little, if any, sales are consummated on the spot, but it is a way of getting the sales message out by way of film, video, and brochures to a large number of people.

Cooperative Advertising.   Advertisements that are jointly sponsored are known as *cooperative,* or *co-op,* advertising. Tour operators, for example, may provide the advertisement to a retail travel agency, which adds its name to the ad. The cost of producing and running the ad is shared by the two companies. Other suppliers, such as airlines and destinations, may offer the same type of deal.

Set a Budget

At this stage of the promotional plan it is appropriate to develop a budget. The objectives have been set, a theme determined, and the media selected. Based upon what has to be done and how it will be done, the amount of money necessary to get it done can be determined.

In a number of cases industry averages are used to approximate how much should be spent or to compare the spending of one facility or destination with that of its peers. The problem here is that figures used are the average for businesses or destinations that have been around for a long time and have built up a reputation and significant trade compared to others that are seeking to enter the marketplace. In the latter case, a larger budget would be necessary. Thus, while averages are useful as an approximate guide, each operation must build its own budget based on what it seeks to accomplish—its objectives—and how it seeks to accomplish them—the promotional mix.

Evaluate the Campaign

It cannot be stressed enough how important it is to evaluate the campaign at each stage of the way. It is a step that is often overlooked. A company may spend thousands of dollars on a campaign only to discover little or no increase in visitors or sales. Something obviously went wrong, but what? No one can say for sure unless the promotional effort is evaluated at each step of the way. It may be that the wrong audience was targeted—did we reach the people we really want to attract? It may be that the wrong objectives were set—did we aim too high, too low? Was the theme appropriate to the objectives—did we succeed in changing people's attitudes about the destination? Did we choose the right media where our message would be seen and understood? Did we budget enough to ensure the success of the message?

ENDNOTES

1. Ronald A. Nykiel, *Marketing in the Hospitality Industry* (New York: Van Nostrand Reinhold Company, 1983), pp. 51–59.
2. Ibid. p. 130.

S T U D Y   QUESTIONS

1. Why is the marketing of tourism different from marketing in the manufacturing industries?
2. What are the differences among a product, selling, and marketing orientation?
3. List the steps in the development of a promotional plan.
4. The promotional campaign by the destination is at least three campaigns. What are they?
5. Compare and contrast the different needs and wants of tourism producers, wholesalers, retailers, and tourists.
6. What are the various stages in the tourist's buying process and what are the promotional objectives at each stage?
7. How does the position of a destination on a marketing strategy grid influence its promotional objective?
8. What should the promotional theme consist of?

9. How does the perception of the market regarding a destination compared to the actual situation influence the destination?

10. Contrast the characteristics of the various forms of promotion.

DISCUSSION QUESTIONS

1. In what ways do the needs of tourists, intermediaries, and producers differ? What kinds of promotional messages, based on needs, would be most effective?

2. How do promotional messages differ (a) at different stages of the tourist's buying process and (b) relative to the strength of the market segment and the competitive position of the destination?

3. How does a tourist's perception of a destination affect the destination's promotional message?

4. Compare and contrast the advantages and disadvantages of using the various advertising media.

11

TRAVEL DISTRIBUTION SYSTEMS

LEARNING OBJECTIVES

At the end of this chapter the reader will be able to:

- Distinguish between direct and indirect distribution systems.
- Determine the advantages to the producer and consumer of each system.
- Outline the appeals of group travel and barriers to be overcome in its promotion.
- Discuss the economics of tour wholesaling and describe the steps involved in planning, marketing, and operating a group tour.
- Describe the importance of the retail travel agent to tourism.
- Discuss how a travel agency operates and makes money.
- Define and correctly use the following terms:

Direct distribution system	Indirect distribution system
Retail travel agent	Tour operator
Tour wholesaler	Speciality channeler
Independent tour	Hosted tour
Escorted tour	Special format tour
Return on equity	Tour specifications
Package	Shell
Preformed group	Tour escort
Guide	Airline Reporting
International Airline Travel	Corporation
Agent Network	
Cruise Lines International	
Association	
National Railroad Passenger	
Association	

TOURISM DISTRIBUTION SYSTEMS

Introduction

The link between tourism suppliers and the customers is known as the *distribution system*. The purposes of the system of distribution are twofold—to give potential travelers the information they need to make a vacation choice, and to allow them to make the necessary reservations once they have decided on their choice.

The various types of distribution systems are diagrammed in Figure 11-1.

Direct Distribution System

The distribution system may be *direct* or *indirect*. A direct system of distribution is one where the supplier—destination, airline, hotel, etc.—communicates directly with the customer. An individual, for example, may call a specific hotel or airline, or write to them requesting a reservation for a specific date. The supplier then answers over the phone or writes back confirming the reservation. The transaction is direct.

Suppliers have experimented with other, less traditional forms of communicating with the traveler. Larger companies provide toll-free 800 telephone numbers that they advertise to the public. This allows the traveler to call the supplier without charge. In a few cases automated ticketing machines have been opened at airports. These machines connect directly with the computer reservations system of an airline and allow the traveler with a credit card the availability of receiving flight information, making a reservation, and receiving both ticket and boarding pass on the spot. These machines have limited exposure at airports, for the airline runs the risk of upsetting the retail travel agents who are being bypassed. If successful, it is likely that automatic ticketing machines will be installed in hotels and elsewhere.

302

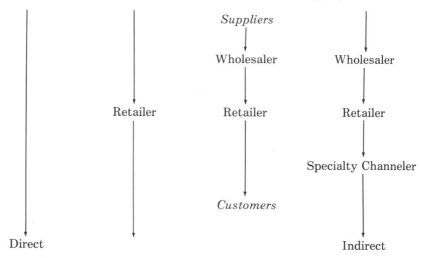

Figure 11-1 Tourism distribution systems.

Technology is available to sell travel through home computers. Mass outlets for selling travel have been utilized in Europe with travel being sold through supermarkets. For simple transactions these direct methods of selling travel can be expected to grow.

For the supplier, the system is simple, profitable, and offers control over the sale. The system is simple in that buyer and seller have direct communication with each other; it is profitable in that all the revenue paid by the customer goes to the supplier; control comes from the fact that the sales representative is an employee of the supplier.

Indirect Distribution System

An indirect distribution system is one where there are one or more intermediaries between the supplier and the customer. The most common intermediaries are discussed in the sections that follow.

Retail Travel Agents.   These are people who sell tours for wholesalers and operators in addition to hotel rooms, car rentals, and transportation tickets. The retailer acts as agent for the supplier and is paid on a commission basis by the supplier for sales made.

Tour Operators or Tour Wholesalers.   These are people who create a package that might include a variety of tourist products such as transportation, lodging, meals, transfers, sightseeing, etc. Wholesalers buy

Figure 11-2 "Following in the footsteps of royalty"—an example of a tour of Prague, developed by Cedok, the National Tourist Office of Czechoslovakia. (Courtesy Cedok.)

these "products" in bulk from the supplier at a reduced price and make money by marking up the package. They can sell the package directly to the tourist (tour operator) or through retailers (tour wholesaler). In the latter case, they would pay a commission to the retail travel agent.

Retail travel agents can package their own tours and sell them to the public and/or through other retailers.

Specialty Channelers.   People who are intermediaries between the retailer and the customer are known as *specialty channelers*. They may represent either the customer or the supplier and include incentive travel firms, meeting and convention planners, association executives, and corporate travel offices. Incentive travel firms put together and sell travel as an incentive to increase sales. They sell their ability to design, promote, and manage incentive travel programs. Other specialty channelers are employees who buy travel services at efficient costs for their organizations.

Supplier Choice.   Why would a supplier choose to give up control of the sale while paying a commission by distributing the product indirectly?

The major reason is cost. For many companies the cost of maintaining a sales network is prohibitive. To set up national and regional sales offices is very expensive and is a fixed cost—the salaries and rents must be paid irrespective of the sales volume produced. By contrast, the cost of selling through intermediaries is variable—a commission is paid only if a sale is made.

Additionally, the intermediary assists the supplier by checking customer credit, taking various individual payments, and paying the supplier in one sum.

Customer Choice.   Numerous reasons exist why the customer would wish to deal with an intermediary. In theory, the middleman offers unbiased professional assistance in selecting from a variety of travel products. For customers calling United Airlines by telephone, the reservationist at United will try to sell United products. A travel agent, on the other hand, will have access to and will be paid a commission on selling a variety of airline flights. The customer is offered a better selection and may find a less expensive and/or more convenient flight.

Both the knowledge and the experience of the intermediary are generally available to the traveler free of charge. In unusual situations where the cost of putting together an individualized itinerary involves a fee, travel agents, for example, will spend time advising clients on where to go, how to get there, what to see, and even how to pack.

The intermediary can often negotiate options for the traveler that the individual tourist cannot get. Because they deal in larger numbers of travelers, intermediaries have clout with suppliers to provide difficult-to-get theater tickets or special discounts, for example.

THE ROLE OF THE TOUR WHOLESALER

Size and Importance

Tour wholesalers combine transportation and ground services into a package that is then sold through a sales channel to the public.

History.   Tour wholesaling began in the mid-nineteenth century. In 1841 Thomas Cook chartered a train to carry several hundred people to a temperance meeting 20 miles away. In 1856 Cook led the first Grand Tour of Europe and, several years later, was offering cruises down the Nile, rail tours to India, and trips to the United States.

It was not until the advent of jet aircraft in 1958 that the packaging of tours increased significantly. Larger aircraft capable of flying greater distances stimulated the development of the package tour as we know it today. Because of the increased capacity of the airlines, prices were lowered. This, in turn, stimulated a demand for low-cost vacations. Tourists were able to travel farther with their two to three weeks of annual vacation. Crossing the Atlantic, for example, was cut from six days by liner and 24 hours by propeller aircraft to seven hours by jet. As a result, tour wholesalers came into the marketplace to put together low-cost package vacations.

Role in Industry.   There are over 1,000 tour operators in the United States today. The tour operator or wholesaler buys in bulk from industry suppliers. Instead of making a reservation for two nights' lodging, a wholesaler may contract for a hundred rooms for the months of June, July, and August. Similar arrangements would be made with airlines, ground transportation, and travel attractions. By buying in bulk the wholesaler gets a better rate than would the regular traveler.

After the wholesaler adds on the costs of doing business, profit, and commission to retailers, the cost savings are passed on to the customer. Typically, a wholesaler gains by making a small profit on each package sold to a large number of customers.

Definition.   Often used interchangeably, the terms *tour operator* and *tour wholesaler* are different. The operator sells packages directly to the public while the wholesaler sells the package through a retail travel agent.

Independent wholesalers make up about three-quarters of all wholesalers. This might be an individual or a corporation such as American Express. The remaining wholesalers are travel agencies that package tours, airlines that have their own wholesaling division, and travel clubs and incentive travel companies that do not sell to the general public.

Operators may specialize by segment of the market catered to, by destination, or by type of transportation used. Over 90 percent of tours sold by independent wholesalers involves air travel. However, some companies may specialize in cruises.

Tours may be independent, hosted, escorted, or special format. An independent tour offers few components—usually hotel plus one other land arrangement such as car hire. Tourists have maximum flexibility regarding departure and return dates. Additionally, they can extend their stay by paying an extra per diem charge.

A hosted tour includes the services of a host at each destination to make local arrangements. Travelers can still choose travel dates and hotel used.

An escorted tour is the most structured. A tour escort accompanies the tour throughout. Tourists begin and end the tour according to the operator's schedule and stay in hotels selected by the operator. Participants have little free time.

Special tour formats include incentive tours, pre- or postconvention tours, and special-interest tours.

Image of Group Tours

Group travel is perceived as an experience rather than "just" a method of travel. It is an experience shared with others; it is organized; it is passive and carefree. Those on tours give up a degree of personal control over the vacation in return for having someone plan and execute the trip for them. Because those planning the trip have experience and buying power, the package is less expensive than if the components were purchased separately by the tourist.

Tour Appeals.   People go on tours for reasons that are practical and emotional. The practical benefits are convenience, expertise, safety, and price.

Tours are convenient in that the vacation can be spent concentrating on the experience rather than on making the arrangements. Having someone else do the driving is important in terms of dealing with city traffic, driving in unfamiliar areas, and spending time reading maps rather than enjoying the scenery. Tours offer the convenience of being picked up and delivered to hotels, attractions, and entertainment. Accommodations and tickets to events are guaranteed. This is particularly important for high-season events or times. Lastly, the idea of the baggage being taken care of is appreciated. This is particularly true for single women and older people.

People who take tours feel that they can see and do more than if they were traveling alone. There is the feeling that the operator has the expertise to select the best places to see. Because of this, participants can actually see more because they do not have to spend time evaluating all of the options.

There is safety in numbers. This is particularly true for older or female travelers and for urban or "off-beat" destinations.

The fixed price of a tour is an important feature. The most important part, however, is not the absolute price but the fact that the costs are known beforehand. There is little or no danger of being halfway through one's vacation and running out of money because of poor budgeting. The tour is prepaid. The only other costs are some meals, sightseeing, and shopping.

People also take tours for emotional reasons—companionship, an opportunity to learn, to share activities, and for security. Tours offer the opportunity to meet new people and make new friends. Many see it as an opportunity to get an overview of a destination—to discover and learn. Adventure touring is important to younger travelers while historical touring is mentioned by older tourists.

Group travel is seen as a way of participating in activities with others who have the same interests. This can include physical-activity tours such as skiing or water sports as well as theater, garden, or historic homes tours. In all of this there is the opportunity to be further educated in a particular area.

The security component comes from the feeling of being an insider even in a strange place. This is an emotional appeal compared to the physical feeling of safety explored above.

Negatives. The negative images that people have about tours fall into four categories—perceptions of the bus, the tour experience, the group concept, and the types of people who take tours.

For a number of people, tours are associated rather negatively with buses. The term "motorcoach" is used by the industry to designate touring buses. Particularly in Europe, most coaches are extremely comfortable with videos, hostesses who serve drinks, and reclining seats. However, despite the fact that such equipment is available in the United States (albeit on a lesser scale), the image brought to mind is too often the school or commuter bus. The bus is seen as too slow, too confining, and too uncomfortable. It is viewed as a cheap and old-fashioned way to travel. Travelers also have a negative image of bus terminals and view this as an undesirable place to start a vacation. Additionally, some people—particularly men—dislike the idea of giving up control to the

Figure 11-3   The cynic's view of group tours! (Courtesy Hong Kong Tourist Association.)

coach driver. They complain about not being able to control the lights, the fans, or where and when to stop.

For people who do not take tours, the tour experience itself it perceived negatively. Touring, to many, is equated with regimentation, inflexibility, and passivity. The tour is seen as a shallow, boring, and impersonal experience. There are those who think that, rather than receiving the advantages of group power, being part of a group involves getting second-class treatment from hotels and restaurants.

Yet another barrier to be overcome in selling tours is the group aspect of the tour. There is a fear of not relating well to other members of the group. A vacation to many people involves having personal space and freedom. Being part of a group limits both.

Finally, many people have a negative perception of the kinds of people who take tours. People who travel as part of a group are seen, stereotypically, as infirm, older, inexperienced travelers. This translates into a personality profile of tourgoers as passive and lacking in self-confidence.

To overcome these negatives, those who package tours need to be more innovative in upgrading both the image and the content of tours. Perhaps even the word "tour" needs to be changed into "adventure holiday," "expedition," "discovery trip," or "excursion." Different modes of transportation can be used in conjunction with each other—air to get the traveler there and coach to see the destination. Hub-and-spoke concepts can be used to bring people to a destination where they can relax on their own. Shorter minitrips can be packaged with more free time, and tours with themes grouped around recreational activities can be developed to appeal to the younger, more active crowd.

Economics

The tour wholesaling business is one that is relatively easy to get into, that places an emphasis on cash flow, has a low return on sales, and a high potential for return on equity invested.

Ease of Entry.   The bus industry was deregulated in 1982, effectively ending control of the tour industry by the Interstate Commerce Commission. Since that time it has become easier for smaller operators to get into the business of wholesaling tours. To be considered a tour, a vacation must meet requirements of duration, price, and number of travelers. For travel agents to receive a commission, the air transportation element of the tour must meet the standards of the Airline Reporting Conference—for domestic tours—and the International Airlines Travel Agent Network—for international tours.

Wholesalers must also take out a performance bond—similar to an insurance policy—to protect travelers, travel agents, and suppliers in the event of bankruptcy by the wholesaler.

Cash Flow.   A wholesaler buys transportation and ground services in bulk. The wholesaler will pay a deposit on services contracted for. As the time of the tour draws closer the percentage of the deposit that is refunded if the tour is cancelled is reduced.

By buying in bulk, the unit cost to the wholesaler is reduced. The ground portion of the tour is marked up, added to any air component, and sold to the public. Commissions flow directly to the travel agent involved in selling the tour. Cash flow is generated by the wholesaler as deposits and final payments for the tour come in. Suppliers do not have to be paid until after they have provided the service being contracted for. The resulting "float" can finance the operation of the wholesaler's business.

When a wholesaler uses the float from one tour to finance a second tour, a reduction in demand can result in cash losses if there is insufficient equity in the business to carry the business downturn.

Return on Sales.   For independent tour wholesalers the average return on sales is about 3 percent. This means that, on a tour selling for $1,000, the net profit is approximately $30. The key to profits is volume—number of tours sold. Out of the revenue received from the traveler, the wholesaler must pay the suppliers and the travel agent who sold the package. This accounts for 85 to 90 percent of the revenue. With what is left—gross profit—the wholesaler must pay for the costs of operating the business. Net profit is what remains after the operating costs are paid.

Return on Equity.   Return on equity is the ratio of net income divided by owner's equity. Because the amount of money invested is relatively small there is an opportunity for a high return on equity.

Tour Preparation

The preparation for a tour begins up to 18 months prior to departure.

Fourteen to Eighteen Months Prior.   Market research is the starting point for any tour, and this is the time to prepare. Based on an analysis of travel research, tourist trends, what the competition is doing, and a survey of retailers and travelers, wholesalers get an indication of what will likely sell.

The best destinations are those that are popular, have adequate facilities, appeal to a broad group, are far away, offer good weather, and have the recommendation of an agent.[1] Popular destinations are easier to sell. Certain destination such as Acapulco, Puerto Rico, and Hawaii have developed a very popular and positive image over the years. The facilities important for a group are:

1. Convenient transportation.
2. Hotels with a variety of function space.
3. A variety of hotel types and prices.

Destinations that offer a wide variety of things to do and see are more attractive because while one part of the group is viewing historic sites others can be off shopping.

Distant destinations can be appealing to both the agent selling the tour and to the traveler. Much of the selling agent's income derives from commissions on the air part of the tour. The greater the distance traveled, the greater the cost of the air fare and the greater the agent's commission. Yet there are also savings for the traveler. One of the advantages of buying a package is the saving on the air fare. The number of dollars saved on a long trip is greater than that on a shorter one.

Finally, a destination should have good weather and the support of the agents selling it. Poor weather can limit the activities that people can

Figure 11-4   Waihirere Maori Club. Tours usually include entrance to local attractions. (Courtesy New Zealand Tourist & Publicity Office.)

undertake during a vacation. Of course, destinations will offer off-season rates in order to entice travel in the low season. Thus, support of the people who will ultimately sell the package is important if the tour is to make money.

Detailed tour specifications can then be developed on departure dates, length of the tour, and transportation and ground services to be used.

Of special importance are considerations of distance, the amount of free time, planning for shopping, and the location of accommodations. The distance that can be covered in a day will vary greatly depending on the terrain and quality of roads. The amount of touring should vary each day, with a long touring day followed by a day of shorter travel. Two- and three-night stopovers help travelers catch up on laundry and rest. Packing and unpacking each day can be both tiring and unsettling.

The number of items to plan compared to the amount of free time available is a matter of cost and convenience. The fewer meals and side trips planned for and included in the basic tour price, the more expensive the add-ons will be for the travelers. This, of course, works against one of the major advantages of buying a package—knowing the price in advance. Yet most people will want to have some time and choice of meals and activities to themselves. The key is that items should not be included in the basic price if travelers have the time to do them on their own, if there are different interests among the group members, and if it is convenient and not too expensive for them to do so.

Certain activities and meals should be included. If an early morning departure is called for, breakfast should be included—preferably a buffet. The same thing is true for dinner after a long day of travel. There should be a group activity shortly into the tour—to allow travelers to get to know each other and to set an upbeat tone for the tour—and one at the end to allow for a grand finale.

Shopping is a very important part of any holiday. Hence, organizers must be aware of early closing times and local holidays.

The choice of hotel is often a balance between cost and convenience. Hotels outside the city may be less expensive, but they are often far from shopping, restaurants, and nightlife.

Twelve to Fourten Months Prior.   Ground services are negotiated and transportation arranged during this time; contracts may also be signed.

Ten to Twelve Months Prior.   This is the period when tour programs are finalized and a selling price reached. Cost figures are tallied and a markup added that will cover overhead and profit. Costs may be either *fixed* or *variable.* A fixed cost is one that must be paid irrespective of the number of travelers. The cost of chartering a coach or hiring a tour escort is a

Figure 11-5   Tour organizers must be aware of shopping hours. (Courtesy New Zealand Tourist & Publicity Office.)

fixed cost. The pro-rated share of such a cost is spread over the anticipated number of travelers. A variable cost is one that is charged per traveler. Charges for hotel rooms, meals, or admission tickets to an attraction are examples of variable costs. Finally, the method of handling reservations is determined during this time.

Tour Marketing

Ten to Twelve Months Prior.   This is the period when brochure production begins. The cost of producing brochures is often shared by suppliers, especially transportation companies. Suppliers may offer *shells* to the wholesaler for personalizing. Shells are brochures that have color photographs with a minimum of copy. The wholesaler adds the copy specific to the tour, outlining the features and statement of conditions. This latter includes such things as what is and is not included, how to make a reservation, procedures for putting down a deposit and final payment, any travel documents required, and a refund policy.

Commission rates and incentives for selling specific numbers of packages can be negotiated with retailers.

Six to Eight Months Prior.   Selling of the tour now begins in earnest. At this point is would be helpful to examine the process by which people choose a tour.

The decision process for many is, in fact, a two-step process. First, the decision is made to travel with a group. Second, the particular tour and/or tour company is chosen. The first step is often to decide which friend or organization to travel with. This seems to be particularly important for singles, especially single women. In fact, it is usually a friend who introduces others to the idea of group travel. In fewer cases do advertisements influence the choice of a tour. Personal experience in using a particular operator and word-of-mouth endorsement from friends and relatives is especially important.

Some differences exist by market segment. Preformed groups are those people who belong to clubs or associations. For these people the destination or company used is secondary to the idea of being with their friends, having fun, and getting away. Travelers who book individually have often formed their own mini-performed group consisting of people who are compatible with each other. One sale can mean four sales. Single older women place a great emphasis on being able to travel safely and securely with others like themselves, whereas for younger single women, adventure and the ability to participate are valued. Price is a more important consideration for this group than for others.

Marketing programs will usually involve the distribution of brochures, media advertising, personal selling, and communication with other wholesalers. There are almost 30,000 retail travel agencies in the United States, and it is obviously costly to distribute brochures to all of them. However, target marketing can reduce the number. Wholesalers can work with retailers who have sold for them before or who are in the geographic areas where the tours would sell—northern cites, for example, for winter tours to the Caribbean. Wholesalers can also identify agencies located in places where the surrounding people have the income to enable them to buy the package.

Media advertising will follow the principles outlined in the previous chapter. Because of the high cost of promotion and distribution, wholesalers in one part of the country may use wholesalers from another part of the country to distribute their tours in that region for a fee.

Marketing efforts may continue up to a few days before the actual tour begins. Since the tour is going anyway, travelers can pick up last-minute bargains if they are flexible as to destination. In Britain, for example, the windows of retail travel agents are often plastered with last-minute savings on tours leaving within the next few weeks. A weekly travel show on British television also offers bargains for the upcoming week. If a plane is chartered and is leaving with ten spaces on board, the wholesaler, at the last minute, will accept reduced prices to bring in some income. If the break-even costs have been met, this extra income, once direct costs have been subtracted, is profit.

Reservations, deposits, and final payments are usually required one to two months prior to departure. Reservations are usually received by telephone from retailers. They are confirmed, recorded, and filed. After the payments have been processed the documents necessary for the tour are sent to the retailer, who will pass them on to the traveler. Suppliers will be paid after the tour.

Tour Operation

Crucial Factors.   For the traveler, the success, or otherwise, of a tour depends upon the tour escort, the extent to which the tour is personalized, the pace of the tour, and the value received.

For many people the tour escort or guide is the person who can make or break a tour. Factors considered important are:

1. How knowledgeable is the guide with the places and sights that are part of the tour?
2. To what extent is the guide able to take care of such problems as poor hotel space, bad meals, and disruptive passengers?
3. How interested is the escort or guide in the group as people as distinct from customers?
4. To what extent is the guide able to create a fun atmosphere?

Group leaders, on the other hand, place a great deal of emphasis on the importance of the driver in giving assistance and even serving as a second host.

The second factor considered important by travelers to the success of the operation of a tour is the degree of personalized service received and the way in which it is delivered. To what extent does the operator, as well as the escort, attempt to get to know the traveler? Some operators extend themselves in such ways as requesting that they be informed of special personal occasions that will occur during the trip. In these instances a birthday cake is arranged, or a gift certificate presented to celebrate a wedding anniversary. Other operators have been known to ask travelers to contact relatives at the tour's destination and to invite them to join the group for one of the tour meals.

The pace of the tour and, in particular, the balance between organized activities and free time is also important. This means less travel time each day, fewer one-night stays, and more opportunities to do individual things at the destinations.

Tour operators are expected to deliver both the physical aspects of the tour—the coach, hotels, meals, and sights—as well as the experience—the fun and flavor of the trip. Thus, it is vital that travelers get what is promised in the brochure. Beyond that, however, is the inclusion of something not mentioned in the brochure—a surprise. It might be an extra outing, a special meal—something perceived to be for free. Some operators say that they advertise 90 percent of what they will deliver. The 90 percent is enough to sell the tour. The extra 10 percent is the surprise or added value. It might be called "planned spontaneity." Often on a vacation it is the unexpected that people most remember. If this can be part of the tour, unknown to the travelers beforehand, it becomes something to talk about afterwards.

Tour Operator Needs

The success of the tour will depend upon the extent to which the operator and supplier meet the needs of each other (and, therefore, the tour group).

In general, tour operators look to suppliers to provide:

1. Services and facilities that are convenient to the main tour route;
2. A staging area for the motorcoach close to the facility entrance to load and unload passengers;
3. A convenient place to service the restroom on the coach;
4. A positive attitude on the part of the staff toward group members.

Supplier Needs

A supplier, at the same time, expects the following from the tour operator:

1. A complete list of those on the tour;
2. Specific arrival and departure times;
3. A complete rooming list, detailing the number of different types of rooms needed;
4. Credit information to set up billing procedures;
5. Confirmation and deposit dates;
6. Notification of any special needs—for handicapped passengers, for example;
7. Complete tour itinerary (this might enable the supplier to suggest additions such as places to eat and sights to see).

Attractions.   It is helpful to the operator if attractions provide a brief description of their facility that might be included in the tour brochure. This helps not only the operator but also the attraction. Brochures from the attraction can be sent to the supplier for distribution to the tour members en route. This increases the anticipation of the tour members prior to the visit.

Figure 11–6   Tour escorts must know the appropriate behavior when visiting centers of worship. Wong Tai Sin Temple, Kowloon Peninsula. (Courtesy Hong Kong Tourist Association.)

Accommodations.   After a day of traveling a tour group wants a friendly reception and some extra amenities. Often a group will get impersonal treatment from staff members who think that, because 40 people arrive at once, they will only expect "group treatment." Thus, the ability to treat each member of a group as an individual is important. Some kind of hospitality reception is appreciated—a wine and cheese or cocktail party can put everyone in a happy mood.

Because group travelers usually travel in pairs, operators will select hotels that offer rooms with two beds—a double-double. Many properties offer either a welcome package or a farewell gift that ties into the destination—a small souvenir or something to eat and/or drink.

The recommendation of the escort is crucial to the continued use of a hotel by an operator. A debriefing by the management of the hotel with the escort before the group vacates the property is vital. Any problems that arise can be taken care of before the group departs. This way the tour members can leave satisfied.

Restaurants.   People on a tour spend approximately one-quarter of their waking hours and more money per day in restaurants than in any other

Figure 11-7 Eating is a big part of any tour. (Courtesy Hong Kong Tourist Association.)

tour component. Success of the meal depends upon the quality of the food, the quality of the service, and the facilities.

Restaurants should be able to serve the group in 60 to 90 minutes. There should be a variety of selections on the menu to accommodate both heavy and light eaters. As with hotels, the level of service given to groups should be the same as that given to other diners. The restaurant should market itself to the operator as the place to be to get a flavor of the area being visited.

Ships and Airlines.   Suppliers who offer special areas and procedures for the boarding of groups are appreciated by the tour operator. Preassigned seating on planes is an important feature.

Motorcoaches.   Operators are concerned with the dependability and safety record of the bus company and the equipment. As mentioned before, the driver is crucial to the success of the tour. Small items such as having the group's name on the outside of the motorcoach adds a personalized touch in addition to making it easier to find the right coach in a parking lot full of them. On board the bus, the quality of the audio system is very important.

Sightseeing.   An operator will often hire the services of a local guide or courier when in a metropolitan area. The driver, tour escort, and local courier must operate as a team with a joint goal of offering a fun experience for the group members. Usually the escort will relinquish control of the tour to the local courier for the duration of the sightseeing trip.

The local courier is expected to offer commentary that is not only factually correct but also entertaining. Some items of local current interest or historical anecdotes can enliven the tour. If free evenings are part of the stop the courier should be able to make appropriate suggestions on things to do and places to eat.

Follow-up

The end of the tour need not be the end of the vacation. Part of the entire experience are the reminiscences afterwards. It was previously noted that word-of-mouth advertising was the most effective means of selling people on group tours. For these reasons follow-up is important. Follow-up can be in the form of "welcome home" letters and/or reunions. Reunions can be tied to the tour itself—with music, food, and drinks linked to the tour that was taken. Tour members can be encouraged to bring along slides and photographs as well as friends, and small prizes can be awarded for photos and slides in different categories. The reunion then becomes the staging area for the next tour.

ROLE OF THE RETAIL TRAVEL AGENT

Introduction

Retail travel agents are the most important travel intermediary. They act as sales outlets for suppliers and wholesalers from whom they receive commission for any sales made. They also act as travel counselor, advising people on when, where, and how to travel; as salesperson actively selling travel, and as clerk, making reservations in response to customer requests.

Historical Development

Thomas Cook.   In 1841 Thomas Cook chartered a train to take people the 20 miles from Leicester to Loughborough to attend a temperance meeting. He is credited with being the first travel agent. Soon came trips to Europe and, in 1866, Cook organized and led a tour of the Civil War battlefields, Niagara Falls, New York City, and Toronto, Canada. In 1872 he escorted a group of travelers around the world. It is said that this trip inspired the Jules Verne book *Around the World in 80 Days.* In 1873 he introduced the "circular note," the forerunner of the present-day traveler's check. The notes were issued originally in denominations of five and ten pounds and could be exchanged for local currency at prevailing exchange rates in any hotels that were part of the Cook system. This meant that people no longer had to travel with large amounts of cash on their person.

United States.   In the United States in the early 1900s the travel agent of the day was the hotel porter. Rail travel was the predominant form of transportation, and most of the travel was undertaken for business purposes. The porter would make reservations for the business traveler staying at the hotel. A commission was paid by the railroad to the porter who would add a delivery charge for going to the railroad station to pick up the ticket.

When the airlines, in the late 1920s, first purchased planes with seats for passengers they saw the railroads as their main competition for the business traveler. They provided ticket stock to the hotel porters and offered them a 5 percent commission for making the sale.

As traffic expanded, the airlines opened offices in hotels where they did a large business. The new breed of travel agent was prohibited by the airlines from opening an office if it would compete with the airline's own sales office. Up until 1959 a travel agency could be opened only if it was sponsored by an airline and its opening approved by two-thirds of the carriers represented by the appropriate domestic or international travel conference.

Travel Agency Growth.   The growth of travel agents can be attributed to two trends that occurred after World War II. These were the growth of international travel and the increase in personal or pleasure travel. Both groups of travelers have an increased tendency to use a travel agent. They have neither the time nor the expertise to make their own travel arrangements.

The recent growth of retail travel agencies can be seen by comparing industry figures from 1978 to 1987. In 1978 14,804 agencies accounted for $19.4 million in industry sales, an average of $1.31 million per agency. In 1987 29,584 agencies were responsible for $64,237,000 in revenue, an average of $2,171,000.

Industry Profile

Every two years *Travel Weekly* publishes a Louis Harris survey of the retail travel industry. Some of the highlights from their 1988 survey indicate that:

- Since airline deregulation in late 1987 the number of travel agency locations in the United States has practically doubled; of all locations, almost one-third are in the East, almost one-half in suburban areas.
- While annual dollar volume of business has grown steadily since 1978, the percentage change from study to study was the lowest in 1987.
- While almost two-thirds of agency locations have average annual revenues of less than $2 million there is an increase in those whose annual revenues total $5 million or more. Seven percent of agency locations fell into this category.
- The share of domestic travel as a percentage of total dollar vol-

ume has risen from 63 percent in 1978 to 70 percent in 1987; the share of international travel has declined from 37 percent to 30 percent in these same years.

- Business-related travel and personal and pleasure travel each account for 50 percent of the industry's volume. The share of the business market has declined and that of pleasure/personal has increased by three percentage points over the past two years.

- Travel agents continue to be influential in affecting decisions made by both pleasure and business travelers. Almost half of all pleasure travelers sought advice on the choice of a particular destination while even larger percentages look for advice on the choice of airline, hotel, package tour, car rental, and side-trip selection. At least four in ten business travelers seek advice on the choice of airline, hotel, and car rental.

- Ninety-five percent of all agencies now have automated reservations systems. Apollo and Sabre are the most popular systems. Thirty-eight percent have an automated accounting system.

- Two-thirds of all agencies are single-location offices not affiliated with groups or consortiums, and they employ, on average, six full-time employees per location.

Regulations Governing Travel Agencies

Although regulations imposed on retail travel agents are not as stringent compared to the days before airline deregulation and the consequent competitive marketing decision, agencies still confront a variety of regulations to get into and stay in business.

Certification. The effect of deregulation can be seen from the fact that approximately one-half of agencies in business today were started after 1980. To be certified for business as a travel agency the business must be appointed or approved by industry conferences. The four major conferences in the United States are:

1. Airline Reporting Corporation (ARC)—for the selling of domestic air tickets.
2. International Airlines Travel Agent Network—for the selling of international air tickets.
3. Cruise Lines International Association (CLIA)—for selling cruises.
4. National Railroad Passenger Corporation (Amtrak)—for selling domestic rail tickets.

Each conference is made up of companies that sell transportation. The ARC consists of domestic airlines. Normally, an agency will apply for an ARC appointment first. To receive an ARC appointment an agency must:

1. Be open for business and actively selling air tickets. Prior to receiving approval, tickets are obtained from the airlines on payment of cash, then sold to customers. After approval has been granted, commissions are received retroactively.
2. The agency must be managed by someone with a minimum of two years' experience in selling tickets and one year's experience in issuing tickets.
3. The agency must be visible from the street, clearly identified as a travel agency, and easily accessible to the general public.
4. The agency must have a minimum bond of $10,000 and a cash reserve of at least $25,000. Accreditation can take up to two years. The cash reserve is necessary to sustain the business during this time.
5. The agency must be actively involved in promoting travel.

Once the ARC appointment has been secured the other appointments are usually issued as a matter of course.

When operating as a business, agencies are regulated as to the amount of ticket stock they can have on hand and the procedures for handling it. Ticket stock is like a blank check and requires stiff security. Agencies are not allowed to change ownership without meeting conference regulations.

Licensing.   In addition to industry appointments a number of states require travel agents to be licensed and to pass examination by state licensing boards.

Customer Protection.   Agents are also held responsible for their actions in running their business. Agents pride themselves as being travel counselors rather than booking agents. Thus, they can be held responsible for the quality of their advice. They must take the age and health of the client and the situation at the destination into account in recommending an appropriate trip.

Situations have arisen where a customer buys a tour package through a travel agent and prior to the vacation the tour wholesaler goes bankrupt. Courts have held that, when the customer was unaware of the existence on any other intermediaries in the purchase of the tour, the retailer was liable for the customer's loss. Agencies can protect themselves by dealing with reputable wholesalers, buying insurance, and explaining and having travelers sign a disclaimer.

Industry Education.   Through such industry groups as the Institute of Certified Travel Agents (ICTA), The American Society of Travel Agents (ASTA), and The Association of Retail Travel Agents (ARTA), professional standards, while not regulated, are encouraged. Both ASTA and ICTA offer home study courses. The ICTA courses lead to the designation CTC, or Certified Travel Counselor.

Running a Travel Agency

Retail travel agents receive income in the form of commissions paid by suppliers and wholesalers. A commission is a percentage of the total sale. The traveler does not pay for the services of a travel agent when a booking is made by the agent.

Commissions

In the past the ATC regulated the percentage of commission paid by the airlines. Deregulation, however, has meant that airlines can pay different percentages of commissions to the agents they deal with. Suppliers can also pay overrides or bonuses for volume sales. A wholesaler may offer a graduated rate schedule to stimulate the retailer to sell more. As the number of bookings increase beyond certain points, the commission percentage increases. Often these overrides are retroactive—the higher percentage commission applies to earlier bookings within a given time frame. It may be, for example, that the basic commission for selling

Figure 11–8   Travel agents are expected to know the location of the best beaches. (Courtesy New Zealand Tourist & Publicity Office.)

a package is 10 percent. An override or incentive commission may be offered of 1 percent for bookings over $15,000; 2 percent for bookings over $20,000; 3 percent over $25,000, etc. An agent selling $26,000 worth of bookings would receive a commission of 13 percent on all bookings under a retroactive override system.

Rebates

In order to attract customers some agencies offer rebates for volume business to them. In this case an agency would split the commission received with the customer, which is usually a company doing a large volume business with the agency. While this is legal for domestic air travel it is against the law to rebate international air travel. It is not uncommon for such rebating to go on, however.

Sources of Income

Almost 60 percent of the average agency's income comes from commissions from selling some form of air travel. American agencies are responsible for selling 70 percent of domestic and 80 percent of international air travel. The average commission received is 10 percent, slightly less than this for domestic air, slightly more for international. The average revenue per air ticket in 1986 was $20.99, indicating an average fare of just under $200.

Income from the cruise lines comprises, on average, 16 percent of travel agency income, and travel agents book 95 percent of all cruises sold in the United States.

Commissions from hotels account for 11 percent of agency income. Agents are responsible for 25 percent of domestic and 85 percent of international sales to hotels.

Car rental business accounts for 8 percent of U.S. travel agency business, and approximately half of all car rental sales are made through travel agents.

Rail travel accounts for only 3 percent of agency business nationwide. Just over one-third of rail ticket sales are made by retailers.

Commissions from package tours can run from 11 to 22 percent. Retail travel agents account for 90 percent of all package tour sales.

Other Income Sources.   Two additional sources of income for agencies are service charges and sales of travel-related products and services.

Over the past few years there has been some discussion among agents about levying a charge for services rendered to travelers. The argument is made that a "travel counselor," in giving professional advice, should charge for that advice. Such a move, some feel, would help professionalize the industry. This argument has received some backing because

Figure 11-9   Tudor Towers, Roturua, New Zealand. Travel agents make commissions from hotels and other suppliers. (Courtesy New Zealand Tourist & Publicity Office.)

low air fares have reduced the dollar amount of commission received. However, the public is not yet ready to pay for an agent making a reservation, but some agencies do charge for drawing up complicated itineraries and making trip cancellations.

There are travel-related services that some full-service agencies provide to increase their income. These include such things as personal, baggage, and trip cancellation insurance; providing travelers checks and foreign currency; and taking passport photos.

Maximizing Profit

According to *Travel Agent* magazine the value of an agency is increased if:

1. It does not depend on one account for more than 10 percent of its gross.
2. The employee turnover rate is less than 20 percent a year.
3. The agency is more than three years old.

4. At least 75 percent of sales are on credit card.

5. At least 20 percent of airline sales are international.

6. The agency's primary automation vendor has paid overrides for each of the last six quarters.

7. The agency does not consider any mega-agency as a major competitor.

8. The percentage of refunds to tickets issued is less than 15 percent.

9. The percentage of nonowner salaries to total expenses is less than 55 percent.

10. The percentage of premises rent to total expenses is less than eight percent.

11. The average ticket price is more than $230.

12. The agency's ticket prices have risen over the past ten months.[2]

Summary

Tourist products and services can either be distributed directly to the traveler or through a variety of intermediaries. The high cost of marketing is a major reason for suppliers to use middlemen in the distribution channel.

Tour wholesalers and operators are major players in distributing travel and tourism. Whether selling through retail travel agents or directly to the public, they offer a variety of group tours for vacationers to enjoy. The advantages of group travel—cost and convenience—will ensure the future growth of this segment of the business.

Retail travel agents are the most important travel intermediary. They receive income from suppliers and wholesalers in the form of commissions and overrides on sales made. Some receive additional income from the traveler when they charge for services rendered in putting together a complicated itinerary or through selling related travel services.

Retail agents will probably continue to be the primary travel distributor because suppliers are so heavily dependent on them for the selling of travel products.

ENDNOTES

1. Ralph G. Phillips and Susan Webster, *Group Travel Operating Procedures* (New York: Van Nostrand Reinhold, 1983).

2. Dawn M. Barclay, "Want to Sell Your Agency? There's No Time Like the Present." *Travel Agent* magazine, September 12, 1988, p. 40.

S T U D Y   QUESTIONS

1. What are the functions of a tourism distribution system?
2. Why would a supplier utilize an indirect form of distribution?
3. Why would a consumer utilize a travel intermediary?
4. What led to the increase in package tours?
5. Why do people go on group tours?
6. What are the negative images that people have regarding group tours?
7. What are the economic characteristics of tour wholesaling?
8. What characteristics should a destination possess to have tour appeal?
9. What factors do travelers consider important in the operation of a tour?
10. What requirements must a retail travel agency satisfy before receiving an appointment from the Airline Reporting Corporation (ARC)?

D I S C U S S I O N   QUESTIONS

1. Compare and contrast a direct tourism distribution system with the various indirect distribution systems.
2. Which would a tourist and a supplier prefer—a direct or an indirect distribution system? Why?
3. Why do people take group tours? What barriers have to be overcome to encourage more people to take them?
4. What is involved in the preparation, marketing, and operation of a group tour?
5. Discuss the development and present-day importance of the retail travel agent to tourism.
6. How do travel agents make money and maximize their earnings?

12

FUTURE TRENDS

At the end of this chapter the reader will be able to:

- Determine how changes in the marketplace will affect the shape of tomorrow's tourism.
- Define and correctly use the following terms:

Generational influence	Family market
Baby boomlet	Baby bust
Baby boomers	World War II babies
Demographic changes	Leisure time availability
Changing consumer tastes	Automation

INTRODUCTION

It is forecasted that tourism will be one of the largest "industries" by the year 2000. The World Tourism Organization estimates an annual growth rate of arrivals in cross-border tourism to be between 4.5 percent and 5.5 percent for the next 20 years. Various trends in the demand for and the supply of tourism substantiate that optimism. Notwithstanding the barriers to continued travel, tourism will continue to grow. Its growth may, however, be in a form different from that experienced today.

INFLUENCES ON DEMAND

The demand for tourism is influenced by the size and structure of the population, the amount and distribution of discretionary income, the amount and distribution of leisure time, and changing consumer tastes.

Population

In terms of absolute numbers of people, the leading *growth* countries of the world in the first half of the twenty-first century will be:

Country	Population in 2033 (in millions)
China	1,516
India	1,311
USSR	366
Nigeria	335
Brazil	333
United States	306
Indonesia	261

Country	Population in 2033 (in millions)
Japan	131
Mexico	117
Philippines	117
France	57
Canada	38

It should be noted that, for many of these countries, the potential for them to generate tourists will be severely limited by factors such as the amount of time and money available to travel. If, however, only a fraction of Chinese, Indians, and Russians travel, their impact will be enormous.

Shrinking Family Market. The major effect in North America, as far as population is concerned, has been a relatively small rate of population growth and vast structural changes. From now until the year 2000, the U.S. population will grow at its slowest rate since the 1930s—0.7 percent a year. There has been a reduction in the size of the traditional family unit together with a shrinking of the importance of the typical family market.

By the year 2000 the proportion of people in each of the major age groups will be as follows:

Group	Age in 2000	% of Population
Baby boomlet	12–23	17
Baby bust	24–35	17
Late baby boom	36–45	21
Early baby boom	46–54	18
World War II babies	55–65	11
Depression babies	66–76	8
World War I babies	77 +	8

The typical family market shrank as a result of the postponement of marriage and childbearing together with a higher incidence of divorce. In 1959 the percentage of wife-husband households was 78 percent; in the mid-1970s it was 70 percent; in the mid-1980s the figure was 60 percent; by 1990 it will be 55 percent. This group will rise numerically, however, as the baby boomers mature into the 25 to 44 age group.

Those couples having children are choosing to have fewer offspring.

In 1910 the average household consisted of 4.5 persons; that number has dwindled to 2.7 and will likely shrink more.

Typically, the presence of children in a family has been a deterrent to international travel. As more people delay marriage and having children, or decide not to have children, there will be an increased propensity for international travel.

More Middle/Older Age Travelers.   There has been an increase in the number of middle and older age groups together with more people retiring earlier. Over half the population of the United States is between the ages of 25 and 44. This group is both willing and financially able to travel. In 1990 this group will control 44 percent of all households and 55 percent of all consumer spending in the United States. By 2011 this group will reach retirement age and will be prime prospects for travel.

In 1900, Americans over 65 comprised 4 percent of the population; in 1990 they will comprise 15 percent of all Americans; by 2030 one in five Americans will be over 65. As more people retire earlier they have the time, the health, and the money to travel. Only one person out of every four works until forced to retire by law. There are, however, barriers to travel that this group experiences. Having grown up during the Great Depression, many still regard travel as a luxury and choose low-cost vacations instead. For widows and widowers the lack of a companion may present a barrier to travel. The travel supplier can take the lead here in

Figure 12–1   More middle- and older-age travelers. (Courtesy Hong Kong Tourist Association.)

arranging groups of single seniors to take trips together. Because of their age, safety and security are major concerns for this group.

More Education. Children in the United States attend school an average of six hours a day, 180 days a year. In Europe and Asia, children average eight hours a day, 240 days a year. It is likely that the United States will follow the trend toward longer school days and a longer school year. Additionally, more people are attending college.

The more education people have, the more curious they become about the world around them. Opening the frontiers of a person's mind will increase the desire to experience more of life and more of the world.

More Working Women. Since 1970 the number of female workers has been increasing more than twice as fast as the number of male workers. In 1986 the nation's pool of 13.8 million professional workers had 29,000 more women than men. More females than males are being graduated from college and more women are choosing business majors than ever before. Multiearner families are more than 55 percent of all families.

This means that more families have more money to travel and more reason to "get away" from the work scene. It also means that there will be an increase in the number of women traveling on business.

Movement to the Sun Belt. The recent past has seen a population movement to the South and West. Regionally, these areas have a higher incidence of people taking trips (as defined by the U.S. Travel Data Center). This movement will continue. As more and more people move to other regions of the country the potential expands for family visits and reunions. The major reason for domestic travel in the United States is to visit friends and family. Population movements will increase the rationale for such trips.

The large number of "snowbirds"—seniors who migrate from the North to the South during the winter months—should also be mentioned in this regard.

Income

In the world's industrialized countries smaller families are becoming the norm. As a result, the average disposable income per household is increasing. As incomes increase the proportion spent on necessities lessens, leaving more money available for discretionary spending. There is an increased tendency to spend this discretionary income on leisure, recreation, and travel—buying experiences rather than possessions.

Leisure

Both travel and tourism are affected greatly by the amount and distribution of leisure time available and by the way people choose to use it.

Weekly Leisure Time.   It is widely reported that the average workweek in the United States is less than 40 hours. There is evidence to suggest, however, that it is much higher and that, in fact, the amount of free time available on a weekly basis has declined over the past 10 to 15 years.

A study by Louis Harris and Associates in 1985 found that the median workweek increased from 43.1 hours in 1975 to 47.3 hours in 1984. Median time for leisure declined in those same years from 24.3 hours a week to 18.1 hours. The same study indicated that, on average, women have 15.6 hours of leisure a week compared to 20.3 hours for men.

There are several reasons for this movement. In times of economic uncertainty, employers tend to have employees work longer hours rather than hire additional employees. More time is devoted to commuting, going to school, and, in the case of women, combining work outside the home with housework in the home. Leisure time is taken up with a variety of do-it-yourself projects as the cost of services continues to rise. Additionally, many people moonlight at a second job. Finally, the United States, as well as many other industrial nations, is experiencing a movement from manufacturing into services with an increase in the numbers of salaried employees who tend to work longer hours with a "fuzzy" relationship between work and leisure. A manager is more likely than a manual worker to take work home in the evening.

Little progress has been made in the United States in "flex time," job sharing, and the four-day workweek.

Because of these factors the amount of free or leisure time available each week may actually be less than it was a decade ago.

Holidays.   In another way the amount of leisure time available for travel and tourism is increasing. For travel purposes the amount of free time on a daily basis is of less concern than that available over extended periods of time.

A major trend in leisure time that is expected to grow is the increase in the number of three-day weekends. People are demanding—and getting—more leisure time in blocks. The three-day weekend allows a greater number of short getaways from the stresses of the workplace. With more families with two spouses in the work force it is often easier to arrange time off for both over a shorter holiday time slot.

On average, American workers have nine vacations days a year. This number is far less than in Europe and is likely to grow as more people enter the ranks of salaried employees.

Consumer Tastes

Despite the pressures noted above it is clear that there is a leisure ethic present among today's citizens. After World War II there was a movement in values to the present, the self, to greater permissiveness, and an interest in social causes. During this time leisure became associated with the so-called good life. While we have seen a weakening of the focus on self and an increased orientation toward the future coupled with a renewed interest in the family, one thing has not changed. That is the idea that we are entitled to periods of leisure.

Given the scope of demographic, economic, and social changes, we can expect the following:

- Increased differentiation of demand. There is a growing need for individualized service packages.

- Increased desire to relate to nature, to experience things first-hand, and to be involved in active pursuits or adventure trips. These may involve visits to off-beat destinations, the use of unusual modes of transportation, or the chance to pursue unusual hobbies or interests.

- Increased desire to learn, which may show itself in a willingness to know foreign cultures.

- Fitness/wellness centers. It is estimated that by the year 2000, about 85 to 90 percent of insurance carriers will expand coverage

Figure 12–2 More people want active vacations. (Courtesy New Zealand Tourist & Publicity Office.)

or offer reduced rates to people who practice "preventative maintenance." There will be an increased demand for pampering associated with fitness clubs. Resorts can sell tourists on the idea of doing something for themselves while saving money through the lowering of insurance rates.

- Leisure will be more highly planned and deliberate.

As consumers increasingly become better educated they will become more critical of the offerings for their important, yet scarce, leisure time. They will place more pressure on tourism suppliers to deliver quality experiences.

Generational Influence.   The term "generational influence" refers to the idea that people who came of age during a particular decade share a common set of values and attitudes. These values and attitudes help shape the buying behavior of that particular group. It is useful to examine the demographic groups in the United States in the year 2000 in light of their generational influences on vacation purchase behavior.

Seven generational groups were identified earlier in this chapter. The *baby boomlets* will have traveled extensively with their parents and will have been socialized to the idea of travel.

The *baby busters* were raised in the socially interactive years of the 1980s. They may prefer to travel independently in the future. However, the convenience of buying a package will appeal to their need to save time, a factor important to them.

The *baby boomers* came of age in the 1970s. Because of their numbers, they faced great competition for jobs. This may have influenced the emphasis on self that is important to this group. By the year 2000 there will be a growing number of time-constrained working parents looking for opportunities to create worthwhile family experiences. Because of frustrations in the workplace there may be a desire for fulfilling hobbies. Leisure and vacation choices may be tied to these in addition to family vacation opportunities. Because of the familiarity and sophistication of this group they will demand a particularly high level of service.

The *early baby boomers* grew up in the accepting years of the 1960s. Over the next 10 years this group will reach the peak of its earning potential. Many will have sent their children to college and will have acquired long-term assets. This group may also include a segment of early semi-retirees. Because of the social environment of acceptance that was prevalent when this group came of age, the less traditional destinations could be very attractive to them.

World War II babies grew up in the 1950s and come to the marketplace with a strong work ethic and the need to "earn" their leisure. Encouraged to take early retirement, this segment may be good prospects for off-season and shoulder-season travel. Their upbringing may make them prone to choose vacation opportunities for social interaction and personal growth.

Depression babies were influenced by the 1940s—a time for patriotism and personal sacrifice. While they will have the time, money, and health to travel, they are averse to credit and seek bargains. Their strong family ties may lead to opportunities for travel with grandchildren whose parents are working. Against this must be noted "grandparent angst"— the feeling of worry coming from the reluctance of one's children to have children of their own. If the trend toward low fertility rates continues, there may be fewer grandchildren around in the year 2000 (and, consequently, less reason to visit family).

World War I babies have never been active travelers. They will offer the travel industries a picture of what the twenty-first century will be like when American society begins to be dominated by older Americans.

Business Travel

The demand for business travel is a function of four factors—economic, regulatory, communications, and automation. Other factors such as marketing policies and political and social developments influence the pattern of, and market shares within, business travel rather than how well it develops.

Economic.   The rate of growth of the economy determines the size and rate of change of the market for business travel. Strong trade, invest-

Figure 12-3   The early baby boomers will look for less traditional destinations. (Courtesy Australian Tourist Association.)

ment, and output growth are positive signs for business travel, whereas high interest rates and unemployment levels bring business volume down. The long-range forecast for the United States remains favorable despite major structural changes in the labor force.

Variations in currency exchange rates are another important economic consideration in the demand for business travel. When there is a significant change in the exchange rate between two countries the balance of trade moves in favor of the country with the weaker currency. When the dollar is weak compared to the British pound, U.S. goods are price-competitive in England and British goods are priced out of the U.S. market. Also, the cost of travel to Britain from the United States is more expensive, while the reverse is true. However, to take advantage of the favorable trade conditions, it is necessary to incur high travel costs. American companies must travel to Britain to take advantage of the strong dollar. For incentive travel and conferences, which are not destination-specific, exchange rate changes can influence the flow of business travel. Countries with weak currencies will get proportionately more business.

It is virtually impossible to predict long-term currency rates. The important consideration, however, is to understand the movements in response to changes in the relative rates of exchange.

Regulatory.   The two major regulatory influences on business travel are the deregulation of travel businesses and the way the government treats business travel expenditures for tax purposes.

The effect of deregulation in the United States has resulted in cheaper fares in many markets, movement of carriers both in and out of the airline industry, and a cutting back of service to smaller towns. As Europe moves toward deregulation in the 1990s, the same trends can be expected.

Recent restrictions on business travel limit the tax deductibility of a meal taken on a business trip to 80 percent of the cost. Further restrictions will cause businesses to rethink marginally productive business trips.

Communications.   The business world is becoming more international or global in scope. As multinationals grow in number and the term "national economy" is replaced by "global economy," we can expect to see an increase in international business travel, particularly in the United States, Europe, and the Far East.

Automation.   The development of increasingly sophisticated automation and communications systems will make reservations systems and information services available to business travelers. They will demand more precise travel information to make arrangements and keep track of company travel costs. Several firms, such as Diners' Club, are already offering this control function to management. As the ability to monitor travel costs increases we can expect such demands by business customers.

Suppliers will have to differentiate their products by offering special services for the woman business traveler, the hotel suite segment, and the "high-tech traveler"—people with high income, high level of education, employed by a high-tech company, between 30 to 45 years of age, very mobile and unpredictable, and with frequent changes in travel plans. Suppliers will stress loyalty programs, which will replace the frequent-flyer and frequent-stay programs that are aimed at the individual. It is likely that such programs will be phased out in the 1990s as accountants "charge" the airlines for the accumulated mileage and as the IRS charges consumers for the value of the benefits. New loyalty programs will be oriented toward the company in the form of volume-related bonus schemes.

What about increasing automation reducing the need to travel? Technology offers the opportunity to send documents through the telephone lines and to conduct a face-to-face meeting through teleconferencing. John Naisbitt has noted that, as part of this "high tech–high touch" trend, as computerization increases in offices, so does the writing of notes by hand. Contact with others will remain necessary to conduct business. Video teleconferencing has been slow to expand because of the high cost and because it inhibits creativity. People feel awkward when part of a video conference.

Incentive Travel and Conferences. The demand for conferences will likely grow with the diversification of meeting facilities into multipurpose event centers.

Travel will remain a major motivator of sales performance in incentive programs. It is likely that the use of incentive travel to motivate employees will expand out of sales to other types of employees who will be rewarded for such things as increasing productivity and reducing turnover. The demand for incentive travel will be greater than that for business travel.

FINAL WORD OF CAUTION

While the picture painted above is one of optimism for the future of travel and tourism, some problems should be noted.

In both North America and Europe the tourism infrastructure is strained and inadequate. In the United States the quality of the road system is inadequate and a great infusion of money is needed to bring the highways up to par.

Similarly, the nation's airspace is becoming overcrowded. In 1988, restrictions were placed on the number of flights arriving at and departing from Chicago's O'Hare Airport. In Europe the air traffic control system is hopelessly outdated. The situated is made worse by the fact that the "system" is, in fact, 42 separate systems. Problems in communication and coordination account for delays of days during the peak holiday season.

Many tourist destinations are slow to face up to the problems of pollution and safety. Raw sewage and improperly disposed of medical supplies have caused the closure of beaches in Europe and the United States.

Crime in the streets has resulted in a fear on the part of many people toward urban destinations.

The future of travel and tourism will depend upon the extent to which decision-makers in both the private and public sectors can take advantage of the opportunities the future will bring while working hard to solve the problems outlined above.

Figure 12–4   Can we preserve the environment for future generations of tourists and locals? (Courtesy New Zealand Tourist & Publicity Office.)

S T U D Y   QUESTIONS

1. What factors affect the demand for tourism?
2. By the year 2033 what five countries will have the largest populations?
3. What have been the major population changes in North America in the last few years?
4. What factors have served to limit the growth of leisure time in the United States?
5. What trends can be expected in tourist demand in the next few years? What is the likely generational influence on leisure travel of:
    a. Baby boomlets, baby busters, and baby boomers?
    b. World War II babies?
    c. Depression babies?
    d. World War I babies?
6. The demand for business travel is a function of four factors. What are they?

D I S C U S S I O N   QUESTIONS

1. How will changes in population, income, leisure, consumer tastes, and business travel affect tourism in the future?

TRAVEL
AND TOURISM
INFORMATION
SOURCES

INDEXING SOURCES

Business Periodicals Index. A cumulative index covering subjects in business.

Predicasts. Articles are indexed by industry and product, by country, and by company.

Predicasts F & S Europe. Covers the Common Market, Iberia, Scandinavia, Eastern Europe, USSR.

Predicasts F & S Index International. Covers Canada, Latin America, Africa, Middle East, Oceania, Japan, and other Asian countries.

Predicasts F & S Index United States. Indexes articles from the United States and foreign sources that affect American business.

Public Affairs Information Service Bulletin. Books, pamphlets, government publications, private and public agency reports and periodicals relating to economic and social conditions, public administration, and international relations.

Reader's Guide to Periodical Literature. Index of the contents of general magazines.

BIBLIOGRAPHIES

Annals of Tourism Research, Menomonie, Wisconsin, Department of Habitational Resources, University of Wisconsin–Stout, "Tourism and the Social Sciences: A Bibliography," Jafar Jafari, (ed.). Vol. 6, No. 2 (April/June 1979), pp. 149–194. Covers work done from 1970 to 1978.

Bibliographie Touristique, Aix-en-Provence, France, Centre d'Études du Tourisme, 18, Rue de l'Opera, 13100 Aix-en-Provence, R. Baretje (ed.). Inventory of the world's literature in tourism by subject, country, and author. Every three months the centre publishes the *Tourist Analysis Review,* an analysis of approximately 160 books or articles dealing with tourism.

Bibliography of Hotel and Restaurant Administration, Ithaca, New York, *The Cornell Hotel and Restaurant Administration Quarterly.* School of Hotel and Restaurant Administration, Statler Hall, Cornell University, Margaret J. Oaksford (ed.), 1982, 275 pp. Listing of 5,500 references.

Bibliography of Theses and Dissertations in Recreation, Parks, Camping and Outdoor Recreation, Alexandria, Virginia, National Recreation and Park Association, 1970, 555 pp. Annotated bibliography of about 4,000 references.

Bibliography of Theses and Dissertations in Recreation and Parks, 1979. Annotated bibliography of 2,798 references that updates the 1970 bibliography listed above.

Bibliography of Tourism and Travel Studies, Reports and Articles, Boulder, Colorado, Business Research Division, College of Business, University of Colorado, C.R. Goeldner and Karen Dicke (eds.), 1980, 762 pp. The nine-volume set contains material on information sources, economics, international tourism, lodging, recreation, transportation, advertising, and statistics.

Book Catalogue of Tourism Research Studies/82, 4th ed., Ottawa, Ontario, Tourism Research and Data Centre, Canadian Government Office of Tourism, 235 Queen Street, Ottawa, Ontario, K1A OH6. Listing of sources produced by primarily Canadian sources.

Journal of Travel Research, Boulder, Colorado, Business Research Division, College of Business, University of Colorado. "The Travel Research Bookshelf," an annotated bibliography of current materials, is a regular feature of the quarterly journal.

HCIMA Research Register. Hotel, Catering and Institutional Management Association, 191 Trinity Road, London, England SW17 7HN. Contains nine major categories of items: Products and Services, Gastronomy, Management, Accounting and Finance, Manpower and Personnel, Marketing, Education, Tourism, and Sectors of Industry.

Leisure, Recreation and Tourism Abstracts (formerly *Rural Recreation and Tourism Abstracts*), Oxford, England, Commonwealth Agricultural Bureaux. Quarterly abstracts arranged by subject.

The Lodging and Restaurant Index, Continuing Education Business Office, Purdue University. Annual index of 28 hospitality publications.

PATA Research Library Bibliography, San Francisco, Pacific Area Travel Association, 1977. Annotated listing of recent or popularly used references.

Tourism: A Guide to Sources of Information, Edinburgh, Scotland, Capital Planning Information, Ltd., 6 Castle Street, Edinburgh, Scotland, EH2 3AT, 1981, 73 pp. Deals primarily with references about the United Kingdom.

Tourism and Vacation Planning: State and Local Government Planning, Springfield Virginia, National Technical Information Service, 1983, 223 pp. Covers economic and socioeconomic studies from 1964 to 1983.

Travel and Tourism Bibliography and Resource Handbook, Jeanne Gay (ed.), Santa Cruz, California, The Travel and Tourism Press, P.O. Box 1188, 1981, 1,328 pp. Includes listings by geographic location, environment-ecology, transportation, leisure, and travel photography.

Travel and Tourism Research: A Guide to Information Sources in the Washington D.C. Area, Boulder, Colorado, Business Research Division, University of Colorado, 1982, 107 pp. Listings under public and private organizations, libraries, publications, available data bases, and embassies.

Travel Data Locator Index, Washington, D.C., U.S. Travel Data Center, 1978, 232 pp. More than 1,000 statistical series covering travel and recreation.

University Research in Business and Economics, Morgantown, West Virginia, Bureau of Business Research, College of Business and Economics, West Virginia University, annual, 298 pp. Covers the publications of members of the Association for University Business and Economic Research and the American Assembly of Collegiate Schools of Business.

PERIODICALS

Annals of Tourism Research, Pergammon Press, Elmsford, New York, quarterly.

ASTA Travel News, American Society of Travel Agents, Inc., New York, monthly.

Canadian Travel News, Southam Communications, Ltd., Don Mills, Ontario, bi-weekly.

Canadian Travel Press, A Baxter Publication, Toronto, Ontario, biweekly.

The Cornell Hotel and Restaurant Administration Quarterly, School of Hotel Administration, Cornell University, Ithaca, New York, quarterly.

Courier, National Tour Association, Inc., 546 East Main Street, Lexington, Kentucky 40508, monthly.

Hotel and Motel Management, Harcourt Brace Jovanovich Publications, Cleveland, monthly.

Hotels and Restaurants International (formerly *Service World International).* Cahners Publishing Co., Boston, seven times a year.

ICTA Journal, Institute of Certified Travel Agents, Wellesley, Massachusetts, twice a year.

International Journal of Hospitality Management, Pergammon Press, Oxford, England, three times a year.

International Tourism Quarterly, The Economist Intelligence Unit, Ltd., London, England, quarterly.

Journal of Leisure Research, National Recreation and Park Association, Alexandria, Virginia, quarterly.

Journal of Travel Research, Business Research Division, College of Business, University of Colorado, Boulder, quarterly.

Leisure Sciences, Crane Russak and Company, Inc., New York, quarterly.

Leisure Studies, E. & F.N. Spon Ltd., London England, three times a year.

Lodging, American Hotel Association Directory Corporation, New York, monthly except August.

Meetings and Conventions, Ziff-Davis Publishing Company, New York, monthly.

Resort Management, Western Specialty Publications, Inc., Memphis, Tennessee, monthly.

The Tourist Review, Association of Scientific Experts in Tourism, St. Gallen, Switzerland, quarterly.

Tourism Management, Butterworth Scientific, Ltd., Guildford, England, quarterly.

Tourism Recreation Research, Centre for Tourism Research, Lucknow, India, twice yearly.

The Travel Agent, American Travel Division, Capital Cities Media, Inc., New York, twice weekly.

Travel Marketing (JAX FAX), 397 Post Road, Box 4013, Darien, Connecticut 06820, monthly.

Travel Printout, U.S. Travel Data Center, Washington, D.C., monthly.

Travel Trade, Travel Trade Publications, Inc., New York, weekly.

Travel Weekly, Ziff-Davis Publishing, Inc., New York, twice weekly.

World Travel, World Tourism Organization, Madrid, Spain, six times a year.

TRADE AND PROFESSIONAL ORGANIZATIONS

Air Transport Association of America, 1709 New York Avenue, N.W., Washington, D.C., 20006.

American Hotel and Motel Association, 1201 New York Avenue, N.W., 6th Floor, Washington, D.C. 20005–3917

American Society of Travel Agents, 1101 King Street, Alexandria, Virginia 22314. Mailing address: Box 23992, Washington, D.C. 20026.

Association of Travel Marketing Executives, 53 Church Street, Stonington, Connecticut 06378.

Institute of Certified Travel Agents, 148 Linden Street, Wellesley, Massachusetts 02181.

International Air Traffic Association, 2000 Peel Street, Suite 200, Montreal, Quebec, Canada H3A 2R4.

International Association of Amusement Parks and Attractions, 7222 W. Cermak Road, Suite 303, North Riverside, Illinois 60546.

International Association of Convention and Visitor Bureaus, 702 Bloomington Road, Champaign, Illinois 61820.

International Association of Scientific Experts in Tourism, Varnbuelstrasse 19, CH-9000 St. Gallen, Switzerland.

National Recreation and Park Association, 3101 Park Center Drive, Alexandria, Virginia 22302.

National Tour Association, 120 Kentucky Avenue, Lexington, Kentucky 40502.

Pacific Area Travel Association, 228 Grant Avenue, San Francisco, California 94108.

Tourism Industry Association of Canada, 130 Albert Street, Ottawa, Ontario, Canada K1P 5GH.

Travel and Tourism Research Association, P.O. Box 8066, Foothill Station, Salt Lake City, Utah 84108.

Travel Industry Association of America, 1899 L Street, N.W., Washington, D.C. 20036.

World Tourism Organization, Capitan Haya, 42, Madrid, 20, Spain.

GOVERNMENT DIRECTORIES

Tourism Compendium, World Tourism Organization, Capitan Haya, 42, Madrid, 20/Spain. Contains a listing of the members and associates (including most government travel organizations).

World Travel Directory, Ziff-Davis Publishing Company, One Park Avenue, New York, 10016. Contains a listing of government agencies involved in tourism.

DATA BASES

Tourism Reference and Data Centre, 3rd Floor West, 235 Queen Street, Ottawa, Ontario K1A OH6, Canada.

The Travel Reference Center, Business Research Division, College of Business, University of Colorado, Boulder, Colorado 80309. Houses the library of the Travel and Tourism Research Association. Computer searches available.

U.S. Travel Data Center, 1899 L Street, N.W., Washington, D.C. 20036. Includes work on *National Travel Survey, Impact of Travel on State Economies, Survey of State Travel Offices, Travel Price Index,* and an *Annual Travel Forum.*

World Tourism Organization, Capitan Haya, 42, E-Madrid, 20/Spain.

Appendix
2

GLOSSARY OF TERMS

Adjoining room   Two or more rooms side by side without a connecting door between them. Rooms can be adjoining without being connecting.

Affinity group   Members of an organization formed for purposes other than travel but operating affinity charter flights.

Aft   Near, toward, or in the stern of a vessel.

Agency rep   A salesperson calling on travel agents.

Agency tour   A familiarization tour, complementary or reduced-rate travel for travel agents to familiarize them with new destinations in order to increase sales.

Air/sea   A cruise or travel program in which one or more transportation legs are provided by air and one or more by sea. Often combined with local hotel operations.

A la carte   (a). A menu or list of items from which guests may select their various choices. This type of meal arrangement is included only in some higher-priced tours. Menu items are sold individually and priced individually. (b). Cooked to order.

All-expense tour   An all-inclusive tour offering all or most services for an established price. Terms and conditions of the tour contract specify all services paid for and included in prepaid tour arrangements.

American Plan (AP)   Hotel accommodations with three meals daily included in the price of the room. Sometimes referred to as "full pension."

Amtrak   Name used by the National Railroad Passenger Corporation, under which it operates almost all U.S. intercity passenger trains (except commuter trains) under contract with the individual railroads.

Appointment   In the travel industry, an official designation to act as sales outlet for a conference group of carriers. Conferences approve travel agents before they are appointed individually by conference members.

APEX   Advance purchase excursion. Airline fare, cheaper than normal, but with restrictions. The ticket must be paid for in advance of the trip and the trip must involve a Saturday night away from home.

Back to back   A manner of operating tours on a consistent continuing basis. A flight with, say, 250 passengers arriving in a city would pick up another 250 passengers who have completed their stay in that city and would continue on or return on that same plane. This scheduling eliminates unnecessary ferrying of aircraft. It also makes it possible to block out or reserve hotel rooms on a continuing basis.

Balance of payments, or trade   When a country exports more than it imports it is said to have a positive balance of payments; when it imports more than it exports there is a negative balance of payments. Tourism is part of the balance of trade under the heading of services. When a tourist from one country visits another country the economic effect for the country visited is the same as exports.

Bareboat charter   A yacht rented without supplies or crew.

B and B   Bed and breakfast. Includes a room and English or Continental breakfast; used throughout the United Kingdom and Europe.

Beam   The width of a vessel at its widest point.

Bermuda Plan (BP)   Room and American breakfast daily.

Berth   A bed on a ship or train; also a space in which a ship may dock.

Blocked space   Guaranteed reservation of rooms or space at hotels, restaurants or attractions made by suppliers to travel agents, wholesalers, or group movers for later resale.

Bond   Used to guarantee the conduct or performance of an individual to an employer and to promise to pay a sum of money to the employer if the bonded person defaults. A guarantee of financial protection for suppliers and clients, purchased by premium, paid by an agent or operator to a bonding or insurance company.

Booking   Making a reservation.

Booking form   A form completed by purchasers of tours, giving the operator full information about the purchaser. It contains a complete statement about what is being purchased and often includes a liability clause to be read, understood, and signed.

Bow   The forward part of a ship.

Briefing tour   A hotel or tourist-board promotion. It sells a destination usually to the travel trade at the trade's location as opposed to selling it at the destination.

Brochure   Printed folder containing descriptions and conditions of a tour.

Bulk fare   Special airline fare made available to tour operators by cooperating airlines, based on a tour operator or operators taking a predetermined number of seats on the same flight.

Bumping   To remove or displace a passenger in favor of someone who has a higher priority or is more important.

Cabana   A room adjacent to a pool area, with or without sleeping facilities, and usually separate from the hotel's main building.

Cabin   Passenger compartment on a ship, or a sleeping room, usually less luxurious than a stateroom.

Carrier   A public transportation company such as an airline or steamship line, railroad, bus line, etc.

Certified Travel Counselor (CTC)   Designation conferred on the completion of a course of study by the Institute of Certified Travel Agents, attesting to professional competence as a travel agent.

Charter flight   A flight booked exclusively for a specific group or groups, on scheduled or nonscheduled airlines, and available to these groups under charter conditions.

Check-in   The hotel day starts at 6:00 a.m.; however, occupancy of rooms by arriving guests may not be possible until after the established check-out time (usually 1:00 p.m.).

Check-out   The time by which a hotel guest is required to vacate a room in order to avoid additional charges.

City package   A package tour that includes transportation, accommodations, and some combination of other tour elements in one particular city.

City pair   The departure and destination points of an air trip.

City terminal   An airline office, other than at the airport, where a passenger may check in for a flight, receive seat assignments, check baggage, and obtain ground transportation to the airport.

Coach   In railway usage, a day-coach for ordinary short-haul travel. In recent years, improved coaches have been introduced with reclining seats for overnight travel. For buses, coach used to refer to a bus on tour as distinct from point-to-point scheduled travel. Also refers to tourist section of an airplane.

Commercial rate   A special rate given by a hotel to a company or other bulk purchaser, usually a flat rate for rooms of a certain quality or better.

Commission   The varying and often regulated amount of money paid by suppliers to travel agents for the sale of transportation, accommodation, and other services.

Concierge   In almost all European and many major hotels throughout the world, the concierge is the person in charge of services such as baggage handling, mailing letters, making reservations, etc., for guests.

Conducted tour   A prepaid, prearranged vacation in which a group of people travel together under the guidance of a tour leader who stays with them from the start to the end of the trip. Also referred to as the *escorted tour.*

Conference   Usually general sessions and face-to-face groups with high participation to plan, get facts, and solve organization and member problems associated with tourism.

Configuration   Interior arrangement of a vehicle, particularly an airplane; for example, number of coach, business-class, and first-class seats in a plane.

Confirmation   Oral or written statement by a supplier that a reservation has been received and will be honored. Oral confirmations have no legal worth; even written confirmations have specified or implied limitations—a hotel is not obligated to hold a reservation if the guest arrives after 6 p.m. unless late arrival is specified.

Congress   European designation for a *convention;* mainly international in scope.

Connecting rooms   Two or more rooms with private connecting doors permitting access without going into the corridor.

Consolidated Air Tour Manual (CATM)   A publication issued jointly by U.S. airlines as a composite of tours offered for sale to the public, usually through retail agents. Issued semiannually.

Consolidator   A person or company specializing in consolidating groups for travel on airline charters. *Consolidators* refer to operators, mainly in large cities, who purchase air tickets at big discounts and resell them to smaller agencies at a higher commission than airlines give them. They also sell directly to the public through advertisements; sell mainly to foreign destinations.

Continental breakfast   At a minimum, a beverage (coffee, tea, or milk) and rolls or toast. Sometimes the breakfast includes fruit juice.

Continental Plan (CP)   Lodging and Continental breakfast.

Contractor   A person, firm, or corporation who provides vehicles, guides, and/or local services to a tour operator or travel agent for the benefit of the passengers. Contractors operate in every stage of a tour, and their contracted services are coordinated by the tour operator into a complete itinerary. Sometimes called *local operator.* A hotel, for example, is a contractor.

Convention   Usually general sessions and committee meetings; mostly information-giving and generally accepted traditional form of annual meeting.

Couchette   On European trains, a space in an unsegregated compartment that can be converted into a sleeping berth.

Coupon   Document issued by tour operators in exchange for which travelers receive prepaid accommodations, meals, sightseeing trips, etc. Also referred to as *voucher*.

Courier   A professional travel escort sent to supervise arrival details and land arrangements for tourists. This term is generally used in Europe.

CTO   City ticket office.

Cruise   A pleasure voyage as opposed to one solely for transport. Sea cruises usually depart from and return to the same port.

Customs   The government agency or office where, upon entry to a country, the traveler must declare all foreign-purchased items to government officials.

Cut-off date   The designated day when the buyer (upon request) must release or add to function room or bedroom commitment. For certain types of groups, rooming lists should be sent to the hotel at least two weeks prior to arrival.

Day use or day rate   Half the normal rates in the day.

Deadheading   A person traveling on a free pass; any vehicle, ship, or aircraft operating without a payload.

Deluxe   Of the highest standard; part of an official rating system; a top-grade hotel with all rooms having private baths and a high standard of service.

Demi-pension or half-pension   Hotel accommodations that include Continental breakfast and either *table d'hote* lunch or dinner in the price of the room. Same as *Modified plan.*

Denied boarding compensation   The penalty payment made to a passenger by an airline that has not honored a confirmed reservation.

Departure tax   A fee collected by a city or national government for departure from the city or county. U.S. Departure tax, also known as "head tax," is added to fare. Most other governments collect upon departure and issue stamps or receipts.

Deposit reservation   A hotel reservation for which at least one night's payment has been received. The hotel must then hold a room for the first night, no matter how late the guest arrives.

Discounting   Price cutting and/or specials designed to increase customer frequency.

Domestic Independent Tour, or Domestic Inclusive Tour (DIT)   Generally used in the United States and Canada.

Double   Room with one large bed for two persons.

Double occupancy rate   The price per person for a room to be shared with another person. The rate most frequently quoted in tour brochures.

Downgrade   To move to a lesser accommodation or class of service.

Dry lease   Rental of a vehicle without operator or crew; a pure dry lease also excludes supplies, fuel, or maintenance.

Duplex   A suite with two floors and connected by private stairway.

Duty-free shop   A store located at an international airport or at a port of exit that sells goods free of taxes to travelers going to another country.

Economy hotel   Tourist or second-class hotel with few or no private baths and limited services.

Efficiency   An accommodation containing some type of kitchen facility.

Elastic demand curve   A demand curve showing that when a price is lowered more items will be sold and revenue will increase. Or, if a price is increased, fewer items will be sold but the percentage decline in number of items sold will not be offset by percentage increase in price. Total revenue decreases.

Elasticity   A measurement of relative sensitivity among two or more variables. Usually refers to *price elasticity*.

English breakfast   A morning meal generally served in the British Isles and Ireland. It usually includes hot or cold cereal, bacon or ham and eggs, toast, butter, jam or marmalade, and a beverage, traditionally tea.

Entry tax (or fee)   A fee collected by a city or national government for entry into that city or country.

Escort   Courier; professional travel escort; also called tour escort, tour leader, or tour manager.

Escorted tour   A prearranged escorted travel program; also a guided sightseeing program.

Escrow account   Agency and tour operator funds placed in licensed financial institutions for safekeeping. Many charter travel regulations require that customers' deposits and prepayments be placed in escrow accounts.

ETA   Estimated time of arrival.

ETD   Estimated time of departure.

Eurailpass   A railroad ticket to provide unlimited rail travel throughout 13 countries of Western Europe. Fares are flat rates for specified number of days and are available at special children's rates as well as for adults.

European Plan (EP).   Hotel accommodations with no meals whatever included in the price of the room.

Excursion fare   Round-trip fare at reduced price. Excursions have limitations as to days of departure, time of day, and length of stay.

Excursionist   A traveler who spends fewer than 24 hours at a destination.

Extension   A trip to be taken before, during, or at the conclusion of a basic tour for which all reservations and arrangements can be made, and usually optional for members of a tour group, at additional cost.

Familiarization tour   An educational program, generally for travel agents or airline personnel, to a destination for inspection of tourist facilities. Usually sponsored in cooperation with airlines, tour operators, and local tourist boards.

Federal Aviation Administration (FAA).   A government agency within the U.S. Department of Transportation. Exercises overall control of airports, equipment, pilots, routes, etc., and issues mandatory requirements and standards to govern civil aviation.

Ferry mileage   The mileage a plane is flown without passengers to where it must pick up tour members. Airlines charge for these air miles; therefore, the fewer ferry miles on the schedule, the lower the operating cost of the charter. This term applies to charter air transportation.

FET   Foreign escorted tour.

Final itinerary   The schedule provided by the travel agent that spells out in great detail the exact program mapped out for the traveler, including flight or train numbers, departure times, etc. This is always delivered shortly before actual departure.

First-class fare   The most expensive and best class of service in air, sea, and rail travel.

First-class hotel   A medium range, comfortable hotel with high standard services provided; most rooms have a private bath.

FIT   Foreign independent tour or foreign inclusive tour. This is a tour to a foreign country made up and planned or tailored to an individual's desires or requirements. It must be a prepaid tour.

Flag carrier   Major airline designated by its government.

Flyer   Printed advertisement, usually mailed to potential customers.

FMC   Federal Maritime Commission.

Forward   Toward or at the bow of a vessel.

Free sale   Allowing another carrier to sell a predetermined number of seats without having to check the seat availability. It is an allotment of seats to another carrier.

Full pension   A predominantly European term referring to hotel accommodations with three meals daily included in the price of the room. Sometimes referred to as *American Plan* or *Full American Plan.*

Galley   The kitchen on a ship.

GIT   Group inclusive tour. A tour-based fare to various destinations, providing a special fare for a minimum of five persons and requiring that all the members must travel on the same flight round-trip, and must travel together during their entire time abroad, and where reservations must be made at the same time.

Gratuities   Payments to service personnel for services rendered.

Greenwich Mean Time (GMT)   Mean solar time at Greenwich, England, used as the basis for calculating standard time for the entire world.

Ground arrangements   All services provided for the traveler by the tour operator after the traveler reaches the first destination and beyond.

Ground operator   A company that provides local travel services to a client at destination; receiving agent.

Group Inclusive Tour (GIT)   A prepaid tour on which passengers complete the trip going and coming as part of an air package; usually organized by a tour operator.

Guaranteed reservation   Hotel reservation that a guest agrees to pay for whether or not used; payment may be guaranteed by a company or a travel agent who has a credit rating with the hotel, or by prepayment.

Guide   Someone who is licensed to take tourists on local sightseeing excursions.

Guided tour   Local escorted sightseeing trip.

Head tax   Amount collected by a government from a passenger who enters or leaves a country.

Hospitality suite   A parlor with connecting bedroom(s) to be used for entertaining.

Hostel   Supervised low-cost accommodation, usually for young people of designated ages.

Hotel package   A special offering, including such things as transportation, transfers, room, board, and use of facilities.

Hotel representative (hotel rep)   A person, firm, or corporation designated by a hotel to provide tour operators, travel agents, and the general public with reservations in hotels and resorts.

Hotel and Travel Index   A worldwide quarterly compilation of hotel facilities, rates, and personnel information.

Hotel voucher   Coupon issued by the tour operator to cover payment for all specified prepaid tour features. Guest surrenders hotel voucher on check-in and the hotel sends voucher and billing statement to tour operator for payment.

ICC   Interstate Commerce Commission.

Incentive (or incentive commission)   Override; extra commission paid by airlines, wholesalers, suppliers, hotels, or government to increase sales.

Incentive travel   Travel offered as a prize to stimulate employees' sales; the business of providing such travel programs.

Incidentals   Charges incurred by the participants of a tour but which are not included in the tour price.

Inclusive tour   A tour that includes all elements of an itinerary, usually making it unnecessary for a passenger to spend money for anything except personal extras during the course of the tour.

Inclusive Tour Charter (ITC)   An aircraft charter carrying an inclusive tour; travel industry term for a tour on which basic transportation is by chartered aircraft.

Inelastic demand curve   A demand curve showing that when price is lowered more items will be sold but not enough to offset the decline in price. Total revenue will decrease. Or, if a price is raised, fewer items will be sold but the percentage decline in the number of items sold will be offset by the percentage increase in price. Total revenue will increase.

Infrastructure   Underground and service installations—for example, power, roads, water supply, communication installations, etc.

In-plant   Travel agency situated in a company's premises, doing business only for that company.

Interline arrangements   The practice of airline employees traveling on another airline.

Intermodal travel   Tour using more than one means of transportation.

I.T. number   Code number on an ARC- or IATAN-approved tour that qualifies agents selling air transportation in connection with those agencies for override commissions.

ITX   Inclusive tour excursion. British and European term for an inclusive tour fare.

Itinerary   An outline of a tour covering daily activities.

Junior suite   Large hotel room with a partition dividing bedroom and sitting area.

Knot   One nautical mile per hour (about 1.15 statute miles per hour).

Lanai   Balcony, patio, or area outside the room to which one has access.

Land arrangements   The term used in a tour program to designate all features, except basic transportation.

Land operator   Company providing local services, such as transfers, sightseeing, etc.

Leg   That portion of a flight between two consecutive scheduled stops; segments.

Lido deck   The deck on which a pool is located on a ship, or the area around the pool.

Load factor   The percentage of carrier capacity sold of the total capacity for sale.

Lower   A lower berth on a ship or train.

Managed tour   Same as *conducted tour.*

Minimum land package   The minimum tour, in cost and ingredients, needed to qualify a passenger for an airline inclusive tour, group inclusive tour, or contract bulk inclusive tour.

Miscellaneous Charges Order (MCO).   Form issued by travel agent or airline to cover miscellaneous ground arrangements. If tour order is not available, an MCO can be issued to cover package tour ground arrangements. Client normally exchanges MCO for hotel and vouchers on arrival at destination (usually on check-in at hotel).

Modified American Plan (MAP)   Room, breakfast, and either lunch or dinner daily.

Net rate   A wholesale rate to be marked up for eventual resale to the consumer. Same as net wholesale rate.

No-show   Guest with confirmed reservation who does not arrive and whose reservation was not cancelled.

Observation car   Railroad car specially made for sightseeing.

Occupancy rate   The percentage of bed-nights sold, compared with total available for sale in a hotel.

Official Airline Guide (OAG)   Monthly listing of all airline tariffs and flight schedules.

Official Hotel and Resort Guide (OHRG)   Worldwide reference directory describing hotels, motor hotels, and resorts.

Official Meeting Facilities Guide (OMFG)   Semiannual directory of worldwide rates, accommodations, and meeting capacities of hotels and resorts.

Off-peak   A fare or hotel rate to be applied at a time that is in the slack season and usually not the busiest.

On request   Term used by hotel reservation services to indicate they cannot confirm the room but must request it directly from the hotel.

Open jaw   An arrangement, route, or fare authorized in a tariff that grants the traveling public the privilege of purchasing round-trip transportation from the point of origin to one destination, at which point another form of transportation is used to a second destination; at this point the passenger resumes the original form of transportation and returns to point of origin; or from such destination to another destination that is in the general direction of the original starting point.

Open ticket   A ticket that does not give the date on which a certain service is to be performed; this leaves the passenger to secure his or her own reservation later.

Optional   Term used in tour literature to indicate a supplemental extra cost.

Overbooking   The deliberate or mistaken confirmation of more reservations than there are seats or rooms.

Override   Extra commission paid by airlines, wholesalers, suppliers, governments, etc., as bonuses or incentives.

Package or package tour   Any advertised tour, or a single-destination tour, including transportation, accommodations, and other tour elements.

Packager   A wholesaler; one who organizes and advertises a tour or package.

Parlor   Room in a suite that is not a bedroom.

Parlor car   Railroad car in parts of the United States with individual swivel seats and food and bar service.

Passenger kilometer   One passenger carried one kilometer.

Passenger mile   One passenger carried one mile.

Pension   French term widely used to designate a modest accommodation, usually of a guest house variety, providing lodging and all meals.

Pitch   The fore-and-aft motion of a ship at sea. Also the space between the back of one airline seat and the back of the seat behind it.

Port   A nautical term meaning *left side*.

Porterage   Baggage-handling service. If a tour includes porterage, a client does not have to pay or tip for its carriage.

Positioning   The movement of a vehicle to the place where it will perform a revenue service. A positioning cruise takes passengers but is primarily for the purpose of moving a ship to another cruise area.

Postconvention tour   An extension of a basic return trip from a convention.

Preconvention tour   An extension supplementing the trip to a convention.

Prepaid extra nights   Additional nights included in hotel voucher over and above the number of nights included in the basic package tour. Rates for extra nights are normally published next to rate for package tour within the tour folder.

Price elasticity   A measure of the degree of sensitivity of quantity sold when a price is allowed to vary.

Principal   A primary producer—airline, hotel, etc.—or a unit of travel merchandise; one who assumes responsibility for a travel program; one who pays commission to another for selling a program.

Promotional fare   A fare below the regular fare, intended to stimulate travel when use of space is low; usually round-trip with conditions.

Pullman   In North America, a railroad sleeping car.

Quad   Room occupied by four persons.

Rack rate   The regular published rates of the hotel.

Rail Travel Promotion Association (RTPA)   A central clearing house for railroad coordination of package tours.

Receiving agent (or receptive agent)   A tour operator or travel agent who specializes in service for incoming visitors.

Reception agency   Receiving agent; travel agent who handles local arrangements.

Reconfirmation   Statement of intention to use reserved space. A passenger must reconfirm reserved space within certain time limits, under airlines rules, or the space may be resold.

Registry   Registration certification showing ownership and national flag of a ship, but not indicating quality of the ship or nationality of her personnel.

Reservation   An arrangement to hold a room, seat, place, etc., for a person; a promise of accommodation.

Rest and Recreation (R&R)   Time allotted to travelers in planned tours for rest or recreation other than that included on the tour.

Return   British and European term for round-trip, as in "return ticket."

Revenue passenger mile (RPM)   One paying passenger carried one mile in commercial airline service.

Rooming list   A list of names submitted by the buyer to occupy the previously reserved accommodations.

Run of the house (ROTH)   Rate used between hotel manager and tour operator when a specific rate is being established for tours and special packages to be offered by the tour operator. This rate is applicable to all rooms used by the tour regardless of location or rack rate.

Scheduled airline   Air carrier offering scheduled service for individual passengers. Scheduled carriers may also operate charter flights.

Service charge   Percentage of a hotel or restaurant bill paid by the guest to take the place of a tip; a travel agent's fee charged to a client.

Shoulder fare, rate, or season   A calendar period between a peak season and an off-season, usually favored by a promotional fare, lower than peak and higher than off-season.

Single   One person occupying one room; one single bed.

Single supplement   Extra charge for single accommodation on a tour.

Single entity charter   An air charter sponsored and paid for by one person, company, or organization, on which none of the passengers are charged.

Space   A reserved seat or room, or a reservation for such.

Space available   Reduced or free passage; customer is given passage if the space is available.

Split charter   An aircraft or other vehicle hired by more than one distinct legal entity; the portion of the aircraft hired for a specific flight or flights. Seat allotments are split among charterers.

Stabilizer   A device used to eliminate or lessen a ship's tendency to roll.

Standby   A special promotional fare offered on a space-available basis.

Starboard   A nautical term meaning *right side*.

Stateroom   Sleeping room on a ship, usually more luxurious than a cabin.

Stern   The rear of a ship or boat.

Stopover   A deliberate stop or the right to leave transportation for a period of time (usually 24 hours or more) at a regular route stop.

Studio   Room with a convertible bed; has a parlor that converts into a bedroom.

Subject to temporary accommodation (STA)   Term used mainly by Bermuda hotels. Indicates confirmation of space, but allows the hotel designated to arrange other accommodations in another hotel in the event that space is not available.

Suite   One or more bedrooms and connecting parlor; combination of rooms.

Supplement   A charge for better or extra service, or the service itself (as in *single supplement).*

Supplemental carrier   An airline certified by government authorities to operate charter flights. Frequently called "non-skeds."

Supplier   A carrier, hotel, sightseeing operator, etc., who produces a unit or segment of travel.

Table d'hote   (a) A nonselective fixed-price menu served at a specific time to all guests; (b) menu on which a price is given for a complete dinner, as opposed to *a la carte* pricing of each item; (c) price of the entree is the total price of the complete meal.

Tariff   A fare or rate from a supplier; a class or type of fare or rate; a published list of fares or rates from a supplier; official publication compiling fares and rates.

Tonnage   Measurement term for describing size of ship.

Tour   Any prearranged (usually prepaid) journey to one or more destinations and back to point of departure.

Tour-basing fare   Reduced-rate excursion fare for buyer of prepaid tour or package.

Tour brochure   A printed folder describing a tour and its conditions.

Tour broker   Persons or company licensed by the ICC to organize and market motorcoach tours.

Tour code number   Number assigned to every package tour by an airline. In order to be eligible for extra commission granted by airlines on package tours, this code number must be officially approved in advance of sale to the public. Sometimes called an "I.T." number, the extra commission is granted to the travel agent selling the tour.

Tour conductor   Professional travel escort.

Tour departure   Date of the start of a particular travel program by any person or group or the operation of a particular tour.

Tour escort   Professional travel escort or leader.

Tour guide   Professional who leads a tour, usually at an attraction or destination.

Tourism   All activities involved with attracting, servicing, and satisfying tourists.

Tourists   Person who travels for reasons other than employment or personal business. The United Nations defines tourist as one who spends more than one night but less than a year away from home for pleasure or business, except diplomats, military personnel, and enrolled students.

Tourist card   A document given to prospective tourists by the issuing country to allow them entry and departure (common in Mexico and Central and South America).

Tourist class   Economical accommodations or airline seating below top grade or first class.

Tourist hotel   Economy or second-class hotel, with few or no private baths and limited service.

Tour leader   A courier or professional tour escort; someone with special qualifications to conduct a travel group.

Tour manager   A professional tour escort who leads a prepaid tour from beginning to end (also known as *tour director*).

Tour operator   A company that creates (packages) and markets inclusive tours, selling them through travel agents or directly to the public, and that may perform tour services or subcontract for such services.

Tour order   Form issued by a travel agent or airline to cover all-inclusive package tour ground arrangements (hotel, sightseeing, etc.). Client normally exchanges tour order for hotel and tour vouchers upon arrival at destination (usually on check-in at hotel).

Tour organizer   Someone who organizes a group of passengers for a special prepaid tour. An organizer need not have conference appointments, but can work through an established travel agency as an outside sales representative.

Tour package   A travel plan that includes most elements of a vacation such as transportation, accommodations, and sightseeing.

Tour shell   Brochures containing graphics or illustrations but no text, to be overprinted by travel agents.

Tour voucher   Voucher issued by tour operator to cover payment for sightseeing or entertainment features. Client surrenders tour voucher to appropriate purveyor in exchange for sightseeing or entertainment feature. Purveyor sends voucher and billing statement to tour operator for payment.

Tour wholesaler   A company that creates and markets I.T.'s and FITs through travel agents; often used interchangeably with tour operator.

Transfer   The service provided for arriving or departing transfers in a given city to transport clients from one air, sea, or rail terminal to another, or between such a terminal and their hotel. Transfers are normally a standard element of an inclusive tour.

Travel agent   A person, firm, or corporation qualified to provide tours, cruises, transportation, hotel accommodations, meals, transfers, sightseeing, and all other elements of travel to the public as a service. Compensation is usually derived from commissions paid by hotel and other ground or air-related services.

Triple   A room occupied by three people.

Twin   A room occupied by two persons and having two single beds.

Universal Air Travel Plan (UATP)   Credit card and carrier-sponsored charge plan.

Upgrade   To change to a better class of service or accommodation.

Upper   The berth on a ship or train that is above another berth.

Value season   The off-season when prices are usually less.

Visa   Official authorization, added to a passport, permitting travel to and within a certain country or region; not all countries require visas.

Vouchers   Documents or coupons issued to clients by tour operators to be exchanged for services such as accommodations, meals, sightseeing, etc.

Wagon lits   Company operating sleeping cars on European railroads.

Waitlist   A list of customers who are waiting for space on a date or time that is sold out.

Walk-in   A guest who arrives without a reservation.

Wet lease   Rental of a vehicle with crew; a pure wet lease includes full operational and cabin crew, supplies, fuel, and maintenance services.

Wholesaler   A company that markets and usually creates I.T.'s and FITs to sell through travel agents.

Youth hostel   Inexpensive supervised lodging for young people.

LISTING OF MAJOR TRADE ABBREVIATIONS

AAA	American Automobile Association. Also operates as AAA Worldwide Travel, which is an AAA-affiliated travel agency organization.
AAR	Association of American Railroads.
ABA	American Bus Association.
ABTB	Association of Bank Travel Bureaus.
ACTO	Association of Caribbean Tour Operators.
ACTOA	Air Charter Tour Operators of America.
AGTE	Association of Group Travel Executives.
AH&MA	American Hotel and Motel Association.
AITO	Association of Incentive Travel Operators.
ALPA	Airline Pilots Association.
ALTA	Association of Local Transport Airlines.
AOCI	Airport Operators Council International Inc.
ARTA	Association of Retail Travel Agents.
ASTA	American Society of Travel Agents.
ARC	Airline Reporting Conference.
ATA	Air Transport Association.
CAAA	Commuter Airline Association of America.
CHRIE	Council on Hotel, Restaurant and Institutional Education.
CLIA	Cruise Lines International Association.

DATO	Discover America Tourism Association.
HSMA	Hotel Sales Managers Association.
IAAPA	International Association of Amusement Parks and Attractions.
IACA	International Air Charter Association.
IACVB	International Association of Convention and Visitor Bureaus.
IAFE	International Association of Fairs and Expositions.
IATA	International Air Transport Association. Now Replaced by International Airline Travel Agents Network.
IATAN	See above.
IATM	International Association of Tour Managers.
ICAO	International Civil Aviation Organization.
ICTA	Institute of Certified Travel Agents.
IHA	International Hotel Association.
IPSA	International Passenger Ship Association.
ISHAE	International Society of Hotel Association Executives.
ISTA	International Sightseeing and Tours Association.
MPI	Meeting Planners International.
NAMBO	National Association of Motor Bus Owners.
NPTA	National Passenger Traffic Association.
NRPA	National Recreation and Parks Association.
NRA	National Restaurant Association.
NTA	National Tour Association.
SATH	Society for the Advancement of Travel for the Handicapped.
SATW	Society of American Travel Writers.
SITE	Society of Incentive Travel Executives.
STTE	Society of Travel and Tourism Educators.
TIAA	Travel Industry Association of America.
USTOA	United States Tour Operators Association.

REFERENCES

Americans Outdoors: The Legacy, The Challenge: The Report of the President's Commission, Washington, D.C.: Island Press, 1987.

BURKART, A.J., and S. MEDLIK, *The Management of Tourism*, London: Heinemann, 1975.

Creating Economic Growth and Jobs Through Travel and Tourism: A Manual for Community and Business Developers, Washington D.C.: U.S. Printing Office, 1981.

CLEVERDON, ROBERT, *International Business Travel: A New Megamarket*, London: The Economist Intelligence Unit, 1985.

CURRAN, PATRICK, J.T., *Principles and Procedures of Tour Management*, Boston: CBI Publishing Company, 1978.

FARRIS, MARTIN T., and FORREST E. HARDING, *Passenger Transportation*, Englewood Cliffs, N.J.: Prentice-Hall, 1976.

FUSSELL, PAUL (ed.), *The Norton Book of Travel*, New York: W.W. Norton & Company, Inc., 1987.

GEARING, CHARLES E., WILLIAM W. SWART, and TURGUT VAR, *Planning for Tourism Development: Quantitative Approaches*, New York: Praeger, 1976.

GEE, CHUCK Y., DESTER J.L. CHOY, and JAMES C. MAKENS, *The Travel Industry*, Westport, Conn.: The AVI Publishing Company, Inc., 1984.

GUNN, CLARE A., *Tourism Planning*, New York: Crane Russak, 1979.

HOWELL, DAVID W., *Passport: An Introduction to the Travel and Tourism Industry*, Cincinnati: South-Western Publishing Co., 1989.

HOWELL, RICHARD L., RALPH HAMBRICK, and SUSAN BLANTON (eds.), *A Reception Services System for International Visitors*, Richmond: Virginia Commonwealth University, 1982.

HUDMAN, LLOYD E., *Tourism: A Shrinking World*, Columbus, Ohio: Grid Publishing, 1980.

International Tourism and Small Business: A Report of the Committee on Small Business, Washington, D.C.: U.S. Government Printing Office, 1987.

The Inn Business, Ottawa: Canadian Government Publishing Centre, 1982.

KAISER, CHARLES, JR, and LARRY E. HELBER, *Tourism Planning and Development*, Boston: CBI Publishing Company, 1978.

LAVENTHOL and HORWATH, LEO A. DALY COMPANY and OSORIO y TERAN, *A Proposal to Prepare a Feasibility Study of Tourism Development in Nicaragua*, undated.

LEHMANN, ARMIN D., *Travel and Tourism: An Introduction to Travel Agency Operations*, Indianapolis: The Bobbs-Merrill Company, 1978.

MATHIESON, ALISTER and GEOFFREY WALL, *Tourism: Economic, Physical and Social Impacts*, London: Longman Group Limited, 1982.

MCINTOSH, ROBERT W., and CHARLES R. GOELDNER, *Tourism: Principles, Practices, Philosophies*, 4th ed., Columbus, Ohio: Grid Publishing, 1984.

ROBINSON, H., *A Geography of Tourism*, London: MacDonald and Evans, 1976.

MILL, ROBERT CHRISTIE, and ALASTAIR M. MORRISON, *The Tourism System: An Introductory Text*, Englewood Cliffs, N.J.: Prentice-Hall, 1985.

MURPHY, PETER, *Tourism: A Community Approach*, New York: Methuen Inc., 1985.

NYIEL, RONALD A., *Marketing in the Hospitality Industry*, New York: Van Nostrand Reinhold Company, 1983.

Partners in Profit: An Introduction to Group Travel Marketing, Lexington, Ky., National Tour Association, Inc., 1987.

PHILLIPS, RALPH G., and SUSAN WEBSTER, *Group Travel Operating Procedures*, New York: Van Nostrand Reinhold Company, 1983.

A Literature Review, The President's Commission on Americans Outdoors, Washington, D.C.: U.S. Government Printing Office, 1986.

REILLY, ROBERT T., *Handbook of Professional Tour Management*, Wheaton, Ill.: Merton House Publishing Company, 1982.

SCHMOLL, G.A., *Tourism Promotion*, London: Tourism International Press, 1977.

SMITH, VALENE, ed., *Hosts and Guests: The Anthology of Tourism*, Philadelphia: University of Pennsylvania Press, 1977.

Tourism U.S.A., Volumes 1–4, Washington, D.C.: U.S. Government Printing Office, 1978.

TRAVEL & LEISURE'S, *World Travel Overview 1986/1987*, New York: American Express Publishing Corporation, 1986.

TRAVEL WEEKLY, *The 1988 Louis Harris Survey*, New York, 1988.

T.R.I.P. Report and NTA Group Travel Summit Proceedings 1986, Lexington, Ky: National Tour Foundation, 1986.

WAHAB, SALAH, L.J. CRAMPON, and L.M. ROTHFIELD, *Tourism Marketing*, London: Tourism International Press, 1976.

WATERS, SOMERSET, *Travel Industry World Yearbook-The Big Picture—1987*, New York: Child & Waters, Inc., 1987.

ZEHNDER, LEONARD E., *Florida's Disney World: Promises and Problems*, Tallahassee: The Peninsular Publishing Company, 1975.

INDEX